Wisdom From the Margins

Wisdom From the Margins

Daily Readings

WILLIAM G. BRITTON

RESOURCE *Publications* · Eugene, Oregon

WISDOM FROM THE MARGINS
Daily Readings

Resource Publications
An Imprint of Wipf and Stock Publishers
199 W. 8th Ave., Suite 3
Eugene, OR 97401

www.wipfandstock.com

PAPERBACK ISBN: 978-1-5326-3448-2
HARDCOVER ISBN: 978-1-5326-3450-5
EBOOK ISBN: 978-1-5326-3449-9

Manufactured in the U.S.A.   04/30/18

Permissions

"What are virtues for the mystic are torment and sickness for the modern man or woman: estrangement, loneliness, silence, solitude, inner emptiness, deprivation, poverty, not-knowing, and so forth . . . . What the monks sought for in order to find God, modern men and women fly from as if it were the devil."

—Jürgen Moltmann

"Retirement is the laboratory of the spirit; interior solitude and silence are its two wings. All great works were prepared in the desert, including the redemption of the world. The precursors, the followers, the Master Himself, all obeyed or have to obey one and the same law. Prophets, apostles, preachers, martyrs, pioneers of knowledge, inspired artists in every art, ordinary men and the Man-God, all pay tribute to loneliness, to the life of silence, to the night."

—A. Gilbert Sertillanges

"In all the historic formulations of the Perennial Philosophy it is axiomatic that the end of human life is contemplation, or the direct and intuitive awareness of God; that action is the means to that end; that a society is good to the extent that it renders contemplation possible for its members; and that the existence of at least a minority of contemplatives is necessary for the well-being of any society."

—Aldous Huxley

"It is not always easy to hear what the marginalized have to tell us. Their truth may be blurred by anger, slurred by pain, or whispered from insecurity or fear. When a person at the center ... makes the effort to listen to those at the margins, however, miracles happen and God's kingdom reappears.... To turn aside from those on the margins of society, the needy and the powerless, is to turn aside from Jesus. Such people show his face to the world.... How ironic it is that God often chooses to whisper to us through the lives of those who have lost their voice in our society, those who have no place, no credibility, no clout...."[1]

—Edwina Gateley

"Contemplation is very far from being just one kind of thing that Christians do: it is the key to prayer, liturgy, art and ethics, the key to the essence of a renewed humanity that is capable of seeing the world and other subjects in the world with freedom–freedom from self-oriented, acquisitive habits and the distorted understanding that comes from them. To put it boldly, contemplation is the only ultimate answer to the unreal and insane world that our financial systems and our advertising culture and our chaotic and unexamined emotions encourage us to inhabit. To learn contemplative practice is to learn what we need so as to live truthfully and honestly and lovingly. It is a deeply revolutionary matter."[2]

—Rowan Williams

Why this book?

"THIS 'CHRISTIAN THING' DOESN'T really work for me." That's what I said to my church friend fifteen years ago. I think it made him uncomfortable, so he dismissed my comment with, "Bill, you're doing fine." Little did he know–and little did I know, just how short I was of "doing fine."

It took crashing and burning in ministry, losing almost everything near and dear to me, and finally hitting bottom, to become desperate enough and determined enough to figure out what was wrong. Eventually I did, and things began to change. First I discovered Christians outside my usual circle of interest who were writing about what to me was a really different approach to spirituality. Then, I started keeping track of what I was finding so I could routinely review the insights. After all, in most cases, these writers had paid dearly to acquire them. Eventually, I discovered that what was helping me was of help to others too, and the dream of a book came to be. The book that you're holding is that book.

God used the insights in this book to save me–to save me from continuing to be the person, the husband, the father, the friend, the pastor that I had always been–the person who wasn't very useful to God or to others–the person whose tombstone was likely to read, "He didn't finish well." All that needed to change–and did.

My prayer is that through these daily readings–these powerful "seeds"–God will save you as well. My prayer is that God will guide you into new ways of thinking and helpful new practices. Not that the truth or the practices are new! No, they're as old as Jewish saints like Abraham and David, and Christian saints like Paul and Peter. They have been practiced by innumerable saints, monks, preachers, mystics, and prophets down through the centuries. We see them illustrated in the ancient life of Saint Francis, the modern life of Pope Francis–and most powerfully, in the life of Jesus Himself.

What's here is "wisdom from the margins." The book could almost be called "what you should hear in church–but often don't" or "the most

3

important things you need to know to live the spiritual life–but were never told." For many readers what's here may often seem unfamiliar or counter-intuitive. It's definitely countercultural. The men and women I'm quoting advocate for those on the margins in our world (the poor, powerless, over-looked, disenfranchised), and they themselves work from the margins. They may very well strike you as unknown, dubious, fringe, unpopular, strange–or even dangerous–guides. But the ideas and practices they're championing were commonplace and appreciated for much of church history–just not now. (It's starting to get better. There is an "alt" movement afoot, and this book is part of it.)

If my contributors are experts that most people ignore, or guides with suspicious credentials, that should be no surprise, since God chose a man from a family of idolaters to be the father of his people (Abraham), a murderer to lead Israel out of slavery in Egypt (Moses), and a wandering mendicant–a rabble-rousing, obscure member of a despised race, who lived in an mostly unknown village, in an unimportant country, and who died a criminal's death, to be the Savior of our world. God works in the margins. We find God in the margins. We hear God from the margins–and from the marginalized. We learn from the marginalized what we need to know for ourselves and others–what we would never know otherwise. You could say wisdom from the margins is the key to our salvation. I hope in this brief exposure to time-tested spiritual truth, you will come to agree with me, and find salvation–salvation worthy of the name–salvation that "works."

Outsiders and the Conversion of the Church

"The movement of Jesus is always from the outside-in: welcoming, inviting, including. Jesus was always including people, bringing them in from the outside. As James Alison has noted, for Jesus there was no 'other.' All were welcome members of his community. By speaking to 'outsiders,' healing those who were not part of the Jewish community, as well as his 'table fellowship' with the outcasts, Jesus was embodying God's hospitality. Jesus's hospitality was the foundation of later patterns of Christian hospitality. In the Middle Ages, St. Benedict, in his set of rules for his religious order gave his monks the dictum, *Hospes venit, Christus venit.* 'The guest comes, Christ comes.' That is, for the Benedictines all guests were to be welcomed as Christ. In the 17th century, St. Alphonsus Rodríguez, a humble Jesuit brother, worked as a porter, or doorkeeper, at the Jesuit college of Majorca, in Spain. His job was to greet all the students, faculty and visitors who rapped on the great wooden door. The humble Jesuit brother had a wonderful way of reminding himself to be cheerful and hospitable to all visitors, and ... welcome them as if they were Jesus himself. Upon hearing someone knocking on the door, he would say, 'I'm coming, Lord!'"[3]

—James Martin

"Those at the edge, ironically, always hold the secret for the conversion of every age and culture. They always hold the projected and denied parts of our soul. Only as the People of God receive the stranger and the leper, those who don't play our game, do we discover not only the hidden and hated parts of our own souls, but the Lord Jesus himself. In letting go, we make room for the Other. The Church is always converted when the outcasts are re-invited into the temple."[4]

—Richard Rohr

"I was a stranger and you invited me in"
Matthew 25:35b NIV

- Who are the "foreigners and strangers" in your world? Do you think of them as treasured and loved by Jesus?

5

- Do you have elevated expectations of how Jesus would appear, should he appear to you? Would you expect it to be obvious?
- In Sunday morning church, do you have the attitude, "The guest comes. Christ comes?"

Abba, don't let me forget when I was a stranger. Don't ever let me forget that feeling.

For more: *Between Heaven and Mirth* by James Martin

Try Softer

"When you stretch, you don't make it happen simply by trying harder. You must let go and let gravity do its work. You give permission, opening yourself to another, greater force. This is not just true when it comes to stretching. As a general rule, the harder you work to control things, the more you lose control. The harder you try to hit a fast serve in tennis, the more your muscles tense up. The harder you try to impress someone on a date or while making a sale, the more you force the conversation and come across as pushy. The harder you cling to people, the more apt they are to push you away.... But for deeper change, I need a greater power than simply 'trying harder' can provide. Imagine someone advising you, 'Try harder to relax. Try harder to go to sleep. Try harder to be graceful. Try harder to not worry. Try harder to be joyful.' There are limits on what trying harder can accomplish. Often the people in the Gospels who got into the most trouble with Jesus were the ones who thought they were working hardest on their spiritual life. They were trying so hard to be good that they could not stop thinking about how hard they were trying. That got in the way of their loving other people.... here is an alternative: Try softer. Try better. Try different. A river of living water is now available, but the river is the Spirit. It is not you.... Don't push the river."[5]

—John Ortberg

"Faith does not need to push the river because faith is able to trust that there is a river. The river is flowing. We are in it."[6]

—Richard Rohr

"Rivers of living water will flow from within them."
John 7:38b NIV

- Is "trying harder" your default mode? Are you constantly "pushing the river?" Is that working?
- What exactly would it look like for you to "try softer?"
- What might you discover by trying softer?

Abba, help me stop pushing and striving and trust the river to do its work.

For more: *The Me I Want To Be* by John Ortberg

Training Not Trying

"We can become like Christ by doing one thing–following him in the overall style of life he chose for himself."[7]

"The way to liberation and rest lies through a decision and a practice."[8]

—Dallas Willard

"Someday, in years to come, you'll be wrestling with the great temptation, or trembling under the great sorrow, of your life. But the real struggle is here, now, in these quiet weeks. Now it is being decided whether, in the day of your supreme sorrow or temptation, you shall miserably fail or gloriously conquer. Character cannot be made except by a steady, long-continued process."

—Phillips Brooks

"Any time you make a choice, you are turning the central part of you, the part of you that chooses, into something a little different from what it was before. Taking your life as a whole, with all your innumerable choices, all your life long you are slowly turning this thing into either a heavenly creature or a hellish creature. That is, either

7

a creature that is in harmony with God, its fellow creatures, and itself, or else into a creature that is in a state of war and hatred with God, its fellow creatures, and itself. To be the one kind of creature is heaven, joy, peace, knowledge, and power. To be the other means madness, horror, idiocy, rage, impotence, and eternal loneliness. Each of us at each moment is progressing to the one state or the other."[9]

—C.S. Lewis

"Everyone who competes in the games exercises self-control in all things.
They then do it to receive a perishable wreath, but we an imperishable.
Therefore I run in such a way, as not without aim;
I box in such a way, as not beating the air;
but I discipline my body and make it my slave,
so that, after I have preached to others,
I myself will not be disqualified."
1 Corinthians 9:24–27 NASV

- Is your approach to the spiritual life characterized by "a practice"–a training regimen like that of an athlete? . . . an imitative approach like that of an apprentice?
- The Lewis quote is hard to hear but also hard to ignore. What's your reaction?
- Are you training your body now for success, or just hoping in that future day of testing to win by just trying really hard?

Abba, by *practicing* may I learn to do "the right thing at the right time in the right way with the right spirit."[10] (John Ortberg)

For more: *Mere Christianity* by C. S. Lewis

Life as Usual Must Go

"There was a new thing at work in me. And I had learned something about how we do change–and how we do not. In particular, I had learned that *intensity* is crucial for any progress in spiritual perception and understanding. To dribble a few verses or chapters of scripture on oneself through the week, in church or out, will not reorder one's mind and spirit—just as one drop of water every five minutes will not get you a shower, no matter how long you keep it up. You need a lot of water at once and for a sufficiently long time. Similarly for the written Word."[11]

—Dallas Willard

"A year or so later I learned a related lesson with regard to prayer. In the tradition in which I was brought up, scripture reading and prayer were the two main religious things one might do, in addition to attending services of the church. But I was not given to understand that these had to be practiced in a certain way if they were to make a real difference in one's life. In particular I did not understand the intensity with which they must be done, nor that the appropriate intensity required that they be engaged in for lengthy periods of undistracted time on a single occasion. Moreover, one's life as a whole had to be arranged in such a way that this would be possible. One must not be agitated, hurried, or exhausted when the time of prayer and study came. Hence one cannot tack an effective, life-transforming practice of prayer and study onto 'life as usual.' Life as usual must go. It will be replaced by something far better."[12]

—Dallas Willard

"Follow my example,
as I follow the example of Christ."
1 Corinthians 11:1 NIV

- Have you concluded that life as usual must go? If so, what has changed?
- Are you spending enough undistracted time in prayer and study for those practices to be life transforming?
- Have you arranged your life in such a way that this untypical approach to life would be possible? If so, how so?

Abba, help me, in the midst of this confused, distracted world, to renounce the practice of life as usual. Lead me into truly life-transforming practices for my good—and the good of others.

For more: *The Divine Conspiracy* by Dallas Willard

Jesus and His Convulsive Earthquake

"Jesus Christ has irreparably changed the world. When preached purely, His Word exalts, frightens, shocks, and forces us to reassess our whole life. The gospel breaks our train of thought, shatters our comfortable piety, and cracks open our capsule truths. The flashing spirit of Jesus Christ breaks new paths everywhere. His sentences stand like quivering swords of flame because He did not come to bring peace, but a revolution. The gospel is not a children's fairy tale, but rather a cutting-edge, rolling-thunder, convulsive earthquake in the world of the human spirit. By entering human history, God has demolished all previous conceptions of who God is and what man is supposed to be. We are, suddenly, presented with a God who suffers crucifixion. This is not the God of the philosophers who speak with cool detachment about the Supreme Being. A Supreme Being would never allow spit on his face. It is jarring indeed to learn that what He went through in His passion and death is meant for us too; that the invitation He extends is Don't weep for Me! Join Me! The life He has planned for Christians is a life much like He lived. He was not poor that we might be rich. He was not mocked that we might be honored. He was not laughed at so that we would be lauded. On the contrary, He revealed a picture meant to include you and me."[13]

—Brennan Manning

"Don't imagine that I came to bring peace to the earth!"
Matthew 10:34a NLT

- Is yours a "comfortable piety?"
- Is the "convulsive earthquake" of Jesus continuing with you?
- Do you need to reacquaint yourself with the Jesus of the gospels?

"Why should I want to be rich, when You were poor? Why should I desire to be famous and powerful in the eyes of men, when the sons of those who exalted the false prophets and stoned the true rejected You and Nailed You to the Cross? ... Let my trust be in Your mercy, not in myself. Let my hope be in Your love, not in health, or strength, or ability or human resources."[14]

—Thomas Merton

For more: *The Furious Longing of God* by Brennan Manning

Imitating Jesus, Not Just Worshiping Him

"One of the earliest accounts of Saint Francis, the 'Legend of Perugia', quotes him as telling the first friars that 'You only know as much as you do'. His emphasis on action, practice, and lifestyle was foundational and revolutionary for its time and at the heart of Franciscan alternative orthodoxy ("heterodoxy"). For Francis and Clare, Jesus became someone to actually imitate and not just to worship as divine. Up to this point, most of Christian spirituality was based in desert asceticism, monastic discipline, theories of prayer, or academic theology, which itself was often founded in 'correct belief' or liturgy, but not in a kind of practical Christianity that could be lived in the streets of the world. Many rightly say Francis emphasized an imitation and love of the humanity of Jesus, and not just the worshiping of his divinity. That is a major shift. Those who have analyzed the writings of Francis have noted that he uses the word doing rather than understanding at a ratio of 175 times to 5. Heart is used 42 times to 1 use of mind. Love is used 23 times as opposed to 12 uses of truth. Mercy is used 26 times while intellect is used only 1 time. This is a very new perspective that is clearly different from (and an antidote to) the verbally argumentative Christianity of his time, and from the highly academic theology that would hold sway from then on.... Francis and Clare's approach has been called a 'performative spirituality' which means that things are only found to be true in the doing of them.... Francis wanted us to know things in an almost 'cellular' and energetic way, and not just in our heads. This knowing is a kind of 'muscle memory' which only comes from practice."[15]

—Richard Rohr

" Faith by itself isn't enough.
Unless it produces good deeds, it is dead and useless."
James 2:17 NLT

- What's wrong with "verbally argumentative Christianity?"
- Does your faith require you to imitate Jesus in specific ways? How so?
- In reality is your Christian life more about ideas and words (right doctrine), or actually imitating Jesus (loving practices)?
- If you only know as much as you do, how much do you know?

Abba, help me practice daily what I believe.

For more: *Eager to Love* by Richard Rohr

Persistent Immaturity in the Church

"Seventeen years of ministerial efforts in a wide range of denominational settings had made it clear to me that what Christians were normally told to do, the standard advice to churchgoers, was not advancing them spiritually. Of course, most Christians had been told by me as by others to attend the services of the church, give of time and money, pray, read the Bible, do good to others, and witness to their faith. And certainly they should do these things. But just as certainly, something more was needed. It was painfully clear to me that, with rare and beautiful exceptions, Christians were not able to do even these few necessary things in a way that was really good for them, as things that would be an avenue to life filled and possessed of God. All pleasing and doctrinally sound schemes of Christian education, church growth, and spiritual renewal came around at last to this disappointing result. But whose fault was this failure? Try as I might, I was unable to pass this outcome off as a lack of effort on the Christians' part.... Leave the irregular, the half-hearted, and the novices aside for the moment. If the steady longtime faithful devotees to our ministries are not transformed in the substance of their life to the full range of Christlikeness, they are being failed by what we are teaching them."[16]

—Dallas Willard

"The average church-going Christian has a headful of vital truths about God and a body unable to fend off sin."[17]

—Dallas Willard

"Dear brothers and sisters, when I was with you
I couldn't talk to you as I would to spiritual people.
I had to talk as though . . . you were infants in the Christian life."
1 Corinthians 3:1 NLT

- Have you ever felt like you couldn't get the Christian life to work? If so, did you assume somehow it was your fault?
- Listen to Willard: "It's not your fault. You could hardly have done better. No one told you what to do." Can you dare to believe that?
- If you were told of new practices that could lead you into "a life filled and possessed of God" would you be willing to give it a try?

Abba, help me make a new, better, wiser start.

For more: *The Spirit of the Disciplines* by Dallas Willard

Only Stopping Will Do

"It's not enough to believe in silence, solitude and stillness. These things must be experienced and practiced. And practiced often enough to be routine, to create new habits. And so I come to a full stop. I sit quietly. I don't petition God, give thanks, or meditate on some divine attribute. I don't look out the window in wonder. Good things to do, but not first–not yet. Because unless I can first remember that *it doesn't depend on me*, that *I can't do what needs to be done*, then all is lost. And until I do this numerous times a day, every day, there's a slim chance I'll ever remember that. Everything argues against stopping–against remembering: the to-do list, the desire to be productive, the expectations of others, ego, habit. And therefore, ruthlessness is required in establishing this essential practice. I have the potential to be used by God in important ways–but I squander that by flitting from one thing to the next without stopping to 'recollect' myself. These are the most important moments of my day. Nothing else I do will be so informative–and formative. Nothing else will save me from myself. Nothing else will prepare me to attend to God and others, and to what's going on with me. Would it be more important to take these moments to love my spouse, feed a homeless child, memorize Scripture, or engage in worship? No, for unless I first submit to utter inactivity–unless my activity flows from my practiced inactivity before God, I cannot trust that my activity will be anything but smoke and noise. No one needs my hurried self–the one that to me seems so indispensable–the one in such a rush to help. Something must be done, but first–only stopping will do."

—William Britton

"God never hurries. There are no deadlines against which he must work. Only to know this is to quiet our spirits and relax our nerves."

—A. W. Tozer

"He who believes
will not be in haste."
Isaiah 28:16 RSV

- What's driving you? What does that say about you?
- Are you "in haste?" If so, why?
- Have you established *practices* to insure that you stop as you should?

Abba, may my stillness make a space for your divine action.

For more: *The Pursuit of God* by A. W. Tozer

Held Fast By the Bonds of Love

"Therefore, banish from your heart the distractions of earth. Turn your eyes to spiritual joys so that you may learn at last to rest in the light of the contemplation of God. Indeed, the soul's true life and repose are to abide in God, held fast by love and refreshed by divine consolations. . . . Little by little as you abandon baser things to rest in the one true and unchangeable Good, you will dwell there, held fast by the bonds of love."[18]

—Albert the Great

"Monasticism aims at the cultivation of a certain quality of life, a level of awareness, a depth of consciousness, an area of transcendence and of adoration which are not usually possible in an active secular existence. This does not ... mean that worldly life is to be considered wicked or even inferior. But it does mean that more immersion and total absorption in worldly business ends by robbing one of a certain necessary perspective. The monk seeks to be free from what William Faulkner called 'the same frantic steeplechase toward nothing' which is the essence of 'worldliness' everywhere."[19]

—Thomas Merton

"There is nothing to live for but God, and I am still full of the orchestras that drown His Voice."

—Thomas Merton

"This is what the Lord says:
'Stand at the crossroads and look; ask for the ancient paths,
ask where the good way is, and walk in it,
and you will find rest for your souls.
But you said, 'We will not walk in it.'"
Jeremiah 6:16 NIV

- Are you learning to abide in God and be refreshed by "divine consolations?" . . . to be held fast by the bonds of love?
- Have you become a victim of the "frantic steeplechase toward nothing?"
- Can you offer yourself up to God as you are, including any "baser things" or distracting "orchestras"–asking God for a deeper experience of his love? Can you do that now?

Abba, help me to turn from the distractions of earth, and put away baser things–including any frenzied living that keeps me from experiencing the consolations of your love.

For more: *The Voices of the Saints* by Bert Ghezzi

The Suffering of Jesus

"Yesterday, on the Cross, He darkened the sun's light, and behold in full day it was as night; today death has lost its dominion, suffering itself a kind of death. Yesterday the earth mourned ... and in sadness clothed itself in a garment of darkness. Today, *the people that walked in darkness have seen a great light. ... O* new and unheard of happening! He is stretched out upon a Cross Who by His word *stretched out the heavens.* He is held fast in bonds Who has *set the sand a bound for the sea.* He is given gall to drink Who has given us wells of honey. He is crowned with thorns Who has crowned the earth with flowers. With a reed they struck His Head Who of old struck Egypt with ten plagues, and submerged the head of Pharaoh in the waves. That countenance was spat upon at which the Cherubim dare not gaze. Yet, while suffering these things He prayed for His tormentors, saying: *Father, forgive them, for they know not what they do.* He overcame evil by goodness. Christ undertook the defense of those who put Him to death: eager to gather them into His net; annulling the charge, and pleading their ignorance. Made the sport of their drunken frenzy, He submitted without bitterness. He suffered their drunkenness, and in His love for mankind called them to repentance. What more could He do?" [20]

—Amphilochius of Iconium

"I wonder maybe if our Lord doesn't suffer more from our indifference, than he did from the crucifixion."

—Fulton Sheen

> *"When they hurled their insults at him,*
> *he did not retaliate;*
> *when he suffered, he made no threats.*
> *Instead, he entrusted himself*
> *to him who judges justly."*
> 1 Peter 2:23 NIV

- From the cross, Jesus prayed, "Father, forgive them for they know not what they do." Imagine how ignorant, even oblivious, those were who put Jesus to death.

- Imagine how often this is true of us as well–not only in our obvious sins, but in our "indifference." Can you admit this about yourself?
- Can you nevertheless believe that you are loved by God, just as you are? Sit with that, and see what emotions arise.

Abba, thank you for your unfailing love–and for not revealing to me the full magnitude of my sin.

For more: *The Voices of the Saints* by Bert Ghezzi

Carving Out Space For Reflection

"Without great solitude no serious work is possible."

—Pablo Picasso

Susan Cain's book *Quiet* "…focuses on introverts, making the case that they have a kind of intellectual advantage. And their edge stems largely from greater amounts of solitude, from the degree to which they've swapped motion for stillness, chatter for calm. They've carved out space for reflection that's sustained and deep. This isn't necessarily a matter of being unplugged, of ditching the hyper-connectedness of our digital lives. It's a matter of ditching and silencing the crowd."[21]

—Frank Bruni

"Cathererine de Haeck Doherty writes, 'All in me is silent and … I am immersed in the silence of God.' It is in solitude that we come to experience the 'silence of God' and so receive the inner silence that is the craving of our hearts."[22]

—Richard Foster

"There are times when solitude is better than society, and silence is wiser than speech. We should be better Christians if we were more alone, waiting upon God, and gathering through meditation on His Word spiritual strength for labour in his service. We ought to muse upon the things of God, because we thus get the real nutriment out of them …."

—Charles Spurgeon

"This solitude confirms my call to solitude. The more I am in it, the more I love it. One day it will possess me entirely and no man will ever see me again."[23]

—Thomas Merton

> "It is good for a man to bear the yoke while he is young.
> Let him sit alone in silence, for the Lord has laid it on him.
> Let him bury his face in the dust—there may yet be hope."
> Lamentations 3:27–29 NIV

- Are you more comfortable with motion or stillness? . . . with chatter or with calm?
- Do you make it a point to carve out space for reflection that's sustained and deep?
- Have you realized yet the value of "ditching" and silencing the crowd?
- Have you experienced the "silence of God" that Foster mentions? Do you long for more of that?

Abba, teach me to sit alone in silence, to carve out space for reflection, to swap motion for stillness and chatter for calm.

For more: *Quiet* by Susan Cain

Your Spirituality Is Showing

"Hank could not effectively love his wife or his children or people outside his family. He was easily irritated. He had little use for the poor, and a casual contempt for those whose accents or skin pigment differed from his own. . . . He critiqued and judged and complained, and his soul got a little smaller each year. Hank was not changing. He was once a cranky young guy, and he grew up to be a cranky old man. But even more troubling than his lack of change was the fact that nobody was surprised by it. . . . It was not an anomaly that caused head-scratching bewilderment. No church consultants were called in. No emergency meetings were held. . . . We did not expect that Hank would progressively become the way Jesus would be if he were in Hank's place. We didn't assume that each year would find him a more compassionate, joyful, gracious, winsome personality.... So we were not shocked when it didn't happen."[24]

—John Ortberg

"True holiness [consists] in the love of God and love of man.... These duties of love to our Creator and our fellow-creatures are regarded as the sum and substance of the moral law ... as the very central point, in which all the means of grace and all the ordinances of religion, terminate."[25]

—James Hervey

"What does the Lord do to ... assist me in seeing how selfish I am? Very simple: He gives me four busy kids who step on shoes, wrinkle clothes, spill milk, lick car windows, and drop sticky candy on the carpet.... Being unselfish in attitude strikes at the very core of our being. It means we are willing to forgo our own comfort, our own preferences, our own schedule, our own desires for another's benefit."[26]

—Charles Swindoll

"The purpose of my instruction
is that all believers would be filled with love."

1 Timothy 1:5 NLT

- Can you trust that God's means of grace are at work when your stuff is wrecked or schedule interrupted?
- Are you more loving with the passing years? Is there anything God wants more for you?
- What practices are helping you to love well?

Abba, destroy the narcissism that so easily causes me to fail at love.

For more: *The Life You Always Wanted* by John Ortberg

When Silence Is Better

"The first service that one owes to others in the fellowship consists in listening to them. Just as love to God begins with listening to His Word, so the beginning of love for brethren is learning to listen to them. It is God's love for us that He not only gives us His Word but also lends us His ear. So it is His work that we do for our brother when we learn to listen to him. Christians, especially ministers, so often think they must always contribute something when they are in the company of others, that this is the one service they have to render. They forget that listening can be a greater service than speaking. Many people are looking for an ear that will listen. They do not find it among Christians, because these Christians are talking when they should be listening. But he who can no longer listen to his brother will soon no longer be listening to God either; he will be doing nothing but prattle in the presence of God too. This is the beginning of the death of the spiritual life, and in the end there is nothing left but spiritual chatter and clerical condescension arrayed in pious words. One who cannot listen long and patiently will presently be talking beside the point and be never really speaking to others, albeit he be not conscious of it. Anyone who thinks that his time is too valuable to spend keeping quiet will eventually have no time for God and his brother, but only for himself and for his own follies."[27]

—Dietrich Bonhoeffer

"Speak only when your words are more beautiful than the silence."
—Arabic Proverb

[Job's friends] ". . . sat on the ground with him for seven days and nights. No one said a word to Job, for they saw that his suffering was too great for words."
Job 2:13 NIV

- Can you listen to others as God listens to you?
- Do you tend to think that by speaking you contribute something and that by silent listening you don't?
- Can you trust God to use your silence as much as, or even more than, what you have to say?

Abba, I will trust your work in my silence as much as in my words.

For more: *Life Together* by Dietrich Bonhoeffer

Suffering's Unwelcomed Gift

"Pain is knowledge rushing in to fill a gap."[28]

"Suffering can be a path to awakening when we engage it with receptivity to the gifts it holds rather than simply attempt to endure it. One of those gifts is that suffering has unique capacity to help us soften and release attachments and move toward a life of non-attachment. Simone Weil said that suffering that does not detach us is wasted suffering. Don't waste suffering. It's always a shame to have to repeat lessons because we don't get their point but suffering is a particularly bad lesson to be slow to get."[29]

—David Benner

"Real holiness doesn't feel like holiness; it just feels like you're dying. It feels like you're losing it. And you are! Every time you love someone, you have agreed for a part of you to die. You will soon be asked to let go of some part of your false self, which you foolishly thought was permanent, important, and essential! You know God is doing this in you and with you when you can somehow smile and trust that what you lost was something you did not need anyway. In fact, it got in the way of what was real."[30]

—Richard Rohr

"In the middle of the pain there is some hidden gift. I, more and more in my life, have discovered that other gifts of life are often hidden in the places that hurt most."[31]

—Henri Nouwen

"Son though he was,
he learned obedience

21

from what he suffered."
Hebrews 5:8 NLT

- Can you imagine embracing suffering that comes your way as a giver of gifts? Can you remember to look for such a gift when you're in those places that hurt most?

- Has suffering in your life caused you to loosen your grip on things? Has it changed your perspective about what is "permanent, important, and essential?"

- When it feels like you're dying or losing it, can you trust God to be at work for your good in the very thing that is "killing" you?

Abba, your Son suffered that he might know me. Help me to embrace the gifts of suffering that I might know him. I know I'm going to want to run from it like the disciples ran from the garden. Strengthen me.

For more: *Spirituality and the Awakening Self* by David G. Benner

---

God, Our Jilted Lover

"Today the heart of God is an open wound of love. He aches over our distance and preoccupation. He mourns that we do not draw near to him. He grieves that we have forgotten him. He weeps over our obsession with muchness and manyness. He longs for our presence."[32]

—Richard Foster

"Search the Scriptures,
for in them you will find
this God of the loveless,
this God of Mercy, Love and Justice,
who weeps over these her children,
these her precious ones who have been carried from the womb,
who gathers up her young upon her wings
and rides along the high places of the earth,

22

who sees their suffering

and cries out like a woman in travail,

who gasps and pants;

for with this God,

any injustice that befalls one of these precious ones

is never the substance of rational reflection and critical analysis,

but is the source

of a catastrophic convulsion within the very life of God."[33]

—Karen Drescher

"Jerusalem, Jerusalem, you who kill the prophets and stone those sent to you, how often I have longed to gather your children together, as a hen gathers her chicks under her wings, and you were not willing."
Matthew 23:37 NIV

- Do you sometimes think of God as if God were an impartial jury foreman about to render a verdict in your case? Can you reject such thinking as misguided?

- Instead, can you think of God as one who has "carried you from the womb," and who gasps and pants in pain like a woman in travail-travailing with a broken heart because his love for you and others is so meekly returned?

- Are you able to think about God as wounded by your little love for him? Can you imagine him "mourning . . . grieving . . . weeping" over you the way a mother would over her suffering child?

Abba, I realize that even my love for you is often so wavering and half-hearted. Keep me from resisting as you gather me into the embrace of your loving arms.

For more: *The Suffering of God* by Terence E. Fretheim

The Perils of Success

"Everyone said I was doing really well, but something inside me was telling me my success was putting my soul in danger." Henri Nouwen

"Sweet success is being able to pay full and undivided attention to what matters most in life … experienced as a fulfilled and calm spirit that doesn't compare itself to the happiness and success of others. It is characterized by an unhurried daily life led without the burden of the drive for victory over others or to get more status and 'stuff.' It is being able to regularly share with those we love a persistent sense of glee in the simple pleasures that derive from being alive and well at this moment in time. … Put simply, toxic success is constant distraction caused by pressure to do and have more; sweet success is attending fully to the now with the confident contentment that enough is finally enough. Overcoming toxic success syndrome is not a matter of giving up the good life, it is a matter of getting it back by freeing ourselves from the short-term illusion that so many of us now call 'success.' It is recovering from the social virus author John de Graaf calls 'affluenza … a painful, contagious, socially transmitted condition of overload, debt, anxiety, and waste resulting from the dogged pursuit of more.'"[34]

—Paul Pearsall

"Care for your soul as if it were the whole world."

—Mark Nepo

"Watch over your heart with all diligence,
For from it flow the springs of life."

Proverbs 4:23 NASB

Reread the first half of Pearsall's definition of "sweet success." What Pearsall as a psychoneuroimmunologist recommends, Jesus lived. This is the kind of life Jesus wants for you.

- Do you feel like your soul could be in danger?
- To what degree does Pearsall's definition of true success describe you?

- Are you caring for your soul "as if it were the whole world?" How, specifically?

Abba, deliver me from the illusions and pathologies of my day. Help me to find rest for my soul as I walk the ancient pathways.

For more: *Toxic Success* by Paul Pearsall

The Invisible Companionship of God

"What are virtues for the mystic are torment and sickness for the modern man or woman: estrangement, loneliness, silence, solitude, inner emptiness, deprivation, poverty, not-knowing, and so forth.... What the monks sought for in order to find God, modern men and women fly from as if it were the devil."[35]

—Jürgen Moltmann

"We seldom read of God's appearing by Himself or His angels or to any of His prophets or saints in a throng but frequently when they are alone."

—Richard Baxter

"The man who fears to be alone will never be anything but lonely, no matter how much he may surround himself with people. But the man who learns, in solitude and recollection, to be at peace with his own loneliness, and to prefer its reality to the illusion of merely natural companionship, comes to know the invisible companionship of God. Such a one is alone with God in all places, and he alone truly enjoys the companionship of other men, because he loves them in God in Whom their presence is not tiresome, and because of Whom his own love for them can never know satiety."[36]

—Thomas Merton

"After telling everyone good-bye,
[Jesus] went up into the hills by himself to pray."
Mark 6:45, 46 NLT

"One day soon afterward Jesus went up on a mountain to pray,
and he prayed to God all night."
Luke 6:12 NLT

"About eight days later Jesus took Peter, John, and James
up on a mountain to pray."
Luke 9:28 NLT

- Why do you think God most often makes himself known to someone who is alone?
- Are you regularly alone before God, or would that represent "torment and sickness" for you?
- What plan can you make to regularly escape the throng as Jesus did, and give God more of your undivided attention?

Abba, help me learn to leave the crowd behind and make myself available to you–simply giving you my affection and undivided attention.

For more: *Experiences of God* by Jürgen Moltmann

The Upside-Down Kingdom

"Here's the way God's kingdom works: it's 'lose your life, and you'll find it.' It's 'the last will be first, and the first will be last.' It's 'life comes out of death, new beginnings out of endings.' The kingdom of God is 'in giving we receive.' It's 'when we rest God works.' It's 'weakness is the way to power.' . . . It's 'the humble who will be exalted. It's those who exalt themselves–they're going to be humbled.' In fact, the meek are going to inherit the earth. It's the broken, it's the meek, it's power under control–in fact God has chosen the poor to be rich in faith (James 2). God's kingdom is small, it's little. Jesus said it's like a mustard seed. You can barely see it. It's imperceptible. . . . It's the weakest and the least among us. God says, 'There's my kingdom. They're indispensable to our whole existence. The kingdom of God identifies with the unimpressive, the insignificant, the orphan, the widow, the elderly, the poor, the sick–these are the ones, these are what you're all about'. ...We want 'God's dream'[His kingdom], but we don't want this! And we end up running after the wrong things."[37]

—Pete Scazzero

"No king is saved by the size of his army;
no warrior escapes by his great strength.
A horse is a vain hope for deliverance;
despite all its great strength it cannot save.
But the eyes of the Lord are on those who fear him,
on those whose hope is in his unfailing love . . .
he is our help and our shield."
Psalm 33:16–20 NIV

- Jesus's Kingdom values aren't the values of our world. Are they increasingly your values, or are you "running after the wrong things?"
- Do you have others that share these counter-cultural, counter-intuitive values with you, so you can encourage one another on the spiritual journey?
- When you go to church, are you taught to embrace these values? If you have a ministry, do they inform it?

Abba, help me more and more to see the constant noise and nonsense of this world for what it is.

For more: *Unexpected News* by Robert McAfee Brown

Patience With Yourself

"Above all, trust in the slow work of God. We are quite naturally impatient in everything to reach the end without delay. We should like to skip the intermediate stages. We are impatient of being on the way to something unknown, something new. And yet it is the law of all progress that it is made by passing through some states of instability–and that it may take a very long time. And so I think it is with you; your ideas mature gradually–let them grow, let them shape themselves without undue haste. Don't try to force them on, as though you could be today what time (that is to say, grace and circumstances acting on your own good will) will make of you tomorrow. Only God could say what this new spirit gradually forming within you will be. Give our Lord the benefit of believing that his hand is leading you. And accept the anxiety of feeling yourself in suspense and incomplete."[38]

—Pierre Teilhard de Chardin

"'What if you discovered that the least of the brethren of Jesus, the one who needs your love the most, the one you can help the most by loving, the one to whom your love will be most meaningful—what if you discovered that this least of the brethren of Jesus … is you?' Then do for yourselves what you would do for others."[39]

—Brennan Manning quoting Carl Jung

"The King will answer and say to them,
'Truly I say to you, to the extent that you did it
to one of these brothers of Mine,
even the least of them,
you did it to Me.'"
Matthew 25:40 NASB

- Think of all the ways you are impatient to reach the end of something or other. Now think about the inevitably slow work of God. Obviously, patience is necessary!

- Teilhard's words make a powerful springboard for prayer. Read though what he says slowly. Let it sink in and turn into prayer, phrase by phrase.

- Think about "accepting" anxiety, and feeling yourself "in suspense and incomplete." Can you do that? How will you?

Abba, help me trust your slow work in me and not give up. May I remember your love for me when incompleteness and anxiety overtake me.

For more: *Hearts on Fire* edited by Michael Harter

Learning Prayer, Prioritizing Prayer

In *The Genesee Diary,* Henri Nouwen records his experiment with life in a Trappist Monastery "I put this question to [my spiritual director] John Eudes: 'How can I really develop a deeper prayer life when I am back again at my busy work? …As long as I remain surrounded by unfinished tasks, my prayer is nearly impossible since I use the time for prayer to wonder about the many things I still have to do. It always seems that there is something more urgent and more important than prayer.' John Eudes' answer was clear and simple: 'The only solution is a prayer schedule that you will never break without consulting your spiritual director. Set a time that is reasonable, and once it is set, stick to it at all costs. Make it your most important task. Let everyone know that this is the only thing you will not change and pray at that time. One hour in the morning before work and a half hour before you go to bed might be a good start. Set the exact time and hold on to it. Leave a party when that time approaches. Simply make it an impossibility to do any type of work, even if it seems urgent, important, and crucial. When you remain faithful, you slowly discover that is is useless to think about your many problems since they won't be dealt with in that time anyhow.…So praying becomes as important as eating and sleeping, and the time set free for it becomes a very liberating time to which you become attached in the good sense.' …It seems very convincing to me [Nouwen says], even obvious. The only task left is this: simply doing it in obedience."[40]

—Henri Nouwen

"Devote yourselves to prayer."
Colossians 4:2a NLT

- Does it seem to you like there is always something more urgent and more important than prayer?

- Would you consider making a reasonable, but essentially inflexible plan for fixed-time prayers?

- Regular daily prayer is as important as eating and sleeping. You probably protect your sleeping and eating time–and you should. Isn't it obvious that you should also plan for and protect your praying time? How will you do that?

Abba, teach me a faithfulness in prayer that results in liberation from my self-imposed, misguided tyranny.

For more: *The Genesee Diary* by Henri Nouwen

Bent and Broken . . . Into Something Better

"Suffering has been stronger than all other teaching . . . . I have been bent and broken, but–I hope–into a better shape."

—Charles Dickens

"We are faced here with a phenomenon which has been widely attested by countless Christians who have lived out their Christian and human existence without looking for any cheap consolation. Countless incurably sick who discovered through their sickness a new awareness of themselves. Countless individuals for whom a new dimension in their life was opened up through their own misfortune, through the loss or even the treachery of someone they had loved. Countless people who, through all disappointments, separations, mis-hits, failures, humiliations, setbacks and disregard, transformed their lives and acquired a new personal quality; through suffering becoming more mature, more experienced, more modest, more genuinely humble, more open for others–in a word, more human."[41]

—Hans Küng

"The way down is the way up. . . . The loss and renewal pattern is so constant and ubiquitous that it should hardly be called a secret at all. Yet it is still a secret, probably because we do not *want* to see it. We do not want to embark on a further journey if it feels like going down, especially after we have put so much sound and fury into going up. . . . The supposed achievements of the first half of life have to fall apart and show themselves to be wanting in some way, or we will not move further."[42]

—Richard Rohr

"I have learned to kiss the waves that throw me up against the Rock of Ages."

—Charles Haddon Spurgeon

"My suffering was good for me,
for it taught me to pay attention to your decrees."
Psalm 119:71 NLT

- No one wants the "gift" of suffering, but we don't usually change or grow much without it. Have you experienced suffering that made you a better person–more loving, patient, humble?
- Is your testimony that you have been "bent and broken . . . into a better shape?"
- Have you learned to "kiss the waves" that throw you up against the Rock of Ages?"

Abba, thanks for the "gifts" I never asked for and didn't want–but desperately needed.

For more: *On Being a Christian* by Hans Küng

Grieving and the Vast Emptiness Of Loss

"You think your pain and your heartbreak are unprecedented in the history of the world, but then you read."[43]

—James Baldwin

"For in grief nothing 'stays put.' One keeps on emerging from a phase, but it always recurs. Round and round. Everything repeats.... How often will the vast emptiness astonish me like a complete novelty and make me say, 'I never realized my loss till this moment?' The same leg is cut off time after time."[44]

—C. S. Lewis

"'All great thought springs from a conflict between two eventual insights: (1) The wound which we find at the heart of everything is finally incurable, (2) Yet we are

31

necessarily and still driven to try!' [quoting Hans Urs von Balthasar] Selah. Our largely unsuccessful efforts of the first half of life are themselves the training ground for all virtue and growth in holiness. This wound at the heart of life shows itself in many ways, but your holding and 'suffering' of this tragic wound, your persistent but failed attempts to heal it, and your final surrender to it, will ironically make you into a wise and holy person. It will make you patient, loving, hopeful, expansive, faithful, and compassionate—which is precisely second-half-of-life wisdom."[45]

—Richard Rohr

"We all want to do something to mitigate the pain of loss or to turn grief into something positive, to find a silver lining in the clouds. But I believe there is real value in just standing there, being still, being sad."

—John Green

"Just as bread needs to be broken in order to be given, so, too, do our lives."[46]

—Henri Nouwen

"Unless a grain of wheat
falls into the earth and dies,
it remains alone; but if it dies,
it bears much fruit."
John 12:24 NASV

- Has your suffering meant experiencing the same loss "time after time?"
- Have you quit trying to understand your loss or heal it? Have you allowed yourself to feel it rather than flee from it?
- Can you trust God to work in the liminal space created by your loss–as you wait for God to bring life out of death in your situation?

Abba, meet me in the pregnant, spacious emptiness created by my loss.

For more: *A Grief Observed* by C. S. Lewis

The Sacrament of the Present Moment

"Jesus is apt to come, into the very midst of life at its most real and inescapable moments. Not in a blaze of unearthly light, not in the midst of a sermon, not in the throes of some kind of religious daydream, but … at supper time, or walking along a road…. He never approached from on high, but always in the midst, in the midst of people, in the midst of real life and the questions that real life asks."[47]

—Frederick Buechner

"God is always coming to you in the Sacrament of the Present Moment. Meet and receive Him there with gratitude in that sacrament."

—Evelyn Underhill

"God wishes to be seen,
and he wishes to be sought,
and he wishes to be expected,
and he wishes to be trusted."

—Julian of Norwich

"Where can I go from your Spirit? Where can I flee from your presence?
If I go up to the heavens, you are there; if I make my bed in the depths, you
are there.
If I rise on the wings of the dawn, if I settle on the far side of the sea,
even there your hand will guide me, your right hand will hold me fast."
Psalm 139:7–10 NIV

- In his infinity and ubiquity, God is able to constantly come to every person made in the image of God. How are you responding to God's hopeful, quiet, persistent advances?

- Do you live trusting that God is always coming to you in the present moment?

- Can you focus, not on the past or the future, but on being present to God in this moment now, and as the moments of this day succeed each other?

Abba, help me learn to structure my days so that I return again and again to these life-giving concepts. Thank you for your nearness, your patience–your persistent, dogged, surprising, unfailing love.

For more: *The Magnificent Defeat* by Frederick Buechner

Shove Back the High Anxiety

"The real problem of the Christian life comes where people do not usually look for it. It comes the very moment you wake up each morning. All your wishes and hopes for the day rush at you like wild animals. And the first job each morning consists simply in shoving them all back; in listening to that other voice, taking that other point of view, letting that other, larger, stronger life come flowing in. And so on, all day. Standing back from all your natural fussings and frettings; coming in out of the wind."[48]

—C. S. Lewis

"The world stands out on either side
No wider than the heart is wide;
Above the world is stretched the sky,
No higher than the soul is high.
The heart can push the sea and land
Farther away on either hand;
The soul can split the sky in two,
And let the face of God shine through.
But East and West will pinch the heart
That can not keep them pushed apart;
And he whose soul is flat—the sky
Will cave in on him by and by."

—Edna St. Vincent Milay

"Evening, morning and noon
I cry out in distress,
and [God] hears my voice."
Psalm 55:17 NIV

- Is it a real problem for you to shove back all your wishes and hopes for the day at its start? If so, with what practice can you address that?

- If you "hit the ground running" in the morning, do you have another way of ensuring that you let "that other, larger, stronger life come flowing in?" . . . that you hear that other voice? What is it?

- Lewis says we need to stand back from all our natural fussings and frettings–we need to "come in out of the wind"–and he means all day. Fixed-time prayer through the day is helpful in this regard, since it can involve shoving back the anxiety repeatedly as the day unfolds. It's a constant battle to prevent the world from "pinching your heart." If you're not praying at fixed times each day, why not try it for a week? Give God an opening and see what He does.

Abba, give me a soul unpinched by the world.

For more: *Mere Christianity* by C. S. Lewis

Healing Shoulder-to-Shoulder[49]

"My belief is that altruism is actually a deep-seated human instinct . . . a mysterious drive to express the best that is in us. When we listen for and hear the cries of the needy, the oppressed, or the sick, something inside us instinctively responds. . . . But we are also driven by a countervailing instinct: the fear of the unknown, of people whose cultures and values we don't understand. This tug-of-war between our fear of strangers and our need to connect with those outside our own experience is the dynamic force that draws men and women to each other, and drives them apart. It's what moves us to travel to foreign lands and meet foreign people, and what compels to erect Berlin Walls and adopt restrictive immigration policies. Service to others is the way we break down the walls that keep us isolated in our own lives and in our own communities. It's how we grow as human beings. . . . You learn about life through interactions with others who are different from yourself, not by looking inward. Doing physical labor side by side with total strangers who needed help taught me lessons that went far beyond anything I had learned in a classroom or in [Quaker] Meeting about the commonality that transcends differences, about the kinship engendered by shared labor. I benefited as much by my efforts as the family I was trying to help. I learned that not only are we our brother's keepers, our brother is *our* keeper too–the keeper of our soul."[50]

—Robert Lawrence Smith

> *"'I don't know,' Cain responded.*
> *'Am I my brother's guardian?'"*
> Genesis 4:9 NLT

- Have you hoped to learn altruism by sermons or by reading?
- Are you involved in helping people in need who are not your family or friends?
- Do you think of yourself as "your brother's keeper?"
- Have you experienced being helped by those you were helping?

Abba, use me to help and to heal others, even as I am helped and healed by them.

For more: *A Quaker Book of Wisdom* by Robert Lawrence Smith

The Bible Story from Below

"The political terms *right* and *left* came from the *Estates General* in France. It's interesting that now we use them as our basic political categories. On the left sat the ordinary people, and on the right sat the nobility and the clergy! (What were the clergy doing over there?!) I think you see the pattern. The right normally protects the community and the status quo. The left predictably looks for change and reform, and there is a certain need for both or we have chaos. In history you will invariably have these two movements in some form, because we didn't have the phenomenon of the middle class until very recently. The vast majority of people in all of history have been poor, as in Jesus' time, and would have read history as a need for change.

The people who wrote the books and controlled the social institutions, however, have almost always been the comfortable people on the right. And much of history has been read and interpreted from the side of the 'winners', or the right, except for the unique revelation called the Bible, which is an alternative history from the side of the enslaved, the dominated, the oppressed, and the poor, leading up to the totally scapegoated Jesus himself.... He tries to put inside and outside together, but is killed by those entrapped and privileged on the inside."[51]

—Richard Rohr

"The chief priests and the Pharisees went to Pilate.
'Sir,' they said, 'we remember that while he was still alive
that deceiver said, "After three days I will rise again.""
Matthew 27:61–63 NIV

- If you were to insert yourself into the Biblical story, would you be more likely with the religious and political authorities on the right (preserving tradition and order), or with Jesus on the left (dissenting and challenging authority)?

- Have you read the Bible as "an alternative history" from the point of view of people on the bottom? If you did, how would that change the way you hear that story?

- Can you imagine the reception Jesus would receive if he did today as he did back then? . . . who would be for him and who against him? . . . what you would do?

Jesus, may I be found, like you, siding with the weak and poor.

For more: *Yes, And . . .* by Richard Rohr

Treating the Poor as Honored Guests

"One afternoon, after several of us had struggled with a 'wino', a 'Bowery bum', an angry, cursing, truculent man of fifty or so, with long gray hair, a full, scraggly beard, a huge scar on this right cheek, a mouth with virtually no teeth, and bloodshot eyes, one of which had a terrible tic, she [Dorothy Day, in her Catholic Worker's soup kitchen] said, 'For all we know he might be God Himself come here to test us, so let us treat him as an honored guest and look at his face as if it is the most beautiful one we can imagine.'"[52]

— Robert Coles

"Into this world, this demented inn, in which there is absolutely no room for Him at all, Christ has come uninvited. But because He cannot be at home in it, because He is out of place in it, and yet must be in it, His place is with those others for whom there is no room. His place is with those who do not belong, who are rejected by power because they are regarded as weak, those who are discredited, who are denied status as persons, who are tortured, bombed, and exterminated. With those for whom there is no room, Christ is present in the world."[53]

—Thomas Merton

"[God] *will rescue the poor when they cry to him;*
he will help the oppressed, who have no one to defend them.
He feels pity for the weak and the needy, and he will rescue them.
He will redeem them from oppression and violence,
for their lives are precious to him."
Psalm 72:12–14 NIV

- Do you share God's pity for the weak and the needy? Have you ever treated a "Bowery bum" as an honored guest? If so, what happened?
- Christ's place is with those "for whom there is no room." He identifies himself with them. He stands with them in solidarity (Mt. 25:40). Do you attempt to treat such people as you would treat Jesus?
- Imagine being denied the status of a person. Imagine what standing with and loving such a person could do for her. Who do you know who is denied the status of a person?

Abba, open my eyes to the invisible. Open my heart to the unwanted. Open my hands to the needy.

For more: *Raids On the Unspeakable* by Thomas Merton

The Crucible of Interruptions

"Jesus ... lived life with the clearest and highest purpose. Yet he veered and strayed from one interruption to the next, with no apparent plan in hand other than his single, overarching one: Get to Jerusalem and die. Otherwise, his days, as far as we can figure, were a series of zigzags and detours, apparent whims and second thoughts, interruptions and delays, off-the-cuff plans, spur-of-the-moment decisions, leisurely meals, serendipitous rounds of storytelling. ... Purposefulness requires paying attention, and paying attention means–almost by definition–that we make room for surprise. We become hospitable to interruption. I doubt we can *notice* for long without this hospitality. And to sustain it we need ... a conviction in our bones that God is Lord of our days and years, and that his purposes and his presence often come disguised as detours, messes, defeats. 'I came to you naked,' Jesus says. 'I came to you thirsty.' 'When, Lord?' we ask, startled. When He wore the disguise of an interruption. Think a moment of all the events and encounters that have shaped you most deeply and lastingly. How many did you see coming? How many did you engineer, manufacture, chase down? And how many were interruptions? ... The span between life as we intend it and life as we receive it is vast. Our true purpose is worked out in that gap. It is fashioned in the crucible of interruptions."[54]

—Mark Buchanan

"And [Moses] looked, and behold, the bush was burning with fire,
yet the bush was not consumed. So Moses said,
'I must turn aside now and see this marvelous sight,
why the bush is not burned up.'"
Exodus 3:2b-3 NASV

- What if Moses hadn't "turned aside?"

- Imagine yourself living as Jesus did, with "zigzags and detours." How would that feel?

- Can you become more hospitable to what happens in "the [vast] span between life as you intend it and life as you receive it?"

"Grant us, we pray you, a heart wide open to all this joy and beauty, and save our souls from being so steeped in care or so darkened by passion that we pass heedless and unseeing when even the thornbush by the wayside is aflame with the glory of God."[55] (Walter Rauschenbusch)

For more: *The Rest of God* by Mark Buchanan

The Embarrassment of Being Ourselves

THE INTERNATIONALLY RENOWNED PRIEST and author, respected professor and beloved pastor Henry Nouwen wrote over 40 books on the spiritual life. He corresponded regularly in English, Dutch, German, French and Spanish with hundreds of friends and reached out to thousands. Since his death in 1996, ever-increasing numbers of readers, writers, teachers and seekers have been guided by his literary legacy in over 22 languages.

"In his review of Nouwen's book *The Road to Daybreak*, Harold Fickett wrote that he found it disappointing to read that the same problems described a decade earlier in [Nouwen's] *The Genesee Diary*–deficient friendships, unrequited love, hurt feelings at perceived slights–continued to plague Nouwen. Fickett went on to explain, 'It's disappointing in exactly the same way it's disappointing to be ourselves–the same person with the same problems who learns and then must relearn again and again the basic lessons of religious faith. Nouwen does not spare himself or us the embarrassment of this perennial truth.'"[56]

—Philip Yancey

"My eyes are ever on the LORD,
for only he will release my feet from the snare.
Turn to me and be gracious to me,
for I am lonely and afflicted.
Relieve the troubles of my heart
and free me from my anguish.
Look on my affliction and my distress
and take away all my sins. . . .
Do not let me be put to shame,

for I take refuge in you."
Psalm 25:15–20 NIV

- Like Nouwen, Fickett and Yancey, are you "the same person with the same problems" you had ten years ago? Welcome to the human race!

- It's "disappointing to be ourselves," but what can we do? We can give up and live in shame, or be one "who learns and then must relearn again and again the basic lessons of religious faith." Can you accept your bad track record and refuse to give up?

- Can you be honest with others about the need for God's grace in your life, not "sparing" them your embarrassment, to encourage them?

Abba, again today I will take refuge in you.

For more: *Soul Survivor* by Philip Yancey

Let Silence Do the Heavy Lifting

"Silence makes us nervous.... We fear that silence may be interpreted as low self-esteem or questionable intelligence.... Many feel silence is a form of nonparticipation, signaling lack of interest.... For fear of being thought clueless, have you dived into a conversation, throwing out opinions, arguing your point, defending your ideas throughout a debate, only to discern later, once you stopped to catch your breath, that there was another, wiser road you could have taken? It is understandable that emerging leaders believe they need to be fast on their conversational feet .... Fierce conversations, however, *require silence*. In fact, the more emotionally loaded the subject, the more silence is required. And, of course, this carries over into our homes, into our personal relationships. Often we are simply trying to intuit something about ourselves, our companions, or the topics themselves. Sometimes we need silence in which to make a decision about the closeness we feel for our companions or the

41

distance we feel from them. Once in a precious while, silence is merely abstinence from self-assertion.... Often my role is to slow down a conversation, and silence is my greatest tool in this. As we talk with people, as we sit with them in silence, what is in the way–anger, numbness, impatience, manipulation, rigidity, blame, ego, cruelty, ambition, insensitivity, intimidation, pride–may fall away. It is in silence that such attributes, emotions, and behaviors reveal themselves as unnecessary. ...My conversations with the people most important to me, silence has become my favorite sound, because that is where the work is being done. Of all the tools I use during conversations and all the principles I keep in mind, silence is the most powerful of all."[57]

—Susan Scott

"When we can stand aside from the usual and perceive the fundamental, change begins to happen.... Silence brings us to back to basics, to our senses, to our selves."[58]

—Gunilla Norris

"Silence is the welcoming acceptance of the other."

—Pierre Lacout

"Fools multiply words"
Ecclesiastes 10:14 NIV

- Can you remember to include silence in your next emotionally loaded conversation?
- In your relationships, can you trust silence to "do the heavy lifting?"
- Will you embrace silence and be brought back to your senses?

Abba, I come today mostly with silence.

For more: *Fierce Conversations* by Susan Scott

Solitude and the Chattering Monkeys

"In solitude I get rid of my scaffolding; no friends to talk with, no telephone calls to make, no meetings to attend, no music to entertain, no books to distract, just me—naked, vulnerable, weak, sinful, deprived, broken—nothing. It is this nothing-ness that I have to face in my solitude, a nothingness so dreadful that everything in me wants to run to my friends, my work, and my distractions so that I can forget my nothingness and make myself believe that I am worth something. But that is not all. As soon as I decide to stay in my solitude, confusing ideas, disturbing images, wild fantasies, and weird associations jump about in my mind like monkeys in a banana tree. Anger and greed begin to show their ugly faces. I give long, hostile speeches to my enemies and dream lustful dreams in which I am wealthy, influential, and very attractive—or poor, ugly, and in need of immediate consolation. . . . The task is to persevere in my solitude, to stay in my cell until all my seductive visitors get tired of pounding on my door and leave me alone."

—Henri Nouwen[59]

"The world is full of people wanting to solve all the problems of the world. But the world would profit much more if people would first confront their own anxieties and the things that cause them 1) to have to fill every silence with meaningless chatter, 2) to stay constantly busy, and 3) to do anything to avoid being still."[60]

—David K. Flowers

"In the history of salvation,
neither in the clamour nor in the blatant,
but the Shadows and the Silence
are the places in which God chose
to reveal himself to humankind."[61]

—Pope Francis

"But Jesus often withdrew to lonely places and prayed."
Luke 5:16 NIV

- Do you avoid solitude? If so, do you know why?

- Are you expecting to find God, or be found by him in the noise of the crowd? . . . of the congregation?
- Are you willing to persevere in your solitude until the "monkeys in the banana tree" give up and leave you alone?

Abba, deliver me from busyness that stems from fear of being still, and into stillness where you are heard.

For more: *The Essential Henri Nouwen* edited by Robert Jonas

The Achilles Heel of Evangelicalism

"I believe silence is the most challenging, the most needed and the least experienced spiritual discipline among evangelical Christians today. It is much easier to talk about it and read about it than to actually become quiet. We are a very busy, wordy and heady faith tradition. Yet we are desperate to find ways to open ourselves to our God who is, in the end, beyond all of our human constructs and human agendas. With all of our emphasis on theology and Word, cognition and service–and as important as these are–we are starved for mystery, to know this God as One who is totally Other and to experience reverence in his presence. We are starved for intimacy, to see and feel and know God in the very cells of our being. We are starved for rest, to know God beyond what we can do for him. We are starved for quiet, to hear the sound of sheer silence that is the presence of God himself."[62]

—Ruth Haley Barton

"'Go out and stand before me on the mountain,' the Lord told him. And as Elijah stood there, the Lord passed by, and a mighty windstorm hit the mountain. It was such a terrible blast that the rocks were torn loose, but the Lord was not in the wind. After the wind there was an earthquake, but the Lord was not in the earthquake. And after the earthquake there was a fire, but the Lord was not in the fire. And after the fire there was the sound of a gentle whisper. When Elijah heard it, he wrapped his face in his cloak and went out and stood at the entrance of the cave."
I Kings 19:11–13 NLT

44

- Do you feel the need for silence? Have you thought about how spending time in silence could benefit you?

- Is your faith tradition "very busy, wordy and heady?" Is it characterized by "theology and Word, cognition and service?" Are you starved for rest, quiet, intimacy?

- Will the level of noise in your life allow you to hear if God comes to you in "sheer silence?" Are you willing to carve out some places for silence?

Abba, as I attend you to in silence, help me to receive your love for me there.

For more: *Invitation to Solitude and Silence* by Ruth Haley Barton

---

Prayer and the Wandering Mind

"I neglect God and his angels for the noise of a fly, for the rattling of a coach, for the whining of a door; I talk on in the same posture of praying, eyes lifted up, knees bowed down, as though I prayed to God; and if God or his angels should ask me when I thought last of God in that prayer, I cannot tell. Sometimes I find that I had forgot what I was about, but when I began to forget it I cannot tell. A memory of yesterday's pleasures, a fear of tomorrow's dangers, a straw under my knee, a noise in mine ear, a light in mine eye, an anything, a nothing, a fancy, a chimera in my brain troubles me in my prayer."[63]

—John Donne

"One of the cardinal rules of prayer is: Pray as you can, don't pray as you can't.... Remember the only way to fail in prayer is not to show up."

—Brennan Manning

"The great thing is prayer. Prayer itself. If you want a life of prayer, the way to get it is by praying."

—Thomas Merton

"When you pray, rather let your heart be without words than your words without heart."

—John Bunyan

"But when you pray, go away by yourself,
shut the door behind you, and pray to your Father in private."
Matthew 6:6 NLT

- John Donne shares very honestly about his problems in prayer, and the humor in his report shows he isn't condemning himself. Perhaps he is just letting these distractions "float on downstream"–not resisting them or really even giving them any mind. What do you think? Can you extend grace to yourself as he does when it comes to prayer?

- If you focus on the "noise of a fly" and other distractions, you'll probably give up in frustration. Can you "show up" according to plan each day, regardless of whether you feel delighted or distracted? What would be the importance of doing that?

- For your heart to be without words isn't necessarily a bad thing. Have you tried to pray by just silently giving God your attention?

For more: *The Works of John Donne* by John Donne

Your Soul as God's Dwelling Place

"The forming of the soul that it might be a dwelling place for God is the primary work of the Christian leader. This is not an add-on, an option, or a third-level priority. Without this core activity, one almost guarantees that he/she will not last in leadership for a life-time or that what work is accomplished will become less and less reflective of God's honor and God's purposes."[64]

—Gordon MacDonald

"Self care is never a selfish act. It is simply good stewardship of the only gift I have–the gift I was put on earth to offer to others."

—Parker Palmer

"The desperate need today is not for a greater number of intelligent people, or gifted people, but for deep people."

—Richard Foster

"I am the vine; you are the branches.
If you remain in me and I in you,
you will bear much fruit;
apart from me you can do nothing."
John 15:5 NIV

- The first quote is meant for pastors, but isn't it true for all of us? The problem is, many of us (pastors included) don't think of the forming of our own soul as our "primary work." Do you think of this as your most important work, or are you more focused on serving God and others?

- Can you imagine offering your best self to your marriage, your family, your neighborhood, your church, your country–to anything–without such a focus?

- Gordon MacDonald and many of us insisted on learning this the hard way. Will you also need to learn by suffering and painful loss, or can you heed these words of warning? Can you make an action plan so that you don't fool yourself now with merely good intentions?

Abba, I know you have taken up residence in me already, and I'll always be your dwelling place. It's only whether I'll be a holy or unholy one, whether an expansive, welcoming one, or a restricted inhospitable one. Help me to welcome you as lovingly as you have welcomed me.

For more: "Cultivating the Soul–Spiritual Formation with Gordon MacDonald"[65]

Perhaps the Biggest Shock of Marriage–Encountering Yourself

"People throw away what they could have by insisting on perfection, which they cannot have, and looking for it where they will never find it."[66]

—Edith Schaefer

"At the heart of every marriage and every committed relationship, there dawns an elemental shock of realization, that we have made vows to a stranger whom we must now get to know; both in ourselves and in the other. Marriage is where we learn self-knowledge; where we realize that parts of our own makeup are even stranger than the stranger we have married or come to live with and just as difficult for another person to live and breathe with or come to know. Marriage is where we realize how much effort we have put into preserving our own sense of space, our own sense of self and our own cherished everyday rhythms. Marriage is where we realize how much we want to be right and seen to be right. Marriage is where all of these difficult revelations can consign us to a sense of imprisonment and distance or help us become larger, kinder, more generous, more amusing, more animated participants in the human drama."[67]

—David Whyte

"Every human relationship, especially where the participants long to experience deep closeness, encounters significant conflict. And there is simply no way through the conflict to true connection without divine power. There is no way through without an energy in the soul that is supplied by God, an energy that is stronger and better than the energy that is already there, fueling the conflict."[68]

—Larry Crabb

"We have a picture of the perfect partner, but we marry an imperfect person. Then we have two options. Tear up the picture and accept the person, or tear up the person and accept the picture."[69]

—Grant Howard

"Love one another."
1 John 3:1b NIV

- Have you experienced the shocking self-revelation to which Whyte refers? If not, why not?

- Have you made peace with your own limitations as a spouse? . . . with those of your partner?

- Is your response to marriage to feel imprisoned or to be challenged to grow?

- Are you "tearing up" the picture, or the person?

Abba, use my marriage to make me larger, kinder, more generous, more amusing and more alive.

For more: *The Three Marriages* by David Whyte

Jesus's Reverse Mission

"One reason we Christians have misunderstood many of Jesus' teachings is that we have not seen Jesus' way of education as that of a spiritual master. He wants to situate us in a larger life, which he calls the 'Reign of God.' But instead we make him into a Scholastic philosopher if we are Roman Catholic, into a moralist if we are mainline Protestant, or into a successful and imperialistic American if we are Evangelical. Yet the initiatory thrust of Jesus' words is hidden in plain sight. Study, for example, his instructions to the twelve disciples, when he sent them into society in a very vulnerable way (no shoes or wallet, like sheep among wolves). How did we miss this? Note that it was not an intellectual message as much as it was an 'urban plunge,' a high-risk experience where something new and good could happen. It was designed to change the disciples much more than it was meant for them to change others! (See Matthew 10:1–33 or Luke 10:1–24.) Today we call it a reverse mission, where we ourselves are changed and helped by those whom we think we are serving. When read in light of classic initiation patterns, Jesus' intentions are very clear. He wanted his disciples–then and now–to experience the value of vulnerability. Jesus invites us to a life without baggage so we can learn how to accept others and their culture. Instead, we carry along our own country's assumptions masquerading as 'the good news.' He did not teach us to hang up a shingle to get people to attend our services.

He taught us exactly the opposite: We should stay in their homes and eat their food! . .. One can only imagine how different history would have been had we provided this initiatory training for our missionaries."[70]

—Richard Rohr

"Don't take any money with you, nor a traveler's bag,
nor an extra pair of sandals."
Luke 10:4 NLT

- Can you imagine how different history would be if the church had followed the instructions (and personal example) of Jesus when it comes to doing ministry?

- Are you willing to "plunge" into a risky experience where something new and good could happen to you?

- Have you been helped in the process of helping others? Is God calling you to your own "reverse mission?"

Abba, lead me out of my comfort zone, and heal me as I heal others.

For more: *Adam's Return* by Richard Rohr

A Self-Aware Reading of Scripture

"We are all interpreting the text to some degree. We are all privileging–deferring to–certain values, doctrines, creedal commitments, traditions, or biblical texts. Something somewhere is trumping something else.... The only question is whether you are *consciously* vs. *unconsciously* using a hermeneutic .... When your hermeneutic is operating unconsciously it causes you to say things like 'this is the clear teaching of Scripture'.... What is interesting to me in this phenomenon is not that we are all engaging in hermeneutics, acts of interpretation. That is a given. What is interesting to me is how *self-awareness*, or the lack thereof, is implicated in all this.... Denying that you are engaged in hermeneutics–betrays a shocking lack of self-awareness, an inability to notice the way your mind and emotions are working in the background and beneath the surface. I think statements like 'this is the clear teaching of Scripture' are psychologically diagnostic. Statements like these reveal something about yourself. Namely, that you lack a certain degree of self-awareness. For example, saying something like 'this is the clear teaching of Scripture' is similar to saying 'I'm not a racist'.... Self-aware people would say things like 'I don't want to be a racist' or 'I try not to be racist' or 'I condemn racism.' But they would never say 'I'm not a racist' because self-aware people know that they have blind spots.... They have unconscious baggage that is hard to notice or overcome. And it's the same with how self-aware people approach reading the bible. Self-aware people know that they are *trying* to read the bible in an unbiased fashion.... [and] to let the bible speak clearly and it its own voice. But self-aware people know they have blind spots. They know that there is unconscious baggage affecting how they are reading the bible, baggage that they know *must* be biasing their readings and conclusions."[71]

—Richard Beck

"Even if I have to die with you, I will never deny you!"
Mark 14:31 NLT

- Is the Bible's meaning usually pretty obvious to you?
- Are you aware of your biases and blind spots?
- What can you do to read with more self-awareness?

Abba, reveal my blind-spots and arrogance, and open my eyes to see when others show me the truth.

For more: "Emotional Intelligence and Sola Scriptura" by Richard Beck

An Hour Well Employed

"Prayer is focused attention to God."

—Peter Scazzero

"In learning to pray, Christians learn . . . a practice–and the good intrinsic to that practice. They learn, that is, to attend to God, to look to God. And they learn that not just intellectually, not just as an idea. In learning to pray, they learn a human activity that engages their bodies as well as their minds, their affections and passions and loyalties as well as their rationality, and that focuses their lives and their common life upon God. To attend to God is not easy to learn–or painless. And given our inveterate attention to ourselves and to our own needs and wants, we frequently corrupt it. . . . In learning to pray, Christians learn to look to God and, after the blinding vision, to begin to look at all else in a new light. In prayer they do not attend to something beyond God that God–or prayer–might be used in order to reach; they attend to God. That is the good intrinsic to prayer, the good 'internal to that form of activity,' simple attention to God."[72]

—Allen Verhey

"How to meditate? Bring yourself back to the point quite gently. And even if you do nothing during the whole of your hour but bring your heart back a thousand times, though it went away every time you brought it back, your hour would be very well employed."[73]

—Francis de Sales

"Lord, teach us to pray."
Luke 11:1b NLT

- Is your prayer aimed at "focused attention to God" or are you often easily distracted by your inveterate attention to yourself and your own needs and wants? If you're easily distracted, can you forgive yourself, admitting you're like everyone else?

- When worries, fantasies, noises, sinful thoughts and the making of plans disrupt your attention to God, are you able to "bring yourself back to the point quite gently"–with no self recrimination, self-defense or further distraction?

- Can you bring your heart back to attentiveness to God, even if in one session it's "a thousand times?"

Abba, I'm encouraged that with each distraction, I have the opportunity to turn to you and attend to you again. I'm glad to do this over and over as long as I must, knowing you're waiting for me there, eager for my return.

For more: *The Art of Loving God* by Francis de Sales

Your Intuitive Prejudice in Favor of Self

"To proportion one's task to one's powers, to undertake to speak only when one knows, not to force oneself to think what one does not think, or to understand what one does not understand…all that is great wisdom."

—A. D. Sertillanges

"We ought to have the humility to admit we do not know all about ourselves, that we are not experts at running our own lives. We ought to stop taking our conscious plans and decisions with such infinite seriousness. It may well be that we are not the martyrs or the mystics or the apostles or the leaders or the lovers of God that we imagine ourselves to be. Our subconscious mind may be trying to tell us this in many ways and we have trained ourselves with the most egregious self-righteousness to turn a deaf ear.…One of the effects of original sin is an intuitive prejudice in favor of our own selfish desires. We see things as they are not, because we see them centered on ourselves. Fear, anxiety, greed, ambition, and our hopeless need for pleasure all distort the image of reality that is reflected in our minds. Grace does not completely correct this distortion all at once: but it gives us a means of recognizing and allowing for it. And it tells us what we must do to correct it. Sincerity must be bought at a price: the humility to recognize our innumerable errors, and fidelity in tirelessly setting them right. The sincere man, therefore, is one who has the grace to know that he may be instinctively insincere, and that even his natural sincerity may become a camouflage for irresponsibility and moral cowardice: as if it were enough to recognize the truth, and do nothing about it!"[74]

—Thomas Merton

"With humility comes wisdom."
Proverbs 11:2b NLT

- Are you aware of the "intuitive prejudice" that distorts your perception of yourself?

- Do you listen to the voice of others or the "voice within" in such a way that your "infinite seriousness" about your spirituality could be questioned?
- How can you refuse to be "instinctively insincere" before God, and thereby learn to practice truthfulness with others about your weaknesses and limitations?

Self-humbling God, help me humbly receive the truth about myself.

For more: *No Man Is An Island* by Thomas Merton

"Trouble" Is God's Middle Name

"The God we are talking about is a risk-taking God. The God of Abraham, Isaac, and Jacob, and of Sarah, Leah, and Rachel, is always in the thick of things, siding with the poor, putting the divine name on the line for a bunch of slaves, and–in Christian terms–getting incarnated in the most unlikely and risky way imaginable, in a first-century Jew who lived at a time (like all times) when people in general didn't like Jews very much and people in power didn't like Jews at all. So if we get in trouble for affirming such a God, we can be sure that Trouble is God's middle name and that such a God will be alongside us in the midst of trouble, rather than off in a remote heaven practicing neutrality. And if we can begin to make that most difficult switch of all–away from the gods of middle-class values and upward mobility and gilt-edged retirements plans–and if we can explore, even tentatively and gingerly, what it would be like to think with and act for those who are the victims, we might just uncover the most 'unexpected news' of all: that God got there before we did."[75]

—Robert McAfee Brown

"Reading the Bible with the eyes of the poor is a different thing from reading it with a full belly. If it is read in the light of the experience and hopes of the oppressed, the Bible's revolutionary themes–promise, exodus, resurrection and spirit–come alive."[76]

—Jürgen Moltmann

"If we are thrown into the blazing furnace, the God we serve is able to deliver us from it, and he will deliver us . . . . But even if he does not . . . we will not serve your gods or worship the image of gold you have set up."
Daniel 3:17–18 NIV

- Does "getting into trouble" seem like an unseemly or obviously un-spiritual thing to you? Do you think of God as "off in a remote heaven practicing neutrality?"
- How can you better read the Bible "in light of the experience and hopes of the oppressed?"
- Do you think of the Bible as mostly supporting things as they are, or as "revolutionary?" Does it matter?

Abba, keep me from a comfort that blinds me to the experience and struggles of others.

For more: *Unexpected News* by Robert McAfee Brown

The Difference between Thinking and Praying

"I don't understand why God loves me–or anyone else, for that matter. But does a minnow have to understand the ocean to swim in it? Does a goose have to understand his instinctive urges to fly south in winter before taking flight? Does a hawk understand the physics of hot air rising to soar atop the currents? Do I really need to understand the height and breadth and depth of God's love to throw myself upon it? Authentic spirituality, it seems to me, does not depend on understanding everything about ourselves and God and then using that knowledge to hoist ourselves to a higher level of experience and achievement. . . . Authentic spirituality confidently assumes that God is up to something good, going ahead of us, calling us, embracing us, and it seeks simply to participate and delight in this."[77]

—Donald McCullough

55

"Prayer begins with being connected to God. One way I find helpful to remind myself of the ever-present God is to say over and over again, 'God, my great friend . . . somehow you're alive in me.' At times, I am sure, you will need nothing more than that. But the essential difference between thinking and praying is the conscious 'connection.' The goal of these prayers is connecting with and resting in God, not trying to learn anything or to make 'progress in the spiritual life.' Remember, God will lead us as God will, and God's faithfulness, goodness, and love for us are infinite."[78]

—William O'Malley

"I pray that you, being rooted and established in love may . . .
grasp how wide and long and high and deep is the love of Christ,
and know this love that surpasses knowledge . . . ."
Ephesians 3:17b-19b NIV

- Are you striving to know more about God? What can you do to make sure learning more leads to loving more, growing more, and changing more—to new practices rather than just new convictions?

- Are your prayers routinely characterized by connecting with and resting in God, even when they're filled with petitions?

- Do you assume "God is up to something good, going ahead of us, calling us?"

- Do you experience God's love mostly as fact or feeling? Does it "surpass knowledge?"

"Abba, take me to you, imprison mee, for I
Except you enthrall mee, never shall be free,
Nor ever chast, except you ravish mee."

—John Donne

For more: *Daily Prayers for Busy People* by William J. O'Malley

Adjusting to God's Slowness

"Impatience is, as it were, the original sin in the eyes of the Lord. For, to put it in a nutshell, every sin is to be traced back to impatience. I find the origin of impatience in the Devil himself.... When the Spirit of God descends, patience is His inseparable companion. If we fail to welcome it along with the Spirit, will the latter remain within us at all times? As a matter of fact, I rather think the Spirit would not remain at all."

—Tertullian

"Tertullian expounds on a truth we rarely talk about–i.e. God's nature to be patient... ..Tertullian's exhortation on patience keeps me anchored in peace and joy since the realization of goals almost always take much longer than I expect."

—Peter Scazzero

"I am always wary of decisions made hastily. I am always wary of the first decision, that is, the first thing that comes to my mind if I have to make a decision. This is usually the wrong thing. I have to wait and assess, looking deep into myself, taking the necessary time."[79]

—Pope Francis

"God is not bound by time, nor is our story. We desperately want our situation solved. We want resolution. But God unfolds the plot in his own time. It is in our months or years of waiting that our story comes to maturity. It is over a lifetime of stories that he turns our desire toward him."[80]

—Dan Allender

"For examples of patience in suffering, dear brothers and sisters,
look at the prophets who spoke in the name of the Lord."
James 5:10 NLT

- "When the Spirit of God descends, patience is His inseparable companion." Are you a patient person?
- Do you allow for the fact that the realization of goals almost always takes much longer than you expect?

- Are you wary of decisions made hastily? . . . of the "first decision?" What does this look like in your actual experience?
- Do you know how to look deep into yourself so that you act with an awareness of your unconscious motives?
- Is there a spiritual discipline you can devise to help you develop a slower, more aware approach to decision making?

Abba, here it is, yet another reason for me to learn to slow down.

For more: *To Be Told* by Dan Allender

The Mob of Men as a Mob of Kings

"You shall love your crooked neighbour, with your crooked heart."

—W. H. Auden

Saint Francis ". . . honored all men; that is, he not only loved but respected them all. What gave him extraordinary personal power was this: that from the Pope to the beggar, from the sultan of Syria in his pavilion to the ragged robbers crawling out of the wood, there was never a man who looked into those brown burning eyes without being certain Francis Bernardone was really interested in him, in his own inner individual life from cradle to grave; that he himself was being valued and taken seriously. . . . He treated the whole mob of men as a mob of kings."[81]

—G. K. Chesterton

"If we are to love our neighbors, before doing anything else we must see our neighbors. With our imagination as well as our eyes, that is to say like artists, we must see not just their faces but the life behind and within their faces. Here it is love that is the frame we see them in."[82]

—Frederick Buechner

"The first gaze is seldom compassionate. It is too busy weighing and feeling itself: 'How will this affect me?' . . . This leads us to an implosion, a self-preoccupation that cannot enter into communion with the other or the moment. In other words, we

58

first feel our feelings before we can relate to the situation and emotion of the other. Only after God has taught us how to live 'undefended', can we immediately stand with and for the other, and in the present moment. It takes a lot of practice."[83]

—Richard Rohr

"When Jesus landed and saw a large crowd [a mob of men],
he had compassion on them,
because they were like sheep without a shepherd."
Mark 6:34 NIV

- Does awareness of your own "crooked heart" inform your loving?
- Who is the "other" for you–neighbor, spouse, family member, stranger? . . . anyone who is not you?
- Are you aware of the problem of "feeling your feelings" before you relate to the situation of someone else?
- How can you *practice* a gaze where "love is the frame" in which you see others?

Abba, help me learn to look with compassion on others so that I honor, love and respect them. Disarm me, undefend me, unpreoccupy me with myself.

For more: *Saint Francis of Assisi* by G. K. Chesterton

From Loneliness to Solitude

"Fellowship with Christ is a table only for two–set in the wilderness. Inwardness is not a gaudy party, but the meeting of lovers in the lonely desert of the human heart. There, where all life and fellowship can hold no more than two, we sit together and he speaks as much as we, and even when both of us say nothing there is our welded oneness. And suddenly we see we cannot be complete until his perfect presence joins with ours."[84]

—Calvin Miller

"The priest looked at her sharply. 'You can offer idleness to God,' he said. 'Unemployment, idleness, whatever. To do nothing in someone's presence is a greater compliment than being busy and preoccupied.'"[85]

—Gail Morgan

"To live a spiritual life we must first find the courage to enter into the desert of our loneliness and to change it by gentle and persistent efforts into a garden of solitude. This requires not only courage but also a strong faith. As hard as it is to believe that the dry desolate desert can yield endless varieties of flowers, it is equally hard to imagine that our loneliness is hiding unknown beauty. The movement from loneliness to solitude, however, is the beginning of any spiritual life because it is the movement from the restless sense to the restful spirit, from the outward-reaching cravings to the inward-reaching search, from the fearful clinging to the fearless play."[86]

—Henri Nouwen

"When Jesus is present, all is well, and nothing seems difficult; but when Jesus is absent, everything is hard."

—Thomas a Kempis

"Turn to me and be gracious to me,
for I am lonely and afflicted."
Psalm 25:16 NIV

- Behind your outward religious life, is there a hidden, intimate spiritual life just between you and Christ–where you meet as if "at a table only for two?"

- Are you working, when loneliness overcomes you, to embrace it as a divine guide into a potent solitude, where you are "alone" but "Jesus is present?"

- Have you determined to keep your most intimate life with God a private matter between you and God, and not to demean it by using it to attempt to impress others?

Abba, meet with me in the lonely desert of my human heart. Teach me how to be unbusy and unpreoccupied in your presence, attending to you in love.

For more: *The Table of Inwardness* by Calvin Miller

What Can't Happen in the Group

"The intrigue of the table in Psalm 23 has marked my life as a pastor. The metaphor mixes itself in glory. The shepherd becomes the sheep and God becomes the shepherd. There is no flock. There are only two. The shepherd and his love walk along and uninterrupted from the pleasant fields through the threatening chasm and back again. Their glory is not the path they walk but their togetherness. And how do we come to the table in the wilderness? Exactly as we would to any other table—hungry. Our hunger is for him whom we really can never know fully in a group, no matter how religious that group is."[87]

—Calvin Miller

"He lays no great burden upon us—a little remembrance of him from time to time, a little adoration; sometimes to pray for his grace, sometimes to offer him your sorrows, sometimes to return him thanks for the benefits he has bestowed upon you and is still bestowing in the midst of your troubles. He asks you to console yourself with him the oftenest you can. Lift up your heart to him even at your meals, or when you are in company—the least little remembrance will always be acceptable to him. You need not cry very loud: he is nearer to us than we think. To be with God, there is no need to be continually in church."[88]

—Brother Lawrence

"The Lord is my shepherd . . .
my cup overflows."
Psalm 23:1b, 5b NIV

- Are you seeking something from God at in the group that you must be alone to find?
- Can you imagine how being "continually in church" could actually be a major hindrance to nearness with God?

- Do you console yourself with God "the oftenest you can?" Have you considered setting specific daily times to recalibrate your relationship with God? . . . to remember who you are to him? . . . to remember to be aware that God is "nearer to you than you think?"

"Amidst the tiredness that overcomes my body and the tensions that linger in my mind, amidst the uncertainties and fears that haunt me in the darkness of the night, let me know your presence, O God, let my soul be alive to your nearness."[89] (John Philip Newell)

For more: *Sounds of the Eternal* by John Philip Newell

Take the Trouble to See, Then Love

"Love springs from awareness. It is only inasmuch as you see persons as they really are here and now and not as they are in your memory or your desire or in your imagination or projection that you can truly love them; otherwise it is not the people that you love but the idea that you have formed of them. Therefore, the first act of love is to see this person. . . . And this involves the enormous discipline of dropping your desires, your prejudices, your memories, your projections, your selective way of looking. . . . When you set out to serve someone whom you have not taken the trouble to see, are you meeting that person's need or your own? So the first ingredient of love is to really see the other. The second ingredient is equally important: to see yourself, to ruthlessly flash the light of awareness on your motives, your emotions, your needs, your dishonesty, your self-seeking, your tendency to control and manipulate. This means calling things by their names, no matter how painful the discovery and the consequences. If you achieve this kind of awareness of the other and yourself, you will know what love is."

—Anthony de Mello[90]

"One of the Pharisees asked Jesus to have dinner with him, so Jesus went to his home and sat down to eat. When a certain immoral woman from that city heard he was eating there, she brought a beautiful alabaster jar filled with expensive perfume. Then she knelt behind him at his feet, weeping. Her tears fell on his feet, and she wiped them off with her hair. Then she kept

kissing his feet and putting perfume on them. When the Pharisee who had invited him saw this, he said to himself, 'If this man were a prophet, he would know what kind of woman is touching him. She's a sinner!'"
Luke 7:36–39 NLT

"Simon the Pharisee did not really see the sinful woman as a human being loved by God. He saw a sinner, an interruption, a person without a right to be at the dinner table. Jesus saw her differently."[91]

—Peter Scazzero

- Think about it, how would you have seen her?
- How can you see yourself and others without bias or illusion?"

Abba, open my eyes to reality.

More: *Emotionally Healthy Spirituality Day by Day* by Peter Scazzero

---

Love With Your Listening

"Listening is an attitude of the heart, a genuine desire to be with another which both attracts and heals."[92]

—J. Isham

"To listen is very hard, because it asks of us so much interior stability that we no longer need to prove ourselves by speeches, arguments, statements, or declarations. True listeners no longer have an inner need to make their presence known. They are free to receive, to welcome, to accept. Listening is much more than allowing another to talk while waiting for a chance to respond. Listening is paying full attention to others and welcoming them into our very beings. The beauty of listening is that, those who are listened to start feeling accepted, start taking their words more seriously and discovering their own true selves. Listening is a form of spiritual hospitality by which you invite strangers to become friends, to get to know their inner selves more fully, and even to dare to be silent with you."[93]

—Henri Nouwen

"You must all be quick to listen,
slow to speak and slow to get angry. . . .
If you claim to be religious
but don't control your tongue,
you are fooling yourself,
and your religion is worthless."
James 1:19b, 26 NIV

- Do you have a strong sense of inner stability that frees you from the need to explain, defend or interpret yourself to others? How could you develop that?

- How often, if ever, do you have a conversation where you don't feel the need "to make your presence known?" What would be the point of that anyway?

- Loving listening is a form of "spiritual hospitality." No wonder then that James says it's a test of our religion. How can you make a plan for upcoming conversations, to extend loving hospitality more effectively?

Abba, help me today to be quick to listen and slow to speak. Help me to receive, welcome and accept what others have to give instead of striving to make my presence known. I ask that people I meet today would feel accepted by me, and by you–valued, heard and loved.

For more: *Bread for the Journey* by Henri Nouwen

Detaching Religion from Power and Money

"Jesus turns with sympathy and compassion to all those to whom no one else turns; the weak, sick, neglected, social rejects. People were and are always glad to pass these sorts by ....And the devout monks of Qumran ...excluded from the very beginning certain groups of men: 'No madmen, or lunatic, or simpleton, or fool, no blind man, or maimed, or lame, or deaf man, and no minor, shall enter into the Community ....' Jesus does not turn away from any of these ...but draws them to himself ...."[94]

—Hans Küng

"We see in the Gospels that it's the lame, the poor, the blind, the prostitutes, the drunkards, the tax collectors, the sinners, the outsiders, and the foreigners who tend to follow Jesus. It is those on the inside and the top who crucify him (elders, chief priests, teachers of the Law, and Roman occupiers). Shouldn't that tell us something really important about perspective? Every viewpoint is a view from a point, and we need to critique our own perspective and privilege if we are to see truth.... Once Christianity became the established religion of the Roman Empire (313), we largely stopped reading the Bible from the side of the poor and the oppressed. We read it from the side of the political establishment and, I am sorry to say, from the priesthood side ... instead of from the side of people hungry for justice and truth. No wonder Jesus said, 'I did not come for the healthy but for the sick' (Mark 2:17). This priority has the power to constantly detach religion from its common marriage to power, money, and self-importance." [95]

—Richard Rohr

"If you show special attention to the man wearing fine clothes and say, 'Here's a good seat for you,' but say to the poor man, 'You stand there' ... have you not discriminated among yourselves and become judges with evil thoughts?"
James 2:3, 4 NIV

- Is anyone in your church given more honor, attention, or influence because of wealth or status?
- Will you support Jesus's agenda to "detach religion from its common marriage to power and money?"
- Are you aware of your "view from a point?"

Abba, make me aware of my prejudices.

For more: *Everything Belongs* by Richard Rohr

Where We Expect God Least, There He Comes

"Once they have seen him in a stable, they can never be sure where he will appear or to what lengths he will go or to what ludicrous depths of self-humiliation he will descend in his wild pursuit of man. If holiness and the awful power and majesty of God were present in this least auspicious of all events, this birth of a peasant's child, then there is no place or time so lowly and earthbound but that holiness can be present there too. And this means ... [there is] no place where we are safe from his power to break in two and recreate the human heart because it is just where he seems most helpless that he is most strong, and just where we least expect him that he comes most fully."[96]

—Frederick Buechner

"If everyone were holy and handsome, with 'alter Christus' shining in neon lighting from them, it would be easy to see Christ in everyone. If Mary had appeared in Bethlehem clothed, as St. John says, with the sun, a crown of twelve stars on her head and the moon under her feet, then people would have fought to make room for her. But that was not God's way for her nor is it Christ's way for Himself now when He is disguised under every type of humanity that treads the earth."[97]

—Dorothy Day

"He was despised,
and we held him in low esteem."
Isaiah 53:3 NIV

- Do you have God figured out? Where do you least expect God to come?

- Are you at least sure it's not in "that person"–maybe because they're poor, dirty, uneducated, powerless?

- It's in weak people and inauspicious situations God is often most strong. Are you weak, even tragically flawed? Are you in a hopeless situation? Doesn't that actually make your life more likely as a staging ground for some work of God? Can you think about your life in that way?

Abba, I want to learn to expect you not only there but *here*, not only then, but *now*, not only for them, but for *me*. I admit I'm an unlikely candidate who seems likely to fail. Help me therefore all the more to look with expectation for your coming in my life.

For more: *Secrets in the Dark* by Frederick Buechner

Detachment from the Insatiable Self

"I know it takes time to develop a life of prayer; set-aside, disciplined, deliberate time. It isn't accomplished on the run. . . . I know I can't be busy and pray at the same time. I can be active and pray; I can work and pray; but I cannot be busy and pray. I cannot be inwardly rushed, distracted or dispersed. In order to pray I have to be paying more attention to God than to what people are saying to me; to God than to my clamoring ego. Usually, for that to happen there must be a deliberate withdrawal from the noise of the day, a disciplined detachment from the insatiable self."[98]

—Eugene Peterson

"Worship is the strategy by which we interrupt our preoccupation with ourselves and attend to the presence of God. [It's the] time and place that we assign for deliberate attentiveness to God . . . because our self-importance is so insidiously relentless that if we don't deliberately interrupt ourselves regularly, we have no chance of attending to him at all at other times and in other places."[99]

—Eugene Peterson

"I have set the LORD continually before me."
Psalm 16:a NASB

- Are you pursuing a life with God while you're on the run? . . . while you're busy, inwardly rushed, or distracted? If so, is that satisfying your thirst for God?

- It's been said, that if you don't have a plan for your ego, your ego has a plan for you. Do you have a plan for dealing with your "clamoring ego"–for detaching from your "insatiable self?"
- Can you interrupt whatever you're doing now and take a few minutes to attend to the presence of God?

Abba, help me to leave spaces to hear from you in each day, to learn to quiet the competing noise within, and to be aware of your presence in every event, every relationship, every space of the day.

For more: *The Contemplative Pastor* by Eugene Peterson

The Never-ending Need For Applause

"Vast amounts of human behavior, though painstakingly disguised, are simply attempts at showing off.... If we begin listening for these kinds of comments, we will discover that attempting to control the way others think of us is one of the primary uses we put words to in contemporary society. Human conversation is largely an endless attempt to convince others that we are more assertive or clever or gentle or successful than they might think if we did not carefully educate them."[100]

—John Ortberg

"The more insecure, doubtful, and lonely we are, the greater our need for popularity and praise. Sadly ... the more praise we receive, the more we desire. The hunger for human acceptance is like a bottomless barrel.... The search for spectacular glitter is an expression of doubt in God's complete and unconditional acceptance of us. It is indeed putting God to the test. It is saying: 'I am not sure that you really care, that you really love me, that you really consider me worthwhile. I will give you chance to show it by soothing my inner fears with human praise and by alleviating my sense of worthlessness by human applause.... The ... experience of God's acceptance frees us from our needy self and thus creates new space where we can pay selfless attention to others. This new freedom in Christ allows us to move in the world uninhibited by our compulsions ...."[101]

—Henri Nouwen

"Therefore each of you must put off falsehood
and speak truthfully to your neighbor ...."
Ephesians 4:25 NIV

- How much does it matter to you what other people think of you?
- In conversation or on social media, do you work hard to cause people to see you in a certain way? What does your answer say about you?
- What would it look like if you stopped trying to "carefully educate" others so they would think well of you? Can you name several things that would change?

Abba, you are enough for me. You suffice. I only really need to please you. Help me to remember this in the midst of all the temptations to do otherwise.

For more: *The Life You've Always Wanted* by John Ortberg

Sitting Down "On the Inside"

"To rest is to give up on the already exhausted will as the prime motivator of endeavor, with its endless outward need to reward itself through established goals. To rest is to give up on worrying and fretting and the sense that there is something wrong with the world unless we are there to put it right .... We are rested when we let things alone and let ourselves alone, to do what we do best, breathe as the body intended us to breathe, to walk as we were meant to walk, to live with the rhythm of a house and a home, giving and taking through cooking and cleaning. When we give and take in this easy foundational way we are closest to the authentic self, and closest to that self when we are most rested. To rest is not self indulgent, to rest is to prepare to give the best of ourselves, and perhaps, most importantly, arrive at a place where we are able to understand what we have already been given."[102]

—David Whyte

"In deference to God, to heart and meaning of his work, there must be from time to time an interruption, a rest, a deliberate non-continuation, a temporal pause, to reflect on God and his work and to participate consciously in the salvation provided by him and to be awaited from him."[103]

—Karl Barth

"Action and contemplation are very close companions; they live together in one house on equal terms; Martha is Mary's sister.... If you separate the two, then you do wrong.... When I am at rest, I accuse myself of neglecting my work; when I am at work, of having disturbed my repose. The only remedy in these uncertainties is prayer; entreating to be shown God's holy will at every moment ...."

—Bernard of Clairvaux

"Truly my soul finds rest in God . . . ."
Psalm 62:1a NIV

- Are you able to work hard, and also to truly rest?
- Do you routinely bring "the best of yourself" to tasks and relationships?
- Do you pause deliberately to "reflect on God and his work" and wait upon him for salvation?

Abba, may my days be characterized by *sitting down on the inside*.[104]
May my soul find deep rest in you.

For more: *Consolations* by David Whyte

Vulnerability as Strength and Solace

"The dropping away of the anxious worried self felt itself like a death itself, a disappearance, a giving away, seen in the laughter of friendship, the vulnerability of happiness felt suddenly as a strength, a solace and a source ...."[105]

—David Whyte

"The gem of inspiration at the heart of L'Arche [a community for people with developmental disabilities] is that mutual relationships with those who are vulnerable open us up to the discovery of our common humanity. In this way, [Jean Vanier] names human imperfection as a gift, and an opportunity. Imperfection and weakness can draw people closer together, for instance in solidarity around someone who has been hurt and needs help. Vulnerability can move others to give more of themselves, or to open up and reveal their own shortcomings. Strength and mastery can be impressive, yet they tend to divide people in competition and the regular disappointment of not measuring up. I am struck by how sharing our weakness and difficulties is more nourishing to others than sharing our qualities and successes... . The weak teach the strong to accept and integrate the weakness and brokenness of their own lives."[106]

—Pamela Cushing quoting Vanier

"Sharing life with marginalized people galvanized Vanier's understanding that to serve others well requires us to move beyond charity and tolerance. He recognized the *hubris* that grows when a helper imagines himself as somehow superior or separate from those he serves. He learned how much better help feels to the person in need when animated by a sense of solidarity and common humanity than help driven merely by a sense of duty."[107]

—Pamela Cushing

"We must help the weak,
remembering the words
the Lord Jesus himself said:
'It is more blessed to give than to receive.'"
Acts 20:3b NIV

- Imagine human weakness and imperfection as a gift or opportunity. Can you welcome your own weaknesses and brokenness as such?
- Can you see how loving solidarity with and care for the poor can help you avoid the pitfall of *hubris*? . . . to remind you that you are just a "homo sapien, standard vintage?" (Ernest Becker)
- Out of your shared weakness, you can "nourish" others. Will you?

Abba, help me move beyond charity and tolerance in my love for others who seem more needy than me.

For more: *Community and Growth* by Jean Vanier

Parenting the Prodigal

"The image here, obviously, is not that of some heavenly General Patton having difficulty tolerating acts of insubordination. Rather, it is the image of the long-suffering parent and, given the roles in child rearing in Israel, it is probably more the image of mother than father. God is pictured as one in great anguish over what the children have done, but her love is such that she cannot let go. Any parent with a prodigal child should know something of what God must feel."[108]

—Terrence Fretheim

"When Israel was a child, I loved him, and out of Egypt I called my son.
But the more they were called, the more they went away from me.
They sacrificed to the Baals and they burned incense to images.
It was I who taught Ephraim to walk, taking them by the arms;
but they did not realize it was I who healed them.
I led them with cords of human kindness, with ties of love.
To them I was like one who lifts a little child to the cheek,
and I bent down to feed them."
Hosea 11:1–4 NIV

"The striking note of Hosea is that, whereas the common human reaction in such a situation would be give up, God's love is such that she cannot let go. The parental pathos is the heart of God! . . . God's Godness is revealed in the way in which,

72

amid all the sorrow and anger, God's salvific purposes remain unclouded and the steadfastness of divine love endures forever. [Abraham] Heschel once again grasps the essential point: 'Over and above the immediate and contingent emotional reaction of the Lord we are informed of an eternal and basic disposition' revealed at the beginning of the passage: 'I loved him' (11:1)."[109]

—Fretheim

- Can you see yourself in Hosea's description of Israel?
- What emotions arise in you when you gaze at "God's Godness" here?
- Can you ask God to give you a love more like his? . . . that doesn't give up? . . . that is motivated with a heart for salvation?

Abba, there is nothing in this world like your love for me. Thank you for your love.

For more: *the Suffering of God* by Terrence Fretheim

The Strongest Force in the Universe

"True spirituality breaks down the walls of our souls and lets in not just heaven, but the whole world."[110]

—John Kirvan

"There are two ways in which a practical moralist may attempt to displace from the human heart its love of the world–either by a demonstration of the world's vanity, so as that the heart shall be prevailed upon simply to withdraw its regards from an object that is not worthy of it; or, by setting forth another object, even God, as more worthy of its attachment, so as that the heart shall be prevailed upon ... to exchange an old affection for a new one. My purpose is to show, that from the constitution of our nature, the former method is altogether incompetent and ineffectual and that the latter method will alone suffice for the rescue and recovery of the heart from the wrong affection that domineers over it."[111]

—Thomas Chalmers

"Christianity is the world's great love religion. If you miss that, you miss its essence and will always end up emphasizing the wrong thing. The heart of its good news is that God comes to us as love, in love, for love, wooing us with love and working our transformation through love.... Love is the strongest force in the universe. Gravity may hold planets in orbit and nuclear force may hold the atom together, but only love has the power to transform persons. Only love can soften a hard heart.... There is nothing more important in life than learning to love and be loved. Jesus elevated love as the goal of spiritual transformation. Psychoanalysts consider it the capstone of psychological growth. Giving and receiving love is at the heart of being human. It is our raison d'être."[112]

—David Benner

"God is love, and all who live in love
live in God,
and God lives in them."
1 John 4:16 NLT

- Do you measure your spiritual maturity by your love? Has loved opened your heart "to the whole world?"
- Hate sin more, or love God more–which approach do you usually hear? . . . do you usually take?
- What do you do on a daily or weekly basis to grow in your love for God? Is it working?

Abba, change everything by your love.

For more: *Surrender to Love* by David G. Benner

February 25   August 25

Waiting For the Water to Settle

"The great irony of my life was that incessant drivenness and constant ambition had produced so little–and then I realized–it was not in spite of the drivenness that I had produced so little, but because of it."

—William Britton

"Waiting patiently in expectation is the foundation of the spiritual life."

—Simone Weil

"God's acquaintance is not made hurriedly. He does not bestow His gifts on the casual or hasty comer and goer. To be much alone with God is the secret of knowing Him and of influence with Him."[113]

—E. M. Bounds

"It is impossible for a believer, no matter what his experience, to keep right with God if he will not take the trouble to spend time with God. Spend plenty of time with Him, let other things go, but don't neglect Him."[114]

—Oswald Chambers

[comparing contemplative prayer and water poured into a basin] "It takes time for the water to settle. Coming to interior stillness requires waiting.... In solitary silence we listen with great attentiveness to the voice that calls us the beloved. God speaks to the deepest strata of our souls, into our self-hatred and shame, our narcissism, and takes us through the night into the daylight of His truth ...."[115]

—Brennan Manning

"Let all that I am wait quietly before God,
for my hope is in him.
He alone is my rock and my salvation,
my fortress where I will not be shaken."
Psalm 62:5, 6 NLT

- If God really loves you, why would God make you wait? Is God waiting for something from you?

- When you meet with God, are you taking enough time for "the water to settle?"

- Could hurry in your life be sabotaging your flourishing? . . . God's work in you?

Abba, I don't want to hurry through my days, or in my relationships. Help me every day to wait patiently to learn what you have for me and my world.

For more: *Power Through Prayer* by E. M. Bounds

Sniffing Out Wrong in the Neighborhood

"Anger is a most useful diagnostic tool. When anger erupts in us it is a signal that something is wrong. Something isn't working right. There is evil or incompetence or stupidity lurking about. Anger is our sixth sense for sniffing out wrong in the neighborhood. What anger fails to do, though, is to tell us whether the wrong is outside or inside us. We usually begin by assuming that the wrong is outside us—our spouse, or our child, or God has done something wrong, and we are angry. But when we track the anger carefully, we often find it leads to wrong within us—wrong information, inadequate understanding, underdeveloped heart."[116]

—Eugene Peterson

"Many well-meaning people cannot succeed in being kind because they are too rushed to get things done. Haste has worry, fear, and anger as close associates; it is a deadly enemy of kindness, and hence of love."[117]

—Dallas Willard

"If you would pray, and worthily, lose the shabby self-concern and your habitual defensiveness. Endure all things unmoved, for the sake of prayer.... The one who makes note of injuries and still expects to pray may as well gather water to store it in a bucket full of holes.... No one who loves true prayer and still gives way to anger or resentment can be protected from the appearance of insanity. For he resembles a man who tears at his eyes in order to see more clearly."[118]

—Scott Cairns

"In your anger do not sin."
Ephesians 4:26 NIV

- Does your anger function more as a gift ("a diagnostic tool") or a trigger for sin (blaming, defending, judging, acting out)?
- When anger rises up in you, can you look at yourself first and ask that often invaluable question, "What does my response say about me?"

- Can you trust God in the midst of your anger, and make space for him to work in you and your situation?

Abba, may I respond less often with anger and more often with humility and love as I critique my motives and remember the limitations of my perspective. I trust in you all day long. Save me from myself.

For more: *Under the Unpredictable Plant* by Eugene Peterson

Reigning in a Critical Spirit

"It is a good discipline to wonder in each new situation if people wouldn't be better served by our silence than by our words."[119]

—Henri Nouwen

"Often we combat our evil thoughts most effectively if we absolutely refuse to allow them to be expressed in words. It is certain that the spirit of self-justification can be overcome only by the Spirit of grace; nevertheless, isolated thoughts of judgment can be curbed and smothered by never allowing them the right to be uttered.... *Thus it must be a decisive rule of every Christian fellowship that each individual is prohibited from saying much that occurs to him.*"[120]

—Dietrich Bonhoeffer

"If we could control our tongues,
we would be perfect and could also control ourselves in every other way.
We can make a large horse go wherever we want by means of a small bit in
its mouth.
And a small rudder makes a huge ship turn wherever the pilot chooses to go,
even though the winds are strong.
In the same way, the tongue is a small thing that makes grand speeches. . . .
People can tame all kinds of animals, birds, reptiles, and fish, but no one can
tame the tongue. It is restless and evil, full of deadly poison.
Sometimes it praises our Lord and Father,
and sometimes it curses those who have been made in the image of God.
And so blessing and cursing come pouring out of the same mouth.

Surely, my brothers and sisters, this is not right!"
James 3:2–10 NLT

- Think about your conversations in "the fellowship." Do you tend to say whatever occurs to you? Can you determine never to speak in defense of yourself or in judgment of another?

- Imagine that your congregation had a "decisive rule . . . that each individual is prohibited from saying much that occurs to him?" Could you keep it?

- Both James and Bonhoeffer admit the difficulty of controlling our words, and Bonhoeffer reminds us we are dependent upon the Spirit–as always. Even so, both men also insist that we should simply eliminate certain kinds of words. Do you have "rules" for your words?

Abba, surround my words in silence. Inform my words with love.

For more: *Life Together* by Dietrich Bonhoeffer

Exquisitely Tender Jesus

"This passage of exquisite tenderness [Matthew 9:36] offers a remarkable glimpse into the human soul of Jesus. It tells how He feels about human beings. It reveals His way of looking out on the world, His nonjudgmental attitude toward people who were *looking for love in wrong places and seeking happiness in wrong pursuits.*"[121]

—Brennan Manning

"When he saw the crowds, he had compassion on them because they were confused and helpless, like sheep without a shepherd."
Matthew 9:36 NLT

"Whenever I allow anything but tenderness and compassion to dictate my response to life–be it self-righteous anger, moralizing, defensiveness, the pressing need to change others, carping criticism, frustration at others' blindness, a sense of spiritual superiority, a gnawing hunger of vindication–I am alienated from my true self. My identity as Abba's child becomes ambiguous, tentative, and confused."[122]

—Brennan Manning

"Good and upright is the LORD,
therefore he instructs sinners in his ways."
Psalm 25:8 NIV

"We're so used to a God–a 'one-false-move God' and so we're not really accustomed to the 'no-matter-whatness' of God–to the God who's just plain old too busy loving us to be disappointed in us. That is, I think, the hardest thing to believe, but everybody in this space knows it's the truest thing you can say about God."[123]

—Gregory Boyle

- When you look upon a crowd–at the mall, a concert, the DMV, a school-board meeting, a block party, a football game, on a city street or in a church service–do you do so with "exquisite tenderness?" If not, what happens instead? Why does that happen?

- Is your response to people often negative (Manning's list)? If so, can you feel that alienating you from your identity as Abba's child?

- What kind of practice can you adopt that would help you increase in "tenderness and compassion?" (For instance, on a busy street, could you look at all the passing faces, and remind yourself how each individual is loved by Jesus Christ?)

Abba, thank you for the example of your son. May his love for me, and my love for him, inform my response to others. Help me practice exquisite tenderness.

For more: *Abba's Child* by Brennan Manning

When Prayer Is "Impossible"

"Prayer and love are learned in the hour when prayer has become impossible and your heart has turned to stone. If you have never had any distractions you don't know how to pray. For the secret of prayer is a hunger for God and for the vision of God, a hunger that lies far deeper than the level of language or affection. And a man whose memory and imagination are persecuting him with a crowd of useless or even evil thoughts and images may sometimes be forced to pray far better, in the depths of his murdered heart, than one whose mind is swimming with clear concepts and brilliant purposes and easy acts of love."[124]

—Thomas Merton

> "Open my lips, LORD,
> and my mouth will declare your praise.
> You do not delight in sacrifice, or I would bring it;
> you do not take pleasure in burnt offerings.
> My sacrifice, O God, is a broken spirit;
> a broken and contrite heart
> you, God, will not despise."
> Psalm 51:15–17 NIV

- Merton's words convey hope. He says when we are tempted to quit in prayer because of cold hearts or evil thoughts–we should persist. He says, in fact, that it's then we may "pray far better."

- Can you continue to pray when your heart feels dead? . . . when your prayer is interrupted over and over again with sinful thoughts?

- What is to be gained or learned by persisting in these times? . . . and what is to be lost by quitting?

"Let me not be afraid to linger here is your presence with all my humanity exposed. For you are God–you are not surprised by my frailties, my continuous failures."[125] (Teresa of Avila)

For more: *Seeds of Contemplation* by Thomas Merton

Marriage and Spiritual Formation

"There is something deeply flawed in me that separates me from the God who wills my salvation; that 'something' seems to be located in and around my will.... The relation of God's will and my will ... is *the* question. The way we answer it shapes our humanity in every dimension.... A few years into marriage, I was surprised to find myself at the center of what has turned out to be the richest experience yet in my will and God's will. I had supposed when I entered marriage that it was mostly about sexuality, domesticity, companionship, and children. The surprise was that I was in a graduate school for spirituality–prayer and God–with daily assignments and frequent exams in matters of the will."[126]

—Eugene Peterson

"Everything helps me to God."

—Jean-Pierre de Caussade

"I don't really understand myself, for I want to do what is right,
but I don't do it. Instead, I do what I hate."
Romans 7:15 NLT

"My Father! If it is possible, let this cup of suffering be taken away from me.
Yet I want your will to be done, not mine."
Matthew 26:39b NLT

- You don't have to attend seminary for training in the life of faith. If you're married, that is your "graduate school for spirituality." Do you think about marriage that way?

- There is no hiding in marriage, so disappointing behavior, annoying habits and character flaws are obvious. Our divine "assignment" is loving without restraint, forgiving with abandon, returning good for evil–and other terribly difficult things. Are you accepting these "daily assignments?" What are the specifics of what this looks like in your home?

- "Everything helps me to God." You don't have to be married. God will use something–life with a spouse, alone, with children, with parents, in church, in a workplace–as your "school for spirituality." Look around. How is God working to shape you at the very heart of who you are in whatever school you're in?

Abba, may I submit to your training of me, no matter how hard.

For more: *The Contemplative Pastor* by Eugene Peterson

Restlessness and Grace

"A score of years ago a friend placed in my hand a book called *True Peace*. ... It had but one thought–that God was waiting in the depths of my being to talk to me if I would only get still enough to hear His voice. I thought this would be a very easy matter, and so began to get still. But I had no sooner commenced than a perfect pandemonium of voices reached my ear, a thousand clamoring notes from without and within, until I could hear nothing but their noise and din. ... It seemed necessary for me to listen to some of them and to answer some of them; but God said, 'Be still and know that I am God.' Then came the concert of thoughts for tomorrow, and its duties and cares; but He said, 'Be still.' And as I listened ... and shut my ear to every sound, I found after a while that when the other noises ceased ... there was a still small voice in the depths of my being that began to speak with an inexpressible tenderness, power and comfort. ... It became to me the voice of prayer, the voice of wisdom, the voice of duty, and I did not need to think so hard, or pray so hard, or trust so hard; but that 'still small voice' of the Holy Spirit in my heart was God's prayer in my secret soul, was God's answer to all my questions, was God's life and strength for soul and body, and became the substance of all knowledge, and all prayer and all blessing: for it was the living GOD Himself as my life, my all. It is thus that our spirit drinks in the life of our risen Lord and we go forth to life's conflicts and duties like a flower that has drunk in, through the shades of night, the cool and crystal drops of dew. But as *dew never falls on a stormy night*, so the dews of His grace never come to the restless soul."[127]

—A. B. Simpson

"Be still, and know that I am God!"
Psalm 46:10a NLT

- Do you think of "being still" as optional?
- Is God waiting for you to "get still enough to hear his voice?"
- How can you actually practice "stillness?"

Abba, help.

An Art to Waiting Well

"One step taken in surrender to God is better than a journey across the ocean without it."

—Meister Eckhart

"…waiting for clarity of call, waiting until God shows us the next right step, waiting for the Spirit to go ahead of us to light the way. When it's not clear to us what is invited, we wait, watch and pray. And we trust that sometimes the Spirit is working just fine without us, as much as we'd like to help. There's an art to the waiting, I've learned. Wait expectantly without expectations. Watch for what wants to unfold now, not for what I want to unfold. Pray that I may see what is being invited without imposing what I think would be the best solution. Waiting is not passive and disinterested. Waiting is not turning away. Waiting is an active, prayerful stance, a time of alert openness, a space of listening from mind-in-heart.… Sometimes the waiting can be especially difficult. Some are longing for clarity for a personal next step. Some are waiting for justice to be served. Others wait for an end to violence in their land or for a future where their families are not hungry or homeless or despised… . Sometimes our desire to help end the pain is so great that we cannot conceive of anything except action. Yet we know that to everything there is a season. It requires deep wisdom and infinite courage to wait until the right action that is ours to do is given to us. It is a struggle to allow ourselves to listen with our whole heart for God's time rather than respond to our own impulse. Sometimes I wish that I could get on with planting the garden–literally and metaphorically–without the quiet winter when the earthworms and microbes ready the soil. And still I know that I cannot *make* things grow; I can only do my small part and wait while earth and sky do the rest."[128]

—Leah Rampy

"I wait for the LORD,
my whole being waits,

83

and in his word I put my hope."
Psalm 130:5 NLT

- Why is it so hard to wait well?
- Are you sensitive to "triggers" that indicate you should wait?
- What have you lost by not waiting well?

Abba, help me to wait.

For more: *Selected Writings* by Meister Eckhart

Disappointed With Church

"Every time I move to a new community, I find a church close by and join it—committing myself to worship and work with that company of God's people. I've never been anything other than disappointed. Everyone turns out to be biblical, through and through: murmurers, complainers, the faithless, the inconstant, those plagued with doubt and riddled with sin, boring moralizers, glamorous secularizers. Every once in a while a shaft of blazing beauty seems to break out of nowhere and illuminate these companies, and then I see what my sin-dulled eyes had missed: Word of God-shaped, Holy Spirit-created lives of sacrificial humility, incredible courage, heroic virtue, holy praise, joyful suffering, constant prayer, persevering obedience."[129]

—Eugene Peterson

"We shall, as we ripen in grace, have greater sweetness towards our fellow Christians. Bitter-spirited Christians may know a great deal, but they are immature. Those who are quick to censure may be very acute in judgment, but they are as yet very immature in heart. He who grows in grace remembers that he is but dust, and he therefore does not expect his fellow Christians to be anything more; he overlooks ten thousand of their faults, because he knows his God overlooks twenty thousand in his own case. He does not expect perfection in the creature, and, therefore, he is not disappointed when he does not find it.... I know we who are young beginners in grace think ourselves qualified to reform the whole Christian church. We drag her before us, and condemn her straightway; but when our virtues become more mature, I trust we shall not be more tolerant of evil, but we shall be more tolerant of infirmity, more hopeful for the people of God, and certainly less arrogant in our criticisms."

—Charles H. Spurgeon

"Behold, My Servant, whom I uphold;
My chosen one in whom My soul delights . . .
A bruised reed he will not break,
and a dimly burning wick he will not extinguish."
Isaiah 42:3 NASB

- Are you disappointed with behavior in your church? . . . the church at large?
- Have you also witnessed wonderful, amazing virtues in each?
- How can you work on being "more tolerant of infirmity?"

Abba, may I be more tolerant of infirmity in the church, more hopeful, more aware of my own twenty thousand faults.

For more: *Leap Over a Wall* by Eugene Peterson

March 6   September 3

Sit Down and Let the Dust Settle Around You

"When we're in full possession of our powers—our education complete, our careers in full swing, people admiring us and prodding us onward—it's hard not to imagine that we're at the beginning, center, and end of the world, or at least of that part of the world in which we're placed. At these moments we need . . . to quit whatever we're doing and sit down. . . . When we sit down, the dust raised by our furious activity settles. . . . We become aware of the real world. *God's* world. And what we see leaves us breathless: it's so much larger, so much more full of energy and action than our ego-fueled action, so much clearer and saner than the plans that we had projected."[130]

—Eugene Peterson

"If you do not control your ego, your ego will control you. If you do not have a plan for your ego, your ego will have a plan for you. You can be the master of your ego, or you can be its slave. It's your choice."[131]

—Vincent Roazzi

"Activity and productivity are not the same thing."[132]

—Rick Warren

"Then Jacob awoke from his sleep and said,
'Surely the Lord is in this place, and I wasn't even aware of it!'
But he was also afraid and said, 'What an awesome place this is!
It is none other than the house of God, the very gateway to heaven!'"
Genesis 28:16,17 NLT

- Are you prone to immerse yourself in the "furious" activity around you?
- Are you learning to "sit down" and let the dust settle around you so that your action is guided by reality rather than illusion?
- How much of your activity for God could be misguided "ego-fueled action?"
- Do you have a plan for your ego?

Abba, I will not hurry through the day, with my adrenaline pumping, striving and pushing in a way that makes it impossible for me to be aware of the real world, of what you're doing, of what you want from me. Deliver me from my addiction to motion, activity and supposed progress. Help me in the course of each day, to sit down and let the dust settle around me.

For more: *Crazy Busy* by Kevin DeYoung

A Frantic Stream of Words

"We are so accustomed to relying on words to manage and control others. If we are silent, who will take control? God will take control, but we will never let him take control until we trust him. Silence is intimately related to trust. The tongue is our most powerful weapon of manipulation. A frantic stream of words flows from us because we are in a constant process of adjusting our public image. We fear so deeply what we think other people see in us that we talk in order to straighten out their understanding.... One of the fruits of silence is the freedom to let God be our justifier. We don't need to straighten others out.... God can care for us–'reputation and all.'"[133]

—Richard Foster

"Much that happens in solitude and silence ends up being 'for others'–as paradoxical as that may seem. Our speech patterns are refined by the discipline of silence, because growing self-awareness enables us to choose more truly the words we say. Rather than speech that issues from subconscious needs to impress, to put others in their place, to compete, to control and manipulate, to repay hurt with hurt, we now notice our inner dynamics and choose to speak from a different place, a place of love, trust and true wisdom that God is cultivating within us. Over time we become safer for other seeking souls, because we are able to be with them and the issues they are dealing with without being hooked by our own anxieties and fears. We are comfortable with our humanity, because we have experienced God's love and compassion in that place, and so it becomes very natural for us to extend love and compassion to others in their humanity."[134]

—Ruth Haley Barton

"Better is a handful of quietness
than two hands full of toil
and a striving after wind."
Ecclesiastes 4:6 ESV

- Are you more often quiet and relaxed, or "striving?" Why would quietness be "better?"

- Can you choose silence, allowing God alone to be your justifier?

- Are you increasingly safe for others because you have experienced God's love and compassion in a place of silent solitude?

"Lord, it is nearly midnight and I am waiting for You in the darkness and the great silence." (Thomas Merton)

For more: *Invitation to Solitude and Silence* by Ruth Haley Barton

---

March 8 September 5

The Restless Self Loves Its Illusions

"While teaching, lecturing, and writing about the importance of solitude, inner freedom, and peace of mind, I kept stumbling over my own compulsions and illusions. What was driving me from one book to another, one place to another, one project to another? ... What was turning my vocation to be a witness to God's love into a tiring job? These questions kept intruding themselves into my few unfilled moments and challenging me to face my restless self. Maybe I spoke more about God than with him. Maybe my writing about prayer kept me from a prayerful life. Maybe I was more concerned about the praise of men and women than the love of God. Maybe I was slowly becoming a prisoner of people's expectations instead of a man liberated by divine promises. ... I had succeeded in surrounding myself with so many classes to prepare, lectures to give, articles to finish, people to meet, phone calls to make, and letters to answer, that I had come quite close to believing that I was indispensable... . While complaining about too many demands, I felt uneasy when none were made. While speaking about the burden of letter writing, an empty mailbox made me sad. While fretting about tiring lecture tours, I felt disappointed when there were no invitations. While speaking nostalgically about an empty desk, I feared the day on which that would come true. In short: while desiring to be alone, I was frightened of being left alone. The more I became aware of these paradoxes, the more I started to see how much I had indeed fallen in love with my own compulsions and illusions, and how much I needed to step back and wonder, 'Is there a quiet stream underneath the fluctuating affirmations and rejections of my little world?'"[135]

—Henri Nouwen

"[Jesus] appointed twelve
that they might be with him . . . ."
Mark 3:14 NIV

- Has being a Christian or a minister become a "tiring job?"
- Is your *doing for God* anchored in your *being with God?*
- Nouwen was hampered by illusions. What about you?
- Is there a still point that anchors your life? What is it?

Abba, may my ministry to others flow out of your ministry to me.

For more: *The Genesee Diary* by Henri Nouwen

March 9   September 6

This Parched and Weary Land

"O God, I have tasted Your goodness, and it has both satisfied me and made me thirsty for more. I am painfully conscious of my need of further grace. I am ashamed of my lack of desire. O God, the Triune God, I want to want You; I long to be filled with longing; I thirst to be made more thirsty still. Show me Your glory, I pray, so I may know You indeed. Begin in mercy a new work of love within me. Say to my soul, 'Rise up, my love, my fair one, and come away.' Then give me grace to rise and follow You up from this misty lowland where I have wandered so long."[136]

—A. W. Tozer

"I drank at every vine
The last was like the first.
I came upon no wine
So wonderful as thirst.
I gnawed at every root

I ate of every plant.
I came upon no fruit
So wonderful as want.
Feed the grape and bean
To the vintner and monger;
I will lay down lean
With my thirst and my hunger."

—Edna St. Vincent Millay[137]

"O God, you are my God; I earnestly search for you.
My soul thirsts for you; my whole body longs for you
in this parched and weary land where there is no water."
Psalm 63:1–3 NLT

- Do the words of Tozer, Millay, and King David resonate with you? If so, why?

- Many people are very satisfied with things as they are. Why wouldn't you want to be among them?

- Only God's grace both satisfies our thirst for Him and creates an even deeper thirst for him. This is how our relationship with God is deepened. Can you ask God now to do a new work in you–upsetting your status quo and replacing what may be a sense of satisfaction with unease and deep thirst instead?

Abba, I too am painfully conscious, not only of past time spent wandering (but not wasted) in the lowlands, but also of present time characterized by lack of truly deep thirst for you. Perhaps I'm even frightened, not knowing what to expect. Help me to trust your love and welcome your work of grace in my soul.

For more: *The Pursuit of God* by A. W. Tozer

When You're "Disappearing"

"I can, with one eye squinted, take it all as a blessing."[138]

—Flannery O'Connor

"It might be liberating for us to think of our outward life being informed as much by our losses and disappearances as by our gifted and virtuoso appearances and our marvelous arrivals. As if the foundational invitation being made to us at the core of our continual living and dying is an invitation to participate in the full seasonality of existence. Not just to feel fully here and fully justified in those haloed times when we are growing and becoming, and seen to be becoming, but also, to be just as present and to feel just as much here when we are in the difficult act of disappearing, often against our wills, making way often, for something we cannot as yet comprehend. The great and ancient art form and its daily practice; of living the full seasonal round of life; and a touchstone perhaps, of the ultimate form of human generosity: continually giving ourselves away to see how and in what form we are given back."[139]

—David Whyte

"Soul is our appetite, driving us to eat from the banquet of life. People filled with the hunger of soul take food from every dish before them, whether it be sweet or bitter."

—Matthew Fox

"It is by going down into the abyss that we recover the treasures of life. Where you stumble, there lies your treasure."

—Joseph Campbell

"If you cling to your life, you will lose it,
and if you let your life go, you will save it."
Luke 17:33 NLT

- Are you continually living *and* dying? Do you hear the "foundational invitation" that comes to you there?
- Have losses and limits (perhaps aging) taught you about "disappearing?" . . . about accepting something against your will? . . . something confusing?

- Can you explain what the words of Whyte, Fox, O'Connor, Campbell and Jesus–perhaps all in unison–mean for your life?

"If I have you God, I will want for nothing. You alone suffice."[140]
Abba, work in me to make this my truth.

For more: *Let Nothing Disturb You* by Teresa of Avila

Why We Can't Slow Down

"The one who hurries delays the things of God."

—Vincent de Paul

"Nothing can be more useful to a man than a determination not to be hurried."

—Henry David Thoreau

"Slowing down can be terrifying because doing nothing productive leaves us feeling vulnerable, emotionally exposed and naked. Overworking hides these feelings of inadequacy or worthlessness, not just from others but also from ourselves. As long as we keep busy, we can outrun that internal voice that says things like:

    I am never good enough.

    I am never safe enough.

    I am never perfect enough.

    I am never extraordinary enough.

    I am never successful enough.

Do you recognize that voice? Far too many of us use workaholism to run from these shaming messages.... Sadly, I've discovered that this distorted concept of identity can be found from Asia to Latin America, from North America to Africa, from the Middle East to Europe."[141]

—Peter Scazzero

"An active life is a good and laudable thing. Action has its seasons too–one of which is inaction."[142]

—Andréana Lefton

> *"This is what the Sovereign Lord, the Holy One of Israel, says:*
> *'In repentance and rest is your salvation,*
> *in quietness and trust is your strength,*
> *but you would have none of it.'"*
> Isaiah 30:15b NIV

- Do you keep busy to outrun that internal voice that shames you with charges that you're not good enough? Are you good enough?
- Does doing nothing productive leave you feeling "vulnerable, emotionally exposed and naked?" Could you feeling that way be something God will use?
- What do you miss when *you* refuse "quietness and trust?"

Abba, help me listen to your loving voice, not those internal voices that sidetrack and shame me.

For more: *Praying with Vincent de Paul* by Thomas McKenna

A Divine Face . . . Streaked With Tears

"Suffering is unbearable if you aren't certain that God is for you and with you."[143]

—Tim Keller

"Although I cannot learn from [Jesus] why a particular bad thing occurs, I can learn how God feels about it. Jesus gives God a face, and that face is streaked with tears. Whenever I read straight through the Bible, a huge difference between the Old and New Testaments comes to light. In the OT I can find many expressions of doubt and disappointment. Whole books–Jeremiah, Habakkuk, Job–center on the theme. Almost half of the psalms have a dark, brooding tone about them. In striking contrast, the New Testament Epistles contain little of this type of anguish. The problem of pain has surely not gone away: James 1, Romans 5 and 8, the entire book of 1 Peter, and much of Revelation deal with the subject in detail. Nevertheless, nowhere do I find the piercing question *Does God Care?* I see nothing resembling the accusation of Psalm 77: 'Has God forgotten to be merciful?' The reason for the change, I believe, is that Jesus answered that question for the witnesses who wrote the Epistles. In Jesus, God presents a face. Anyone who wonders how God feels about suffering on this groaning planet need only look at that face. James, Peter, and John had followed Jesus long enough for his facial expressions to be permanently etched on their minds. By watching Jesus respond to a hemorrhaging woman, a grieving centurion, a widow's dead son, an epileptic boy, an old blind man, they learned how God felt about suffering. By no means did Jesus solve the 'problem of pain'—he healed only a few in one small corner of the globe— but he did provide an answer to the question, *Does God care?*"[144]

—Philip Yancey

"Christ suffered for you . . . ."
1 Peter 2:21b NIV

- Is your understanding of the invisible God shaped by your understanding of the flesh-and-blood person of Jesus? If so, how?
- A big part of "the problem of pain" is feeling forgotten or forsaken by God. Does remembering Jesus strengthen you against such feelings, even in the worst of times?
- What words of comfort would you offer a suffering friend?

Abba, what a revelation is Jesus your son. Thank you for him.

For more: *The Bible Jesus Read* by Philip Yancey

A Dialogue of Love That Never Stops

"This is the real end of meditation—it teaches you how to become aware of the presence of God; and most of all it aims at bringing you to a state of almost constant loving attention to God, and dependence on Him."[145]

—Thomas Merton

"I love to penetrate beyond the veil of the soul to this inner sanctuary where we live alone with God. He wants us entirely to himself, and is making there within us a cherished solitude. Listen to everything that is being sung ... in his heart. It is Love, the infinite love that envelops us and desires to give us a share ... in all his blessedness. The whole Blessed Trinity dwells in us, the whole of that mystery which will be our vision in heaven. Let it be our cloister. You tell me that your life is passed there. So is mine. I am 'Elizabeth of the Trinity'—Elizabeth disappearing, losing herself, allowing herself to be invaded by the Three. Let us live for love, always surrendered, immolating ourselves at every moment, by doing God's will without searching for extraordinary things. Then let us make ourselves quite tiny, allowing ourselves to be carried, like a babe in its mother's arms, by him who is our all.... In the morning let us wake in Love. All day long let us surrender ourselves to Love, by doing the will of God, under his gaze, with him, in him, for him alone.... And then, when evening comes, after a dialogue of love that has never stopped in our hearts, let us go to sleep still in love. And if we are aware of any faults, let us simply abandon them to Love, which is a consuming fire ...."[146]

—Elizabeth of the Trinity

"I am my beloved's and my beloved is mine . . . ."
Song of Solomon 6:3 NIV

- Can you imagine giving constant loving attention to God? . . . living a day steadily aware of God's gaze?
- How are you becoming more aware of God's presence in your day?
- Can you simply abandon yourself and your faults to Love?

Abba, before I die, may I experience at least one entire day where a dialogue of love between us never stops.

For more: *Voices of the Saints* by Bert Ghezzi

Political Jesus

"According to New Testament scholars Marcus Borg and John Dominic Crossan, the Triumphal Entry was ... an act of political theater, an anti-imperial demonstration designed to mock the obscene pomp and circumstance of Rome. ... Borg and Crossan argue that *two* processions entered Jerusalem on that first Palm Sunday; Jesus' was not the only Triumphal Entry. Every year, the Roman governor of Judea would ride up to Jerusalem ... to be present in the city for Passover–the Jewish festival that swelled Jerusalem's population from its usual 50,000 to at least 200,000. The governor would come in all of his imperial majesty to remind the Jewish pilgrims that Rome was in charge. They could commemorate an ancient victory against Egypt if they wanted to. But real, present-day resistance (if anyone was daring to consider it) was futile. Pontius Pilate's imperial procession [was] 'A visual panoply of imperial power: cavalry on horses, foot solders, leather armor, helmets, weapons, banners, golden eagles mounted on poles, sun glinting on metal and gold.' ... According to Roman imperial belief, the emperor was not simply the ruler of Rome; he was the Son of God. For the empire's Jewish subjects, Pilate's procession ... was the embodiment of a rival theology. Heresy on horseback. This is the background ... against which we need to frame the Triumphal Entry of Jesus. ... As Pilate clanged and crashed his imperial way into Jerusalem from the west, Jesus approached from the east, looking (by contrast) ragtag and absurd. His was the procession of the ridiculous, the powerless, the explicitly vulnerable. 'What we often call the triumphal entry was actually an anti-imperial, anti-triumphal one, a deliberate lampoon of the conquering emperor entering a city on horseback through gates opened in abject submission.' Elsewhere, Crossan notes that Jesus rode 'the most unthreatening, most un-military mount imaginable: a female nursing donkey with her little colt trotting along beside her.'"[147]

—Debbie Thomas

"They ... went out to meet him, shouting, ...
'Blessed is the king of Israel!'"
John 12:13 NIV

96

- Are you comfortable with this Jesus who mocks and confronts the political powers?

- Imagine the concepts being redefined here: power, foolishness, triumph.

- As a follower of Jesus today, are you comfortable with "speaking truth to power?" . . . public agitating?

Abba, your Son is awesome.

For more: *The Last Week* by Marcus Borg and John Dominic Crossan

---

Your Heart Is Always Revealing Itself

"Sadi of Shiraz tells this story about himself: 'When I was a child I was a pious boy, fervent in prayer and devotion. One night I was keeping vigil with my father, the Holy Koran on my lap. Everyone else in the room began to slumber and soon was sound asleep, so I said to my father, 'None of these sleepers opens his eyes or raises his heart to say his prayers. You would think that there were all dead.' My father replied, 'My beloved son, I would rather you too were asleep like them than slandering.'"[148]

—Anthony de Mello

"Every time you find yourself irritated or angry with someone, the one to look at is not that person but yourself. The question to ask is not, 'What's wrong with this person?' but 'What does this irritation tell me about myself?'"[149]

—de Mello

"Many desert stories speak of judgment as the worst obstacle for a monk. Abba Joseph said to Abba Pastor: 'Tell me how I can become a monk.' The elder replied: 'If you want to have rest here in this life and also in the next, in every conflict with another say, 'Who am I?' and judge no one.'"[150]

—Kathleen Norris

"By judging others, we blind ourselves to our own evil and to the grace which others are just as entitled to as we are."[151]

—Dietrich Bonhoeffer

"A good person produces good things from the treasury of a good heart,
and an evil person produces evil things from the treasury of an evil heart.
What you say flows from what is in your heart."
Luke 6:45 NLT

- What is your response to the story about the Muslim father and son? What would you say is the intended lesson?

- When you become irritated and critical, can you learn to stop and ask, "What does my response tell me about myself?"

- Are you aware of your own evil and how much God has forgiven you? Can you extend that grace to others like yourself who, like you, don't deserve it?

Abba, teach me to judge no one, but when I do, may my irritations with others lead me into regular self-examination, greater self-awareness, and greater compassion.

For more: *The Cost of Discipleship* by Dietrich Bonhoeffer

Coming to a Full Stop For Contemplation

"Once, when I was the only guest one Sunday night at a women's monastery, the sisters invited me to join them in statio, the community's procession into church. The word, which means 'standing' in Latin, is one of the many terms from the Roman Army that ancient Christian monastics adopted for their own purposes. To get into position, to station oneself, to take a stand. To wait in line, in a posture that invites individual watchfulness, to 'recollect' oneself before reentering church.... I didn't realize it at the time, but ... not being able to amble into church on my own to find a choir stall pushed me into recognizing what the sisters already sensed, that Christ is actively present in their worshiping community. Not as a static idea or principle, but a Word made flesh, a listening, active Christ who in the gospels tells us that he prays for us, and who promises to be with us always. Walking slowly into church in that long line of women taught me much about liturgical time and space. I found to my surprise that the entire vespers service had more resonance for me because of the solemn way I had entered into it."[152]

—Kathleen Norris

"In some contemplative circles, a related meaning attaches to 'statio.' Statio refers to the practice of pausing between activities. It may be related to Merton's 'recollecting' of oneself (one's communion with one's soul), or what Richard Foster describes as 'reorienting our lives like a compass needle.' It's simply taking a moment to commit to God whatever has just transpired, and looking to him to be in whatever is next. Such a practice can be very brief, and yet pay big dividends in greater awareness of our ever-present God throughout the day—and all the benefits that accrue from that."

—William Britton

"Enter his gates with thanksgiving
go into his courts with praise"
Psalm 100:4 NLT

- Is your church experience given more resonance because of how you enter into it?
- Do you attempt to "recollect" yourself before the service begins?
- What do you do to be intentionally present to Christ who is also present in the course of a typical day?

Abba, help me to constantly recalibrate my soul for communion with you.

For more: *Amazing Grace* by Kathleen Norris

Our World's Great Rhythms

"I remember one morning when I discovered a cocoon in the bark of a tree just as a butterfly was making a hole in its case and preparing to come out. I waited awhile, but it was too long appearing and I was impatient. I bent over it and breathed on it to warm it. I warmed it as quickly as I could and the miracle began to happen before my eyes, faster than life. The case opened; the butterfly started slowly crawling out, and I shall never forget my horror when I saw how its wings were folded back and crumpled; the wretched butterfly tried with its whole trembling body to unfold them.... It needed to be hatched out patiently and the unfolding of the wings should be a gradual process in the sun. Now it was too late. My breath had forced the butterfly to appear all crumpled, before its time. It struggled desperately and, a few seconds later, died in the palm of my hand.... I realize today that it is a mortal sin to violate the great laws of nature. We should not hurry, we should not be impatient, but we should confidently obey the external rhythm."[153]

—Nikos Kazantzakis

"Most people can and must come to life in their own way and time, and if we try to help them by hastening the process, we end up doing harm.... When we understand that our efforts to help other people can be unhelpful, or worse, we may start to avert our eyes from their struggles and pains, not knowing what to do and embarrassed by our own ineptitude.... Instead of fixing up, or letting down, people who have a problem, we [should] ...stay present to each other ...stifling any impulse to fix each other up. We offer each other support in going where each needs to go, and learning what each needs to learn, at each one's pace ...."[154]

—Parker Palmer

"Everyone should be ... slow to speak ...."
James 1:19 NIV

- Can you resist the urge to "fix" someone?
- Can you stay lovingly present rather than averting your eyes?
- Can you trust God and others to do what only they can do?

For more: *A Hidden Wholeness* by Parker Palmer

The Wine We Are Becoming

"We never know the wine we are becoming while we are being crushed like grapes."

—Henri Nouwen

"Most of the Psalms were born in difficulty. Most of the Epistles were written in prisons. Most of the greatest thoughts of the greatest thinkers of all time had to pass through the fire. Bunyan wrote Pilgrim's Progress from jail. Florence Nightingale, too ill to move from her bed, reorganized the hospitals of England. Semi paralyzed and under the constant menace of apoplexy, Pasteur was tireless in his attack on disease. During the greater part of his life, American historian Francis Parkman suffered so acutely that he could not work for more than five minutes as a time. His eyesight was so wretched that he could scrawl only a few gigantic words on a manuscript, yet he contrived to write twenty magnificent volumes of history. Sometimes it seems that when God is about to make preeminent use of a man, he puts him through the fire."[155]

—Tim Hansel

"Contradictions, sickness, scruples, spiritual aridity, and all the inner and outward torments are the chisel with which God carves his statues for paradise."[156]

—Alphonsus Liguori

"Character cannot be developed in ease and quiet. Only through experience of trial and suffering can the soul be strengthened, vision cleared, ambition inspired, and success achieved."

—Helen Keller

"And I saw the river over which every soul must pass to reach the kingdom of heaven and the name of that river was suffering–and I saw the boat which carries souls across the river and the name of the boat was love."

—Saint John of the Cross

"It was fitting for Him for whom are all things,
and through whom are all things,
in bringing many sons to glory, to perfect the author of their salvation
through sufferings."
Hebrews 2:10 NASB

- Think of people you know and all the reasons that people suffer. Do you think you can somehow escape suffering?
- Jesus suffered in order to be perfected. Some things can only be accomplished by suffering. Can you embrace suffering in your life as not only inescapable, but necessary–even good?
- Do you see your life as a good life, even if you are being "crushed like grapes?"

Abba, thank you for the boat of your love that carries me across the river of suffering.

For more: *You Gotta Keep Dancin'* by Tim Hansel

"Slow Jesus"

"Jesus moved slowly, not striving or rushing. He patiently waited through his adolescent and young adult years to reveal himself as the Messiah. Even then, he did not rush to be recognized. He waited patiently for his Father's timing during his short ministry. Why is it then that we hate 'slow' when God appears to delight in it?"[157]

—Peter Scazzero

"Jesus walked a lot.... This gave him time to see things. If he had been moving more quickly–even to reach more people–these things might have become a blur to him. Because he was moving slowly, they came into focus for him, just as he came into focus for them.... While many of his present-day admirers pay close attention to what he said and did, they pay less attention to the pace at which he did it."[158]

—Barbara Brown Taylor

"Jesus' brothers said to him, 'Leave Galilee and go to Judea,
so that your disciples there may see the works you do.
No one who wants to become a public figure acts in secret.
Since you are doing these things, show yourself to the world.'
. . . Jesus told them, 'My time is not yet here.'"
John 7:3–4, 8 NIV

- Dallas Willard famously remarked that the best word to characterize Jesus was "relaxed." Jesus ministered under a microscope and the shadow of his violent death. No one really understood him. The power brokers of his day eventually all turned on him. It was in this context that he was "relaxed." What does that reveal about him?

- And yet, as his followers, we seem to "hate slow." We *don't* relax. Do you hate slow? Can you relax? What do your answers reveal about you?

- What is one way you could slow down for the next few days?

"Lord, grant me the grace to do one thing at a time today, without rushing or hurrying. Help me to savor the sacred in all I do, be it large or small. By the Holy Spirit within me, empower me to pause today as I move from one activity to the next."[159] (Scazzero)

Emotionally Healthy Spirituality Day by Day by Peter Scazzero

---

Contemplatives in the World

"In all the historic formulations of the Perennial Philosophy it is axiomatic that the end of human life is contemplation . . . that a society is good to the extent that it renders contemplation possible for its members; and that the existence of at least a minority of contemplatives is necessary for the well-being of any society."[160]

—Aldous Huxley

"I used to think of monasteries as hopeless throwbacks to the past, a case of let the last monk or sister standing turn out the lights. Now I look upon them as windows to the future–a future we desperately need in our society. One that stresses community over competition, consensus over conflict, simplicity over consumption, service over self-aggrandizement and quiet over the constant chatter in our lives."[161]

—Judith Valente

"The day consists primarily in prayer.... We are contemplatives who live in the midst of the world.... If we were not in constant union with God, it would be impossible for us to endure the sacrifices that are required to live among the destitute."[162]

—Mother Teresa

"In repentance and rest is your salvation,
in quietness and trust is your strength,
but you would have none of it."
Isaiah 30:15b NIV

- Do you see how contemplatives are necessary for the well-being of any society? Do you have any in your life from whom to learn?

- Can you imagine a community that stresses "community over competition, consensus over conflict, simplicity over consumption, service over self-aggrandizement and quiet over the constant chatter in our lives?" Shouldn't that be the church?

- Does your church regularly call its members to these values? Do you practice any of them?

- Like many others, Mother Teresa insisted that service to others must be undergirded by a contemplative lifestyle. Does what you do for God flow out of a practice of quietness and trust where you are strengthened by God's presence?

Abba, may I be a contemplative in this world, practicing these ancient values, for my good, and the good of my world.

For more: *Atchison Blue* by Judith Valente

Living Simply in the Valley of Malls

"Each of us needs to withdraw from the cares which will not withdraw from us."[163]

—Maya Angelou

"'What do I need?' is simplicity's fundamental question, a question that rubs against our natural proclivity for acquiring things, a questions few of us feel ready to address. America's favorite weekend activity is not participating in sports, gardening, hiking, reading, visiting with friends and neighbors. It's shopping. More often impelled by acquisitiveness than by necessity, we set out to buy or just to look and dream. We gain a false and fleeting sense of self-esteem from our ability to purchase expensive things for ourselves and our children. The vibrancy of our busy malls has made them virtual community centers. We leave boredom and emptiness behind as we browse through their glittering corridors of stuff. Yet many of us have learned that acquiring too much stuff can get in the way of happiness, that it can obscure what is best in us, lead us back to boredom and emptiness, corrupt our children's values. We often step out of the mall blinking in the sunshine at the end of an almost-vanished afternoon feeling unsatisfied, regretful, grumpy.... Montaigne wrote, 'All other things—to reign, to hoard, to build—are, at most, inconsiderable props and appendages. The great and glorious masterpiece of man is to be able to live to the point. Simplicity helps us to live to the point, to clear the way to the best, to keep first things first."[164]

—Robert Lawrence Smith

"So complex is the human spirit that it can itself scarce discern the deep springs which impel it to action."

—Sir Arthur Conan Doyle

"All sins are attempts to fill voids."

—Simone Weil

"Watch out! Be on your guard against all kinds of greed;
life does not consist in an abundance of possessions."
Luke 12:15 NIV

- Do you discern the deep springs which impel you away from simplicity and towards acquisitiveness? Are you trying to fill a void? What would that be?
- Are you "on your guard against all kinds of greed?"
- Have you found a way to withdraw from cares that "will not withdraw from you?"

Abba, help me heed Jesus's stern warning. Free me of a need to acquire and own–from seeking meaning in an abundance of things.

For more: *A Quaker Book of Wisdom* by Robert Lawrence Smith

The Least Informed People in the World

"Americans are the best entertained and the least informed people in the world."[165]

—Neil Postman

"We live in a society whose whole policy is to excite every nerve in the human body and keep it at the highest pitch of artificial tension, to strain every human desire to the limit and to create as many new desires and synthetic passions as possible, in order to cater to them with the products of our factories and printing presses and movie studios and all the rest....Advertising treats all products with the reverence and the seriousness due to sacraments."[166]

—Thomas Merton

"The contemplative life should liberate and purify the imagination which passively absorbs all kinds of things without our realizing it; liberate and purify it from the violence done by the influence of social images. There is a kind of contagion that affects the imagination unconsciously much more than we realize. It emanates from things like advertisements and from all the spurious fantasies that are thrown at us by our commercial society. These fantasies are deliberately intended to exercise a powerful effect on our conscious and subconscious minds. They are directed right at our instincts and appetites and there is no question but that they exercise a real transforming power on our whole psychic structures. The contemplative life should liberate us from that kind of pressure, which is really a form of tyranny."[167]

—Merton

"Consumption distracts people. You cannot control your own population by force, but it can be distracted by consumption. The business press has been quite explicit about this goal."[168]

—Noam Chomsky

"Orwell saw, to his credit, that the act of falsifying reality is only secondarily a way of changing perceptions. It is, above all, a way of asserting power."[169]

—Adam Gopnik

"Be transformed by the renewing of your mind."
Romans 12:2a NIV

Think about the "bread and circuses" used to amuse and distract the ancient Roman population and make them docile and easily controlled. Now think about your own TV viewing habits. Do they have the same effect?

- Advertisers believe that media manipulation will affect you "more than you realize." Is it realistic for you believe otherwise?

- What practices you can adopt to liberate yourself from this kind of tyranny?

Abba, help me see through the illusions and artificiality of my day.

For more: *Falling Free* by Shannon Martin

View from the Bottom

"I conceive of God … as a means of liberation and not a means to control others."[170]

—James Baldwin

"Most of the people who have ever lived on this planet have been oppressed and poor. But their history was seldom written except in the Bible. … Only in modern times and wealthy countries do we find the strange phenomenon of masses of people having an establishment mentality. This relatively new thing called 'the middle class' gives many of us just enough comfort not to have to feel the pinch or worry about injustice for ourselves. Most of us in the Northern Hemisphere have a view from the top even though we are nowhere near the top ourselves....In the early Christian Scriptures, or the 'New' Testament, we clearly see that it's mostly the lame, the poor, the blind, the prostitutes, the drunkards, the tax collectors, the sinners—those on the bottom and the outside—that really hear Jesus' teaching and get the point and respond to him. It's the leaders and insiders (the priests, scribes, Pharisees, teachers of the law, and Roman leaders) who crucify him....After Jesus' death and resurrection, the first Christians go 'underground'. They are the persecuted ones, meeting in secrecy in the catacombs.... The Church was largely of the poor and for the poor. The turning point, at which the Church moved from the bottom to the top, is the year 313 A.D. when Emperor Constantine supposedly did the Church a great favor by beginning to make Christianity the established religion of the Holy Roman Empire....As the Church's interests became linked with imperial world views, our perspective changed from the view from the bottom and powerlessness (the persecuted, the outsiders) to the view from the top where we were now the ultimate insiders (with power, money, status, and control)."[171]

—Richard Rohr

"Once you were not a people"
1 Peter 2:10a NIV

- What is your location in our world—top or bottom?
- Do you have friends on the bottom? What does your answer say about you?
- Does your faith seem more about dominating or liberating others?
- How can you better understand the often harsh realities of those of the bottom?

Jesus, convert us, your comfortable people.

For more: *Scripture as Liberation* by Richard Rohr

Listen to Your Body

"Hearts can be hardened–or 'tensed up'–in the same way that muscles can, and as a matter of fact the two things usually go together.... If you can get really well relaxed in the body, it is practically impossible to hold any attitudes of inner tension.... When you adopt an attitude of generosity, unselfishness, trust, rejoicing in another's good, love, respect, fellowship–then your muscles tend to relax. And if you can relax them first, then it is also easier to find these outgoing dispositions in your soul."[172]

—Beatrice Bruteau

Peter Scazzero lists common ways our body tells us we're out of loving union with God:

- "I feel anxiety in the tenseness and tightness in my body.
- I am not present or listening intently.
- I feel pressure, with too much to do in too little time.
- I am rushing.
- I give quick opinions and judgments.
- I am fearful about the future.
- I am overly concerned with what others think.
- I am defensive and easily offended.
- I am preoccupied and distracted.
- I am resentful of interruptions and abrupt.
- I am manipulative, not patient.
- I am unenthusiastic or threatened by the success of others.
- I talk more than I listen."[173]

—Peter Scazzero

"Abide in Me, and I in you.
As the branch cannot bear fruit of itself
unless it abides in the vine,
so neither can you unless you abide in Me."
John 15:4 NASB

- Scazzero's list is a profound body-focused diagnostic tool. What is your body telling you about your present experience of loving union with God?

- It's hard to live in loving union with God and others. Will you accept God's guidance to you, as he talks to you through your body?

- Has God been talking to you lately in this manner? Have you been listening?

- Have you considered relaxing your body as the prelude to addressing "the dispositions in your soul" rather than vice versa?

Abba, anxiety, defensiveness, talking too much, hurrying, criticizing others–these are the "trouble lights" in my O.S. that I'd rather not notice, but if you're going to talk to me this way, I want to listen. Help me do that.

For more: "Your Body is a Major, Not Minor Prophet"[174] by Peter Scazzero

---

Our Need to Impress

"For fourteen years he had kept silent about it."[175]

—James Campbell

"I will go on to visions and revelations from the Lord. I know a man in Christ who fourteen years ago was caught up to the third heaven [and] this man . . . heard inexpressible things, things that no one is permitted to tell. I will boast about a man like that, but I will not boast about myself, except about my weaknesses. . . . I refrain, so no one will think more of me than is warranted by what I do or say, or because of these surpassingly great revelations."
2 Corinthians 12:1b-7a NIV

"In a 'supassingly great' manner, the apostle Paul was transported to heaven where he saw powerful 'visions' and heard 'inexpressible [secret] things.' In all his days of ministry, he never tried to use this to enhance his reputation, and he refuses to do so now. (:5) Even here, he refers to himself only indirectly as 'a man in Christ.' This comes up now only because the Corinthian church was immaturely infatuated with the 'superapostles' in their midst (:11). Paul's experience put him in a special class. No one else had such credentials! Even so, *For fourteen years [Paul] had kept silent about it.*"[176]

—James Campbell

"We might commit ourselves to pondering the things that take place during solitude in our heart, as Mary did, at least for a time, rather than sharing them too quickly or using them immediately as tools for ministry. This is a way of keeping some things precious and sacred.... [like] we protect the privacy of our interactions with intimate friends."[177]

—Ruth Haley Barton

- Could you keep silent about something so impressive for fourteen years? Paul did. What does this says about him?
- Are you quick to share things that make you look good: your impressive morning devotional times, your tithing history, a substantial prayer life, some "power encounter," a long fast, years of keeping the Sabbath, etc.? What does it say about us when we share such things?
- When you share something sacred, it changes it. What is gained instead, by keeping something sacred a secret?

Abba, deliver me from my need to impress or be admired. Let your approval suffice for me.

For more: *Paul the Mystic* by James M. Campbell

March 26   September 23

The Limitations of Public Approval

"Who enjoys tranquility? The one who doesn't take seriously either praise or lack of it from people."[178]

—Thomas a Kempis, paraphrased by Donald Demaray

"One of the most important gifts that came my way in those days of misery [removal from ministry], I now realize, was the loss of public approval.... It forcibly separated me—the *essential* me—from the public's perception of me.... To learn, not just in my head but in the depths of my being, that I was someone different from and always more than the perception of others was like being in a hot, stuffy room and having the windows thrown open.... [Now] I'm not much impressed with the cheering or overly worried about the jeering. I am who I am thank God. And yes, *thank* God, because who I am is a child of God, a beloved of God, a man in whom God takes delight. I had known this before, to be sure, but I didn't know how much I still needed to learn it until I came to the limitations of public approval. Enduring these limitations was something I wouldn't have wished on my worst enemy; now it's something that, if not for the dishonor of it, I would covet for my dearest friends."[179]

—Donald McCullough

"I care very little if I am judged by you or by any human court;
indeed, I do not even judge myself. . . .
It is the Lord who judges me. . . .
He will bring to light what is hidden in darkness
and will expose the motives of the heart.
At that time each will receive their praise from God."
1 Corinthians 4:3–5 NIV

- Have you come to the place in your life where you know not to give any weight to either the praise or criticism of others?
- Have you come to the place where being God's beloved and having God's approval is enough?
- What, if anything, keeps you from sensing God's approval?
- If you do sense it, what has that done for you?

Abba, may I always look to you for approval, and sense your unwavering love for me in the depths of my being. Keep me from bondage to the opinions of others.

For more: *The Consolations of Imperfection* by Donald McCullough

Silence in a World of Noise

"It seemed to him that he knew exactly what it felt like to sit in a room like this, in an armchair beside an open fire with your feet in the fender and a kettle on the hob, utterly alone, utterly secure with nobody watching you, no voice pursuing you, no sound except the singing of the kettle and the friendly ticking of the clock.... To do anything that suggested a taste for solitude, even to go for a walk by yourself, was always slightly dangerous. There was a word for it in Newspeak: *ownlife*, it was called, meaning individualism and eccentricity."[180]

—George Orwell

"The ordinary, daily practice of silence is a prophetic stance in our world of noise. It is one of the greatest gifts we can offer the world."

—Kathleen Norris

"Intentional silence serves as a necessary and valuable counterweight to a society filled with thoughtless and excessive words."

—Peter Scazzero

"Let us labor for an inward stillness–
An inward stillness and an inward healing.
That perfect silence where the lips and heart
Are still, and we no longer entertain
Our own imperfect thoughts and vain opinions,
But God alone speaks to us and we wait
In singleness of heart that we may know
His will, and in the silence of our spirits,
That we may do His will and do that only!"

—Henry Wadsworth Longfellow

*"Tremble and do not sin; when you are on your beds,
search your hearts and be silent."*
Psalm 4:4 NIV

- Do you know what it feels like to sit in a silent room alone? Do you avoid such experiences?
- In Orwell's created world, to have your *ownlife* was considered "slightly dangerous." Look at Norris's quote again and consider why that would be.
- Is experiencing solitude and silence a priority in your life? Is it reflected in some plan or schedule?

Abba, as I seek you in the silence of solitude, may I encounter reality, experience sanity and discover wisdom. I want to have my *ownlife*, not one choreographed for me by those who control the noise and nonsense–the disinformation, the mythology–of my world.

For more: *The Power of Silence* by Robert Sara and Nicolas Diat

---

Ignoring Springs and Digging Wells

"Of all ridiculous things the most ridiculous seems to me, to be busy ...."[181]

—Søren Kierkegaard

"When I give something I do not possess, I give a false and dangerous gift, a gift that looks like love but is, in reality, loveless–a gift given more from my need to prove myself than from the other's need to be cared for. One sign that I am violating my own nature in the name of nobility is a condition called burnout. Though usually regarded as a result of trying to give too much, burnout in my experience results from trying to give what I do not possess–the ultimate in giving too little! Burnout is a state of emptiness, to be sure, but it does not result from giving all I have; it merely reveals the nothingness from which I was trying to give in the first place."[182]

—Parker Palmer

"Remaining in loving union with Jesus is a matter of life and death for us as well as for everyone who looks to us for nourishment."

—Peter Scazzero

"My people have committed two sins:
They have forsaken me,
the spring of living water,
and have dug their own cisterns,
broken cisterns that cannot hold water."
Jeremiah 2:13 NIV

- Ministry is exhausting, but "burn out" something else. Have you ever felt burned out? Do you have insight now into what happened?

- Do you see nourishing your soul as a matter of life and death for you? . . . how failing do to so can make you "dangerous?"

- Is busyness, drivenness, exhaustion, or a misguided sense of self-sufficiency keeping you from nourishing your soul?

- Do you have a specific plan to cultivate loving union with God, "the spring of living water?" If not, how could you begin?

Abba, when I come to the end of my rope–when my well is empty–when I'm running on fumes–when my experience of you is tired or second-hand . . . may I remember then to address the "nothingness" in my inner life before I attempt to do anything else. And may I remember my need even when it seems like I'm doing fine.

For more: *Let Your Life Speak* by Parker Palmer

The Longest Journey–
The Journey Inward

"We have become adept at exploring outer space, but we have not developed similar skills in exploring our own personal inner spaces. In fact the longest journey is the journey inward."

—Dag Hammarsjold

"All travelers, somewhere along the way, find it necessary to check their course, to see how they are doing. We wait until we are sick, or shocked into stillness, before we do the commonplace thing of getting our bearings. And yet, we wonder why we are depressed, why we are unhappy, why we lose our friends, why we are ill-tempered. This condition we pass on to our children, our husbands, our wives, our associates, our friends. Cultivate the mood to linger.... Who knows? God may whisper to you in the quietness what He has been trying to say to you, oh, for so long a time."[183]

—Howard Thurman

"Honoring our different rhythms involves respecting and negotiating our needs and preferences at work, with friends, at church, in our marriage, our extended families, and even our parenting. To begin listening to your inner rhythms, consider the following questions: Do you know when it is time to be with people and when it is time to be alone? Do you know when it is time to rest or time to play? What are your most optimal work hours? How much sleep to you need? When is it time to eat? Is it time for you to wait on something or is it time to move on? How does the pace of your life feel? What can you do to establish an enjoyable routine and healthy balance in this season of your life? And finally, what are the one or two changes you can make in order to get more in step with your God-given inner rhythms?"[184]

—Geri Scazzero

> *"Surely I have composed and quieted my soul;*
> *Like a weaned child rests against his mother,*
> *My soul is like a weaned child within me."*
> Psalm 131:2 NASB

- Are you cultivating the "mood to linger" so you can hear from God?
- Are you learning to know and listen to your inner rhythms?
- How can you linger and listen better than you do now?

Abba, teach me to practice a healthy balance on this tight-rope walk that is my life.

For more: *I Quit!* by Gerri Scazzero

What People Need Most from You

"Sabbath-keeping is the primary discipline that helps us to live within the limits of our humanity and to honor God as our Creator. It is the kingpin of a life lived in sync—with the rhythms that God himself built into our world—and yet it is the discipline that seems hardest for us to practice. Sabbath-keeping honors the body's need for rest, the spirit's need for replenishment, and the soul's need to delight itself in God for God's own sake. It begins with the willingness to acknowledge the limits of our humanness and then taking steps to live more graciously within the order of things.... I am not God. God is the only one who can be all things to all people. God is the only one who can be two places at once. God is the one who never sleeps. I am not. This is pretty basic stuff but many of us live as though we don't know it.... There is something about being gracious and accepting and gentle with ourselves at least once a week that enables us to be gracious and accepting and gentle with others. There is a freedom that comes from being who we are in God and resting into God that eventually enables us to bring something truer to the world than all of our doing. Sabbath-keeping helps us to live within our limits because on the Sabbath, in so many different ways, we allow ourselves to be the creature in the presence of our Creator. We touch something more real in ourselves and others than what we are all able to produce. We touch our very being in God. Surely that is what the people around us need most."[185]

—Ruth Haley Barton

"Then Jesus said, 'Let's go off by ourselves to a quiet place and rest awhile.'
He said this because there were so many people coming and going
that Jesus and his apostles didn't even have time to eat."
Mark 6:31 NLT

- Have you acknowledged the limits of your humanity?
- Can you rest in God? Can you be gentle with yourself?
- What message are you sending to others who observe your lifestyle?
- Do people find in you what they need most?

Abba, ground me as I rest in you.

For more: *Sacred Rhythms* by Ruth Haley Barton

Experiencing God's Experience of Me

Jürgen Moltmann encourages us to think about not only how we experience God, but how God experiences us. "This is not to say that the relationship between God and us is a reciprocal one between equals; rather that for a relationship to be a relationship at all, it must be a two-way affair. The question, 'How does God experience me?' Suggests a fresh way to look at ourselves and our way of being in the world. What is God's experience of me? God's experience of me must seem strange, disappointing, amusing, hurtful, and occasionally delightful. Once the initial question has been entertained by the believer, its effects go on reverberating in the soul. Because I am capable of reflection and self-transcendence (I can go beyond myself), I can also experience God's experience of me. I can 'see' what I am like from God's point of view. I can learn to know myself in the mirror of God's love, suffering, and joy. When I reflect on how God experiences me I begin to learn more about myself; and the more I understand God's experience of me and my world, the more deeply the mystery of God's passion comes home to me."[186]

—Alan Jones

"God's love is the water we drink, the air we breathe, and the light we see. All natural phenomena are different material forms of the love of God. . . . God's love surrounds us, but we do not feel it, anymore than we feel the pressure of the atmosphere."[187]

—Ernesto Cardenal

"On the great love of God I lean,
Love of the Infinite, Unseen,
With nought of heaven or earth between.
This God is mine, and I am His . . . ."

—Horatius Bonar

118

"I led them with cords of human kindness,
with ties of love.
To them I was like one who lifts
a little child to the cheek,
and I bent down to feed them."
Hosea 11:4 NIV

- Try to imagine what God's experience of you is like.

- Can you get past thinking of God's experience of you as mostly strange, disappointing, amusing, or hurtful–no matter your track record?

- Can you attempt to look at yourself from God's eyes? . . . to see yourself "in the mirror of God's love?"

Abba, I will lean only on your great love.

For more: *Soul Making* by Alan Jones

Everyone Around You Is Exhausted . . . Are You?

"The world is run by exhausted people."

—Peter Scazzero

"If the strings of an instrument are always taut, they go out of tune."

—Coelho

"I have sat on dozens of boards and commissions with many fine, compassionate, and generous people who are so tired, overwhelmed, and overworked that they have neither the time nor the capacity to listen to the deeper voices that speak to the essence of the problems before them. Presented with [complex problems] .. . our impulse, born of weariness, is to rush headlong toward doing anything that will make the problem go away. Maybe then we can finally go home and get some rest. But without the essential nutrients of rest, wisdom, and delight embedded in the problem-solving process itself, the solution we patch together is likely to be an obstacle to genuine relief. Born of desperation, it often contains enough fundamental inaccuracy to guarantee an equally perplexing problem will emerge as soon as it is put into place."[188]

—Wayne Muller

"When we get too busy, everything becomes either a trudge or a scramble, the doldrums or sheer mayhem. We get bored with the familiar, threatened by the unfamiliar. Our capacity for both steadfastness and adventure shrivels. We just want to be left alone. One measure for whether or not you're rested enough … is to ask yourself this: How much do I care about the things I care about? When we lose concern for people, both the lost and the found, for the bride of Christ, for friendship, for truth and beauty and goodness; when we cease to laugh when our children laugh (and instead yell at them to quiet down) or weep when our spouses weep (and instead wish they didn't get so emotional); when we hear news of trouble among our neighbors and our first thought is that we hope it isn't going to involve us—when we stop caring about the things we care about—that's a signal we're too busy."[189]

—Mark Buchanan

"In repentance and rest is your salvation . . . ."
Isaiah 30:15b NIV

- How often are you done before the day is?
- Is your life "one enormous obligation?" Are you a slave?
- Are you too exhausted to "care about the things you care about?"

Abba, lead me into quietness and rest.

For more: *Sabbath* by Wayne Muller

The Prayer of Consent

"What God asks of us is a will which is no longer divided between Him and any creature. It is a will pliant in His hands which neither seeks nor rejects anything, which wants without reserve whatever He wants and which never wants under any pretext anything that He does not want.... Happy are those who give themselves to God! ... Placing our will entirely in the hands of God, we want only what God wants, and thus we find His consolation in faith and consequently hope in the midst of all suffering.... Happy are those who throw themselves with bowed heads into the arms of the 'Father of mercies' and the 'God of all consolation.'"[190]

—Francis Fenelon

"Contemplative prayer is a deepening of faith that moves beyond thoughts and concepts. One just listens to God, open and receptive to the divine presence in one's inmost being as its source. One listens not with a view to hearing something, but with a view to becoming aware of the obstacles to one's friendship with God.... In contemplative prayer the Spirit places us in a position where we are at rest and disinclined to fight.... Little by little, we enter into prayer without intentionality except to consent ... and consent becomes surrender ... and surrender becomes total receptivity.... And, as the process continues, total receptivity becomes effortless, peaceful.... It is free and has nothing to attain, to get, or desire .... So, no thinking, no reflection, no desire, no words, no thing ... just receptivity and consent."[191]

—Thomas Keating

"To obey is better than sacrifice,
and to heed is better than the fat of rams."
1 Samuel 15:22b NIV

- Can you imagine wanting only what God wants?

- In prayer, do you listen to become aware of the obstacles to your friendship with God?

- Are you willing to adopt an approach to prayer that is permeated by only receptivity and consent? What would that look like?

Abba, may I be that one, who throws himself with bowed head into the arms of the God of all consolation.

For more: *Devotional Classics* by Richard Foster and James Bryan Smith

---

Holding Your Breath to Listen

"Quiet chooses to be silent. It holds its breath to listen. It waits and is still."[192]

—Frederick Buechner

"The power of silence and solitude has been recognized throughout the history of spiritual formation. It is the purposeful separation of ourselves from the world in order to place ourselves with God. The great advantage of the evil one is his ability to assault our senses with the material world in which we live as if to drown out the distant chords from eternity's symphony. One can only surmise that it was for this reason that Lewis' Screwtape announces to his nephew Wormwood that one of hell's goals is to 'make the whole universe a noise in the end.' Only in silence can we move past the deafening roar of the world and hear the music of God."[193]

—James Emery White

"Unless I am silent I shall not hear God, and until I hear him I shall not come to know him. Silence asks me to watch and wait and listen, to be like Mary in readiness to receive the Word. If I have any respect for God I shall try to find a time, however short, for silence. Without it I have not much hope of establishing that relationship with God or hearing and responding which is going to help me root the whole of my life in prayer."[194]

—Esther de Wall

"The silence of solitude is nothing but dead silence when it does not make us alert for a new voice sounding from beyond all human chatter."[195]

—Henri Nouwen

"Guard your steps as you go to the house of God
and draw near to listen

rather than to offer the sacrifice of fools."
Ecclesiastes 5:1 NASB

"Fools multiply words."
Ecclesiastes 10:14a NIV

- Is *your* world "a universe of noise?"
- Is your religious experience mostly about the power of words: preaching, teaching, evangelizing, praying, singing, sharing, testifying?
- Do you know what it is to "hold your breath and listen" to hear "a new voice sounding from beyond all human chatter?"
- Will you plan to make a time for silence in your daily schedule?

For more: *Seeking God: The Way of St. Benedict* by Esther de Wall

---

The God of Justice and Justification

"What this book [*Good News About Injustice*] obliges us to do is ask ourselves some basic and uncomfortable questions that living in a comfortable culture may never have allowed us to ask before. First, what sort of God do we believe in? Is he concerned exclusively with individual salvation? Or does he have a social conscious? Is he (in Dr. Carl Henry's memorable phrase), 'the God of justice and of justification?' How is it that so many of us staunch evangelical people have never seen, let alone faced, the barrage of biblical texts about justice? Why are we often guilty of selective imagination? Second, what sort of creature do we think a human being is? Have we ever considered the unique value and dignity of human beings, made in the image of God, so that abuse, torture, rape and grinding poverty, which dehumanize beings, are also an insult to the God who made them? Third, what sort of person do we think Jesus Christ is? Have we ever seen him as described in John 11, where first he 'snorted' with anger (v. 33, literally) in the face of death (an intrusion into God's good world) and then 'wept' (v. 35) over the bereaved? If only we could be like Jesus, indignant toward evil and compassionate toward its victims! Fourth, what sort of a community do we think the church is meant to be? Is it not often indistinguishable from the world because it accommodates itself to the prevailing culture of injustice and indifference? Is it not intended rather to penetrate the world like salt and light, and so to change it, as salt hinders bacterial decay and light disperses darkness?"[196]

—John Stott

"'[Your father] defended the cause of the poor and needy . . .
Is that not what it means to know me?' declares the Lord."
Jeremiah 22:15–16 NLT

- Are you moved by "the barrage of biblical texts" about justice? If not, why not?
- Like Jesus, are you compassionate toward the victims of evil? Are you part of the struggle to bring them justice?
- In what ways might you or your church be failing to treat others as unique in value and dignity?

Abba, forgive me for when I have accommodated myself to the prevailing culture of injustice and indifference. Change me.

For more: *God Who Stands and Stays* by Carl Henry

April 5   October 3

The Duty and Dance of Listening

"The first duty of love is to listen."

—Paul Tillich

"An essential part of true listening is the discipline of bracketing, the temporary giving up or setting aside of one's own prejudices, frames of reference and desires so as to experience as far as possible the speaker's world from the inside, step in inside his or her shoes. This unification of speaker and listener is actually an extension and enlargement of ourselves, and new knowledge is always gained from this. Moreover, since true listening involves bracketing, a setting aside of the self, it also temporarily involves a total acceptance of the other. Sensing this acceptance, the speaker will feel less and less vulnerable and more and more inclined to open up the inner recesses

124

of his or her mind to the listener. As this happens, speaker and listener begin to appreciate each other more and more, and the duet dance of love is begun again.... true listening no matter how brief, requires tremendous effort. First of all it requires total concentration. You cannot truly listen to anyone and do anything else at the same time.... If you are not willing to put aside everything, including your own worries and preoccupation's for such a time, then you are not willing to truly listen."[197]

—M. Scott Peck

"To be listened to is, generally speaking, a nearly unique experience for most people. It is enormously stimulating. It is small wonder that people who have been demanding all their lives to be heard so often fall speechless when confronted with one who gravely agrees to lend an ear."

—Robert C. Murphy

"The greatest compliment that was ever paid me was when one asked me what I thought, and attended to my answer."

—Henry David Thoreau

"To answer before listening–
that is folly and shame."
Proverbs 18:13 NIV

- Are you striving to be good listener?

- Do you normally answer before listening or listen before answering? What does your answer say about you?

- It's so rare for others to feel truly heard. Imagine how powerfully you can love others with your listening.

Abba, my impatience, agenda and self-importance all cause me to fail at my duty to love well by listening. Help me be that person others await and so desperately need.

For more: *The Road Less Traveled* by M. Scott Peck

The Unfriendliness That's Killing Your Church

"The Technical Assistance Research Program study for the White House Office of Consumer Affairs found that 96 percent of unhappy customers never complain about rude or unfriendly treatment, but 90 percent of those unhappy customers will not return to the place where that unfriendliness was manifest. Further, each one of those unhappy customers will tell nine other people about the lack of friendliness and courteousness, and 13 percent will tell more than twenty other people.... Every church thinks it's friendly. But what that means is ... they are friendly to each other ... to people they know ... to people they like ... to people who are like them. That's not friendliness; that's a clique or, at best, a club. To prove the point, another recent LifeWay Research survey found that while three out of every four churchgoers say they have significant relationships with people at their church, they admit they don't make an effort with new people. In fact, only one in every six even try. That's not very friendly.... If you are going to reach the nones [the religiously unaffiliated], they are going to come to you *as a none.* That means they will come as couples living together, as gay couples, pregnant outside of marriage, addicted, skeptical. Is that going to raise an eyebrow? Or is it taken in stride in a way that makes the person feel instantly at ease? At Meck [the author's church], it's just another day of normal."[198]

—James Emery White

"I was a stranger,
and you invited Me in."
Matthew 25:35 NIV

- Stand back and watch people interacting before and after the worship service. Are some people being ignored–standing alone in silence during the time of greeting–"abandoned?"

- Do *you* make a point of regularly speaking to people you haven't met?

- When you attend church are you looking for opportunities to show the love of Jesus to people you don't know–or just to connect with friends?

- Have you been included–or even worse, in the "inner circle"–too long to remember how hard it is to "break into" a new church?

Abba, use me to embrace others–known and unknown–with your love.

For more: *The Rise of the Nones* by James Emery White

Patience With Others . . . and Yourself

"I am sure than when St. Paul spoke of 'the fruit of the Spirit,' he had in mind such processes that as we find in nature. A tree which brings forth good fruit is able to do so because over many years it has been brought under the influence of cultivation, fertilization, sunshine, rain, caressing winds, [and] cleansing from blight, and so it acquires the power to bear good fruit. A farmer cannot get his result by suddenly becoming very busy for a season and doing these things."[199]

—Shirley Carter Hughson

"The person ... who looks for quick results in the seed-planting of well-doing will be disappointed. If I want potatoes for dinner tomorrow, it will do me little good to go out and plant potatoes in my garden tonight. There are long stretches of darkness and invisibility and silence that separated planting and reaping. During the stretches of waiting there is cultivation and weeding and nurturing and planting still other seeds."[200]

—Eugene Peterson

"He will be like a tree firmly planted by streams of water,
Which yields its fruit in its season . . . ."
Psalm 1:3 NASB

- Healthy growth takes both time *and* work, but it definitely does take time. Does your work honor the principle that God cannot be rushed?
- Are you ever guilty of impatiently trying to force things to change?

- What might God be doing in you or your situation during "long stretches of darkness and invisibility and silence?"
- With these things in mind, think about people on the journey of faith. What should be your attitude towards fellow pilgrims? What should be your attitude towards yourself? Can you relax and trust God's timing?

Abba, help me walk rather than race, receive rather than grasp, and relax rather than strive. Help me step into the flow of your divine life rather than living a frenzied version of my very human life. Help me focus on being with you and leave the results to you.

For more: *The Spiritual Letters of Shirley Carter* by Shirley Carter Hughson

---

God Is Present . . . Are You?

"As long as we are working hard, using our gifts to serve others, experiencing joy in our work along with the toil, we are always in danger of believing that our actions trigger God's love for us. Only in stopping, really stopping, do we teach our hearts and souls that we are loved apart from what we do. During a day of rest, we have the chance to take a deep breath and look at our lives. God is at work every minute of our days, yet we seldom notice. Noticing requires intentional stopping, and the Sabbath provides that opportunity. On the Sabbath we can take a moment to see the beauty of a maple leaf, created with great care by our loving Creator. . . . Without time to stop, we cannot notice God's hand in our lives, practice thankfulness, step outside our culture's values or explore our deepest longings. Without time to rest, we will seriously undermine our ability to experience God's unconditional love and acceptance. The Sabbath is a gift whose blessings cannot be found anywhere else."[201]

—Lynne Baab

"And now we're all tired. We dream of that day when our work will be done, when we can finally wash the dust of it from our skin, but that day never comes. We look in vain for the day of our work's completion. But it is mythical, like unicorns and dragons. So we dream . . . . [But] God, out of the bounty of his own nature, held this day apart and stepped fully into it, then turned and said, 'Come, all you who are weary and heavy-laden, Come, and I will give you rest. Come, join me here."'[202]

—Mark Buchanan

"You can't wait
for the Sabbath day
to be over . . . ."
Amos 8:5 NLT

- Have you been stopping long enough to notice that God is continually coming to you in love?

- Could intentionally stopping help you be more in touch with your world–inner and outer?

- When is the last time you really stopped for at least one whole day? Are you too stressed, distracted, or simply exhausted to experience God's love–or to love others well?

Abba, help me to keep a weekly Sabbath, and as I do, transform the other six days too.

For more: *Sabbath Keeping* by Lynne Baab

April 9

October 7

Look at God Looking at You . . . and Smiling

"To please God . . . to be a real ingredient in the divine happiness . . . to be loved by God, not merely pitied, but delighted in as an artist delights in his work or a father in a son–it seems impossible . . . but so it is."[203]

—C. S. Lewis

"St. Ignatius encourages people to imagine themselves alongside Jesus. It's different than imagining yourself with God, who is often imagined more as a 'presence.' Imagining yourself with Jesus means something more specific. . . . This may mean something as simple as sitting joyfully with [Jesus] in prayer and imagining [Jesus] sitting joyfully with you.... Laugh with the God who smiles when seeing you, rejoices over your very existence, and takes delight in you, all the days of your life.... In his book *Armchair Mystic*, Mark Thibodeaux, a Jesuit spiritual writer, distinguishes between four stages of prayer. The first is *talking at God* (which includes petitionary prayer, that is, asking for help). The second is *talking to God* (which includes expressing your feelings and emotions, frustrations and hopes to God). The third is *listening to God* (a more contemplative way of reflecting on what is going on in your daily life as well as being attentive to the inner movements of your soul during prayer). The final way is *being with God* (this is closer to 'centering prayer,' a prayer of presence).... One of my favorite suggestions for a meditation is Anthony deMello's statement: 'Look at God looking at you ... and smiling.' DeMello's image is essentially an invitation into a prayer of joy and contentment, into what you might call private, one-on-one time with a smiling God, into seeing the world the way that God does."[204]

—James Martin

"You are ... God's special possession ...."
1 Peter 2:9a NIV

- Can you think of Jesus as smiling at you? Do you?
- Do you think of God as rejoicing in you, like an artist in his work? ... like a mother in her son?
- Are you able to stop and simply be present to God? Do that now, and imagine Jesus smiling when he sees you.

Abba, let me taste more of your love.

For more: *Armchair Mystic* by Mark Thibodeaux

Man as a Consort of God

"To the prophet, God does not reveal himself in an abstract absoluteness, but in a specific and unique way—in a personal and intimate relation to the world. God does not simply command and expect obedience; He is also moved and affected by what happens in the world and he reacts accordingly. Events and human actions arouse in Him joy or sorrow, pleasure or wrath. He is not conceived as judging facts, so to speak, 'objectively', in detached impassibility. He reacts in an intimate and subjective manner.... Quite obviously in the Biblical view, man's deeds can move Him, affect Him, grieve Him, or, on the other hand, gladden and please Him. This notion that God can be intimately affected, that He possesses not merely intelligence and will, but also feeling and *pathos*, basically defines the prophetic consciousness of God.... The God of Israel is a God Who loves, a God Who is known to, and concerned with, man. He not only rules the world in the majesty of His might and wisdom, but reacts intimately to the events of history.... God does not stand outside the range of human suffering and sorrow. He is personally involved in, even stirred by, the conduct and fate of man. Man is not only an image of God; he is a perpetual concern of God. The idea of pathos adds a new dimension to human existence. Whatever man does affects not only his own life, but also the life of God insofar as it is directed to man. The import of man raises him beyond the level of mere creature. He is a consort, a partner, a factor in the life of God."[205]

—Abraham Heschel

"But then I will win her back once again.
I will lead her into the desert
and speak tenderly to her there . . . ."
Hosea 2:14 NLT

• Does a God of pathos challenge your understanding of God?

• Can you think of God as a lover? . . . hurt by your rejections? . . . gladdened by your love?

- "It behooves us to be careful what we worship, for what we are worshipping we are becoming."(Emerson) How does your vision of God shape you?

Abba, may I bring you much joy.

For more: *Between God and Man* by Abraham Heschel

Nonconformity to Idolatry

"Religion begins as a breaking off, as a going away. It continues in acts of nonconformity to idolatry."[206]

—Abraham Heschel

"In the eyes of their contemporaries, the prophets were mad. Hosea, Elisha, and Jeremiah were all considered demented, individuals who ... should be put 'in the stocks and collars.' (Heschel) We call people 'mad' when they see things from a perspective different from our own. We have a vested interest in doing so, for it they are right, we are wrong. Since we do not gladly entertain the notion that we are wrong, we are more than ready to denounce such people as crazy, mad fools. To be sure, the prophets do engage in some very strange activities: they call kings to account for injustice, which is a very unhealthy things to do in a royal society; they excoriate religious leaders for being co-opted, which is equally unhealthy in a society that allows religious leaders to deal with their own deviants; they announce the fulfillment of God's will through pagan leaders, which is considered unpatriotic by leaders of both church and state ...."[207]

—Robert McAfee Brown

"If the prophets Isaiah and Amos were to appear in our midst, would they accept the corruption in high places, the indifferent way in which the sick, the poor, and the old are treated? ... Would they not be standing amidst those who protest against the war in Vietnam, the decay of our cities, the hypocrisy and falsehood that surround our present Administration, even at the highest levels?"[208]

—Heschel

"O my people, your leaders mislead you;
they send you down the wrong road."
Isaiah 3:12b NLT

- Where do political or religious leaders today need to be called to account for injustice?

- Would voices of dissent more likely originate inside or outside traditional structures like your church? Do you think such critics would fare better in our day than prophets like Jeremiah did in his?

- Are there prophets today? Might you have dismissed them as outliers?

- How will you avoid reflexively rejecting criticism from those with a perspective different than yours–who may, after all, be offering a divine perspective?

"O Lord, we confess our sins, we are ashamed of the inadequacy of our anguish, of how faint and slight is our mercy." (Heschel)

For more: *Saying Yes and Saying No* by Robert McAfee Brown

Listening to the Voice of Depression

"Much has been said about the 'voice of depression.' It is a voice that speaks despairingly about the whole of one's life no matter how good parts of it may be–a voice so loud and insistent that when it speaks, it is the only sound one can hear.... *Lincoln's Melancholy,* by Joshua Shenk, is a probing examination of our sixteenth president's journey with depression. What was then called 'melancholy' first appeared in Lincoln's twenties, when neighbors occasionally took him in for fear he might take his own life. Lincoln struggled with this affliction until the day he died .... Lincoln's need to preserve his life by embracing and integrating his own darkness and light made him uniquely qualified to help America preserve the Union. Because he knew dark and light intimately–knew them as inseparable elements of everything human–he refused to split North and South into 'good guys' and 'bad guys,' a split that might have taken us closer to the national version of suicide. Instead ... a month before the end of the Civil War, Lincoln appealed for 'malice toward none' and 'charity for all'. ... In his appeal to a deeply divided America, Lincoln points to an essential fact of our life together: if we are to survive and thrive, we must hold its divisions and contradictions with compassion, lest we lose our democracy. Lincoln has much to teach us about embracing political tension in a way that opens our hearts to each other, no matter how deep our differences. That way begins 'in here' as we work on reconciling whatever divides us from ourselves–and then moves out with healing power into a world of many divides, drawing light out of darkness, community out of chaos, and life out of death."[209]

—Parker Palmer

"We were under great pressure,
far beyond our ability to endure,
so that we despaired of life itself."
2 Corinthians 1:8 NLT

- Have you learned to expect something like a "gift" from the often debilitating experience of depression?
- If so, what was the gift? Was it worth it?
- As we discover divisions and contradictions in ourselves and others, we must respond with compassion–starting with ourselves. Can you do that?

Abba, save me from, and through, the voice of depression.

For more: *Lincoln's Melancholy* by Joshua Shenk

Surrendering to "Reduced Circumstances"

"Asceticism ... is a way of surrendering to reduced circumstances in a manner that enhances the whole person. It is a radical way of knowing exactly who, what, and where you are, in defiance of those powerful forces in society—alcohol, drugs, television, shopping malls, motels—that aim to make us forget."[210]

—Kathleen Norris

"People encounter God under shady oak trees, on riverbanks, at the tops of mountains, and in long stretches of barren wilderness. God shows up in whirlwinds, starry skies, burning bushes, and perfect strangers. When people want to know more about God, the son of God tells them to pay attention to the lilies of the field and the birds of the air, to women kneading bread and workers lining up for their pay. Whoever wrote this stuff believed that people could learn as much about the ways of God from paying attention to the world as they could from paying attention to scripture.… People can learn as much about the ways of God from business deals gone bad or sparrows falling to the ground as they can from reciting the books of the Bible in order. They can learn as much from a love affair or a wildflower as they can from knowing the Ten Commandments by heart."[211]

—Barbara Brown Taylor

"Then Jesus, full of the Holy Spirit, returned from the Jordan River. He was led by the Spirit in the wilderness where he was tempted by the devil for forty days. Jesus ate nothing all that time and became very hungry."
Luke 4:1, 2 NLT

- When God takes things you normally count on out from under you ("reduced circumstances") can you image how that could *enhance* you?" Can you trust God in such times?

- What forces in your life make you "forget exactly who, what, and where you are?"

- Are you able to pay attention and learn from simple things—easily overlooked things—less obviously "religious" things? Are you doing that?

Abba, whether I *choose* less (things, activity, talk) or less is chosen *for* me (opportunity, health, affirmation), I pray that you would work in that empty space to teach me who, what and where I am.

For more: *Dakota: A Spiritual Geography* by Kathleen Norris

A Disciplined Refusal to Act

"A waiting person is a patient person. The word 'patience' implies the willingness to stay where we are and live the situation out to the full in the belief that something hidden there will manifest itself to us. Patient living means to live actively in the present and wait there. Impatient people expect the real thing to happen somewhere else, and therefore they want to get away from the present situation and go elsewhere. For them the moment is empty. But patient people dare to stay where they are."[212]

—Henri Nouwen

"Another will is greater, wiser and more intelligent than my own. So I wait. Waiting means that there is Another whom I trust and from whom I receive. My will, important and essential as it is, finds a Will that is more important, more essential. . . . In prayer we are aware that God is in action and that when the circumstances are ready, when others are in the right place and when my heart is prepared, I will be called into action. Waiting in prayer is a disciplined refusal to act before God acts. Waiting is our participation in the process that results in the 'time fulfilled.'"[213]

—Eugene Peterson

"Do not leave Jerusalem until the Father sends you
the gift he promised, as I told you before." Acts 1: 4 NLT

- Are you always trying to go somewhere else because the moment or place you're in seems empty?

- Have you ever determined not to act, and instead to wait in the painful place between where you are and where you want to be–to wait upon God there?"

- What do you have to lose by trusting in and waiting upon God? Before you act, can you at least give God plenty of time to act?

Abba, keep me from moving on before what you're doing manifests itself. Cure me of impatience (my hurried self), impulsivity (my thoughtless self), and anxiety (my fearful self).

For more: *Earth and Altar* by Eugene Peterson

Change the World, But First Yourself

"You don't need to fix your friends or family. You don't need to solve all the problems that confront you. If you can simply learn to not be controlled by fear–your own or that of others–you will be a non-anxious presence in the lives of others, and there is nothing they need more. So how do you do this? By confronting your own anxieties and fears head-on. An anxious person cannot be a non-anxious presence, obviously. The world is full of people wanting to solve all the problems of the world. But the world would profit much more if people would first confront their own anxieties and the things that cause them 1) to have to fill every silence with meaningless chatter, 2) to stay constantly busy, and 3) to do anything to avoid being still."[214]

—David K. Flowers

"He who attempts to act and do things for others or for the world without deepening his own self-understanding, freedom, integrity, and capacity to love, will not have anything to give to others. He will communicate to them nothing but the contagion of his own obsessions, his aggressivity, his ego-centered ambitions, his delusions about ends and means."[215]

—Thomas Merton

"Here lies the center of Merton's critique of our activism....Activism ultimately places our own unmet longings at the center of our efforts. It therefore does not help others in a wholesome way."[216]

—Henri Nouwen

"Let him who would move the world, first move himself."

—Socrates

"Hypocrite! First get rid of the log in your own eye;
then you will see well enough
to deal with the speck in your friend's eye."
Matthew 7:5 NLT

- It's much easier to focus on fixing another person than to look within. In many instances, Jesus wants us to leave the other person to him. Is there someone in your life right now that you're trying to "fix?"
- Are you aware of the dangers for activists mentioned by Merton and Nouwen?
- Are you seeking to deepen your own self-understanding and capacity to love as an integral part of your attempt to help others or impact the world?

Abba, keep me from a life of action that springs from anxiety, ambition or illusion. Help me walk with you, loving mercy . . . acting justly.

For more: Thomas Merton: Spiritual Master edited by Lawrence S. Cunningham

---

Detachment and Loving Well

"Love flourishes only in freedom. Relationships based on the illusions born of insecurities inevitably will become coercive, and nothing destroys love faster then coercion. How could it be otherwise? Love is a gift, one that cannot be given under compulsion or taken by force. Love cannot happen if others are treated as mere extensions of ourselves, as slaves of our needs and desires. Only through detachment—the separation of ourselves from others and others from ourselves—can we find the freedom that makes room for the mutual attentiveness and mutual honoring and mutual delight and mutual serving that are the foursquare foundation of authentic love."[217]

—Donald McCullough

"All great spirituality teaches about letting go of what you don't need and who you are not."

—Richard Rohr

"I have loved you
even as the Father has loved me.
Remain in my love. . . .

138

Love each other in the same way
I have loved you."
John 15:9, 12 NLT

- Does such "detachment" from others seem like a good and proper thing, or a selfish, misguided thing? Are you able to give others freedom to solve their own problems? . . . to fail? What does your answer say about you?

- Have you ever had someone try to control you or manipulate you "for your own good?" Did you feel loved?

- Is your love ever coercive or manipulative–really about some need of yours? If so, can you put your finger on what that need of yours might be?

- God loves us greatly, but allows us to make lots of mistakes, and often, to suffer the consequences. He respects our freedom, and waits for us to choose to love him. All this could be otherwise. Do you think it's good the way it is? Why or why not?

Abba, help me to love others, not because of some need of my own, but for their good. Help me to love enough to release control of those I love, even when sometimes it means watching them struggle and fail–even when I think I have the answer–even when I think they can't do without me.

For more: *The Consolations of Imperfection* by Donald McCullough

---

When No One Is Applauding

"Deep rivers move in silence . . . shallow brooks are noisy."

—Samuel Butler

"I long to accomplish a great and noble task; but it is my chief duty to accomplish small tasks as if they were great and noble."

—Helen Keller

"Because our daily tasks afford us constant opportunity to engage in the ministry of small things it is through this work that we become most intimately acquainted with God....Small things are the genuinely big things in the kingdom of God. It is here we truly face the issues of obedience and discipleship. It is not hard to be a model disciple amid camera lights and press releases. But in the small corners of life, in those areas of service that will never be newsworthy or gain us any recognition we must hammer out the meaning of obedience. Amid the obscurity of family and friends, neighbors, and work associates, we find God."[218]

—Richard Foster

"It is in the ordinary duties and labors of life that the Christian can and should develop his spiritual union with God."[219]

—Thomas Merton

> "Whoever can be trusted with very little
> can also be trusted with much,
> and whoever is dishonest with very little
> will also be dishonest with much."
> Luke 16:10 NIV

- Do you normally think of your daily tasks at home and work as opportunities for important ministry? . . . as opportunities for profound personal transformation? . . . as opportunities to "find God?"

- Are you content to work in obscurity, ministering for God in a way that no one but God may ever notice? What does your answer say about you?

- Sometimes it's hard for me when I realize, "I'm invisible. No one notices me. No one is applauding." Can you relate? Do you think this painful experience can be beneficial?

Abba, as much as I hate to admit it, I like the sound of applause. Help me, whether I choose obscurity or have it thrust upon me, to submit myself to its good work in my life.

For more: *The Challenge of the Disciplined Life* by Richard Foster

Do Nothing . . . and Then Rest

"How beautiful it is to do nothing, and then rest afterward."

—Spanish proverb

"For many of us the thought of doing nothing is terrifying. We can't imagine what life would be like if we were not slaving away at our projects. Not to have our projects waiting for us is like trying to live with parts missing. We have become so dependent upon the security of the next project that they are no longer *our* projects. We are owned by them. Workaholics often experience some depression when they complete a task. Instead of dealing with the natural feeling of letdown, we overlap completion with a new beginning. Hence, like the relationship addict, we never have to deal with separation or beginnings and endings. In fact, we never have to deal with anything."[220]

—Anne Wilson Schaef

"The press of busyness is like a charm. It is sad to observe how its power swells, how it reaches out seeking always to lay hold of ever-younger victims so that childhood or youth are scarcely allowed the quiet and the retirement in which the Eternal may unfold a divine growth."[221]

—Søren Kierkegaard

"I asked the boy beneath the pines.
He said: The master's gone alone
Herb-picking somewhere on the mount,
Cloud-hidden, whereabouts unknown."[222]

—Chia Tao–8th century

*"In six days the Lord made the heavens and the earth,
and on the seventh day he rested and was refreshed."*
Exodus 31:17 NIV

- Can you imagine living without slaving away at your projects? Are you dependent upon the security of your next project to anesthetize yourself to painful feelings or realities?

- Are you able to "do nothing . . . and then relax?" . . . to disappear to "whereabouts unknown?"
- If it's "quiet and retirement in which the Eternal may unfold a divine growth," are you determined to regularly retire quietly by yourself– "gone alone?"

Abba, thank you for the seventh day. By means of it I am freed of my seemingly uncurable need for production, haste, and importance.

For more: *Meditations for Women Who Do Too Much* by Anne Wilson Schaef

---

Who's Right? Who's Wrong?

"Could our minds and our hearts be big enough just to hang out in that space where we're not entirely certain about who's right and who's wrong? Could we have no agenda when we walk into a room with another person, not know what to say, not make that person wrong or right? Could we see, hear, feel other people as they really are? It is powerful to practice this way, because we'll find ourselves continually rushing around to try to feel secure again–to make ourselves or them either right or wrong. But true communication can happen only in that open space."[223]

—Pema Chödrön

"The dualistic mind is essentially binary. It is either/or thinking. It knows by comparison, by opposition, by differentiation. It uses descriptive words like good/evil, pretty/ugly, intelligent/stupid, not realizing there may be 55 or 155 degrees between the two ends of each spectrum. It works well for the sake of simplification and conversation, but not for the sake of truth or even honest experience. Actually, you need your dualistic mind to function in everyday life: to do your job as a teacher, a doctor, or an engineer. It is great stuff as far as it goes, but it doesn't go far enough. The dualistic mind cannot process things like infinity, mystery, God, grace, suffering, death, or love. When it comes to unconditional love, the dualistic mind can't even begin to understand it."[224]

—Richard Rohr

"All of you,
clothe yourselves with humility
toward one another."
1 Peter 5:5 NIV

- Can you identify examples of dualistic thinking in your world? . . . in yourself?
- Is your desire to love well strong enough for you to exist in that space where you're not entirely certain about "who's right and who's wrong?"
- Is there a practice you can adopt to grow in humility, particularly when it comes to dualistic thinking?

Abba, grant me a heart that cares more about loving people than showing them they're wrong.

For more: *The Naked Now* by Richard Rohr

Depression as a "Trapdoor" to God

"I used to be ashamed of my depression, but now I see it's a secret trapdoor to God. When it hits, I sink down into that black hole and often find Jesus there.... Now when I am asked [who Jesus is], I am most inclined to say, 'Jesus is the one who sits down close to me in my black hole of despair, offering himself until it passes.'"[225]

—Jim Palmer

"Grace is only truly appreciated and expressed in the actual, immediate experience of real life situations. Finally, it can only be 'lived into.'"[226]

—Gerald May

"Oh, night that guided me,
Oh, night more lovely than the dawn,
Oh, night that joined Beloved with lover,
Lover Transformed in the Beloved!"

—John of the Cross

*"Three times I pleaded with the Lord to take it [Paul's "thorn in the flesh"]
away from me. But he said to me, 'My grace is sufficient for you, for my
power is made perfect in weakness.' Therefore I will boast all the more gladly
about my weaknesses,
so that Christ's power may rest on me. That is why, for Christ's sake,
I delight in weaknesses, in insults, in hardships, in persecutions, in difficulties.
For when I am weak, then I am strong."*
2 Corinthians 12:8–10 NIV

- Do you have some weakness, hardship, persecution, addiction or other difficulty that causes you to sink down into "a black hole of despair?"

- Can you imagine Jesus sitting down close to you in that dark, painful place and "offering himself until it passes?" Do that now.

- We often despise our weaknesses, and ourselves for being weak, but the apostle Paul says he is glad for his weaknesses and delights in his difficulties. The next time you visit your own painful "black hole" of trouble, can you wait there for God to make himself known to you in a new and saving way–offering you, not necessarily healing, but the gift of himself? . . . a new sense of God's presence? . . . the experience that God is enough?

Abba, thank you for desiring to make yourself known to me in the midst of my most painful experiences. Help me notice, listen, learn, submit, give thanks, be comforted, and be changed.

For more: *Divine Nobodies* by Jim Palmer

God Suffers With Us in Our Suffering

"God desires closeness; intimacy is God's goal. Further, God is one who chooses to be so present in the finitude and frailty of a human being–indeed, a powerless human being as power is usually conceived. He is one who startles the nations, for who would have believed that the arm of the Lord was revealed in such a one as this (Isa. 53:1)? In and through such individuals, God thereby identifies with frail people. And it is thereby shown that God is not a suffering-at-a-distance God; God enters into the suffering of all creatures and experiences their life."[227]

—Terrence Fretheim

"So I weep, as Jazer weeps . . . I drench you with tears!
The shouts of joy over your ripened fruit and your harvests have been stilled.*

. . .

No one treads out wine at the presses, for I have put an end to the shouting.
My heart laments for Moab like a harp, my inmost being for Kir Hareseth."
Isaiah 16:9–11 NIV

"To hear such mourning on the part of God for a non-Israelite people is striking indeed. Most of this language is also used to describe the weeping and wailing of the Moabites, so that the impression created is that of a God whose lamentation is as deep and broad as that of the people themselves. As with Israel, God is the one who has occasioned the judgment in the first place (e.g., Jer. 48:38); but once the judgment has occurred, God joins those who mourn."[228]

—Terrence Fretheim

- God "has occasioned the judgment . . . but once the judgment has occurred, God joins those who mourn." Contemplate that. Isn't it amazing?

- Have you ever mourned over some disobedience of yours and the divine chastening that followed? Did you realize that God was there, in his love for you, mourning with you–still loving you?

- God "identifies with frail people"–and not only with "his people" (Israel, the church), but with all people (e.g., Moab). Does your attitude towards unbelievers reflect God's attitude? Can you have compassion even for those God might be judging?

Abba, soften my heart towards *all* those you love.

For more: *The Suffering of God* by Terrence Fretheim

Putting Painful Longings in Perspective

"First, our desires … are related not only to our fallenness but also, and more profoundly, to our humanness. In other words, it's okay to desire. Second, when we look carefully at what we deeply desire, we come to realize that what we want is simply not available, not until Heaven.… Both errors in responding to our longings–hiding them in a flurry of Christian activity and focusing on them to find satisfaction–deny the simple truth that we legitimately want what we cannot have in this world. We were designed to live in a perfect world uncorrupted by the weeds of disharmony and distance. Until we take up residence in that world, however, we will hurt. It is, therefore, not only okay to desire, it is also okay to hurt."[229]

—Larry Crabb

"To grit your teeth and clench your fists in order to survive the world at its harshest and worse–is by that very act, to be unable to let something be done for you and in you that is more wonderful still. The trouble with steeling yourself against the harshness of reality is that the same steel that secures your life against being destroyed secures your life also against being opened up and transformed."[230]

—Frederick Buechner

"It is easy to be attracted to the idea of grace–which one dictionary defines as 'divine love and protection bestowed freely on people'–but much harder to recognize this grace when it comes as pain and unwelcome change.… For grace to be grace, it must give us things we didn't know we needed and take us to places where we didn't want to go."[231]

—Kathleen Norris

> *"Scorn has broken my heart*
> *and has left me helpless;*
> *I looked for sympathy, but there was none,*
> *for comforters, but I found none."*
> Psalm 69:20 NIV

- Does your faith allow you, or perhaps even encourage you, to feel emotions like loneliness, sadness, and disappointment?

- Do you purposely attempt to feel your feelings, or do you distract yourself from them in a flurry of activity?

- Why has God make you such an emotional being? Of what benefit could your emotions be to you?

Abba, help me to listen to the wisdom hiding within my most painful emotions.

For more: *Inside Out* by Larry Crabb

Love in Dreams

"Those who are hardest to love need it most."

—Socrates

"Early in *The Brothers Karamazov*, a wealthy woman asks Staretz Zosima how she can really know that God exists. The Staretz tells her that no explanation or argument can achieve this, only the practice of 'active love.' He assures her that really there is no other way to know God in reality rather than God as an idea. The woman confesses that sometimes she dreams about a life of loving service to others–she thinks perhaps she will become a Sister of Mercy, live in holy poverty and serve the poor in the humblest way.... But then it crosses her mind how ungrateful some of the people she is serving are likely to be. They will probably complain that the soup she is serving isn't hot enough or that the bread isn't fresh enough or the bed is too hard and the covers too thin. She confesses to Staretz Zosima that she couldn't bear such ingratitude–and so her dreams about serving others vanish, and once again she finds herself wondering if there really is a God. To this the Staretz responds with the words, 'Love in practice is a hard and dreadful thing compared to love in dreams.'"[232]

—Jim Forest

"If I gave everything I have to the poor
and even sacrificed my body . . .
if I didn't love others,
I would have gained nothing."
1 Corinthians 13:3 NLT

- We often think of God and love in comforting ways. Dostoyevsky suggests that love is "a hard and dreadful thing" and that without such love, we'll fail to know God as more than an idea.

- Have you ever known God only as "an idea"–believing all the right things but not really practicing the hard love that is God's signature?

- You don't have to join a convent or monastery to practice hard love. Who around you is the hardest to love and most in need of your love?

Abba, I like easy not hard, superficial not real, and peace not conflict. Apparently, I also prefer illusion to reality. Lord, teach me to love.

For more: *The Course of Love* by Alain de Botton

The Constant Purification of Motives

"Jesus tells us to give alms, and fast, and pray secretly (Matthew 6:1–6, 16–18). These are the three religious disciplines honored by most historical religions. Whenever you perform a religious action publicly, it enhances your image as a good, moral person and has a strong social payoff. Jesus' constant emphasis is on interior religiosity, on purifying motivation and intention. He tells us to clean the inside of the dish instead of being so preoccupied with cleaning the outside, with looking good (Matthew 23:25–26). The purifying of our intention and motivation is the basic way that we unite our inner and our outer worlds. (Please read that twice!) All through the spiritual journey, we should be asking ourselves, 'Why am I doing this? Am I really doing this for God, for truth, or for others? Or am I doing it for hidden reasons?' The spiritual journey could be seen as a constant purification of motive until I can finally say, 'I have no other reason to do anything except love of God and love of neighbor. And I don't even need people to know this.'"[233]

—Richard Rohr

"And your Father,
who sees what is done in secret,
will reward you."
Matthew 6:18 NASB

- Are you preoccupied with looking good at church? If so, why? Are you as good as you look? Do you feel free to be transparent?

- Do you ask, "Why am I doing this?" Are you aware of your ego's need for a strong social payoff? Are you aware of your hidden motives?

- Sometimes I think, "I hope someone will share this about me at my funeral." I don't mind if it's a secret until then–after all, I want to be (and be known!) as a modest person. I don't feel the need to advertise what few things might make me look good . . . but, I *do* want credit, even if I'm dead! Is it just me, or can you relate?

Abba, I admit I want credit. I admit I want to be admired. I admit that, even though your approval should be everything, I seem to need more. Help me to focus less on what others think of me and more on what you and others need from me.

For more: *Eager to Love* by Richard Rohr

Experiential Knowledge of Spiritual Things

"The Franciscan priest Richard Rohr has written some thirty books, many of which are variations on the same theme. Not long into this book [Eager to Love] he says as much in a footnote. The idea that 'our deepest identity is hidden from us,' and that the purpose of authentic religion is to help us recover our true identity in God, is 'the core message of this entire book, and really my only message in all of my books' .... In this version of that theme, Rohr returns to his Franciscan roots to help us recapture the 'experiential heart of the gospel,' ... which stands in stark contrast to spirituality that's little more than theological concepts, religious ritual, and institutional conformity. Authentic spirituality [requires] ... 'mysticism' ... –experiential knowledge of spiritual things, as opposed to book knowledge, secondhand knowledge, or even church knowledge."[234]

—Daniel Clendenin

"If they [Christians] are to live as true members of Christ and radiate the divine influence among the men with whom they are in contact, they will be obliged to develop rich interior lives of union with God ....[235]

"To be a Christian then, is to be committed to a deeply mystical life.... By faith one not only consents to propositions revealed by God, one not only attains to truth in a way that intelligence and reason alone cannot do, but one assents to God Himself. One *receives* God. One says 'yes' not merely to a statement *about* God, but to the Invisible, Infinite God Himself."[236]

—Thomas Merton

"And all of us, with our unveiled faces like mirrors
reflecting the glory of the Lord,
are being transformed into the image that we reflect
in brighter and brighter glory;
this is the working of the Lord who is the Spirit."
2 Corinthians 3:18 NJB

If we're not careful, we can be "experts" on God who have no intimate relationship with God–no transforming "assent" to God's Invisible, Infinite person.

- Do you talk more *about* God than *with* God?

- Is your experience of God "secondhand?"

- What are you doing to "develop a rich interior life of union with God?"

Abba, I forever renounce faith as merely mental construct, ethic, or commitment–and instead commit to seeking and assenting to you in all your nearness.

Your Power to Crush Or to Bless

"'Look, Daddy! What's that?' I stopped talking with my neighbor and looked down.

'A beetle,' I said.

David was impressed and pleased with the discovery of this fancy, colorful creature.

My neighbor lifted his foot and stepped on the insect, giving it an extra twist into the dirt.

'That ought to do it,' he laughed.

David looked up at me, waiting for an explanation, a reason. I did not wish to embarrass my neighbor, but then David turned, picked up the hose, and continued spraying the raspberries.

That night, just before he turned off the lights in his bedroom, David whispered. 'I like'd that beetle, Daddy.'

'I did too,' I whispered back."[237]

—Christopher de Vinck

"At root, the spiritual life consists in choosing the way of littleness. I become less so that Jesus might become greater. Its essence is *No–No* to ourselves, our impulses and cravings, our acts of self-promotion and self-vindication, our use of power for its own sake. It calls us to deny ourselves possessions, rights, conquests that we're temped to claim just because we can. It is growing, day by day, into the same attitude that Christ had, and by exactly the same means: emptying ourselves, giving ourselves. It is refusing to grasp what we think is owed us and instead embracing what we think is beneath us. Simply behold, in love and wonder, what you have strength to crush. Exercise power–power you might use otherwise–to serve, bless, protect."[238]

—Mark Buchanan

"It will be good for those servants
whose master finds them watching when he comes.
. . . He will dress himself to serve,

151

will have them recline at the table
and will come and wait on them."
Luke 12:37 NIV

- Choosing "the way of littleness" is counter-cultural. Are you attempting it?
- The phrase "growing day by day" reminds us that spiritual growth is incremental. What can you do daily to increasingly practice the way of littleness?
- Do you think of yourself as having strength to crush others? Think about your relationships with this in mind.

Abba, I want to serve, bless, and protect, not harm.

For more: *The Rest of God* by Mark Buchanan

Hitting Bottom, Engulfed in Darkness

"I have learned things in the dark that I could never have learned in the light, things that have saved my life over and over again ...."[239]

—Barbara Brown Taylor

"When we have hit bottom and are emptied of all we thought important to us, then we truly pray, truly become humble and detached, and live in the bright darkness of faith. In the midst of the emptying we know that God has not deserted us. He has merely removed the obstacles keeping us from a deeper union with Him. Actually we are closer to God than ever before, although we are deprived of the consolations that we once associated with our spirituality. What we thought was communion with Him was really a hindrance to that communion.... The theology of the dark night is simplicity itself. God strips us of natural delights and spiritual consolations in order to enter more fully into our hearts."[240]

—Brennan Manning

"To come to the pleasure you have not, you must go by a way in which you enjoy not."

—John of the Cross

"God disciplines us for our good,
that we may share in his holiness."
Hebrews 12:10 NIV

- We might think we want a deeper union with God until we learn what God does to remove obstacles that hinder that. He may empty us of all we thought was important, and leave us feeling deserted and deprived of pleasures we depend on. Is your desire for deeper union with God greater than your desire to escape this painful path of transformation?

- Imagine how confusing and unpleasant this can be, especially for someone who is unaware of this necessity. Are you aware of the likelihood that such an experience is in your future? If you minister to others, are you warning them?

- We have probably learned and perhaps teach others that learning doctrine is the key to spiritual formation. Is this your approach? Can you see why this approach is not enough in itself? If so, what are the implications for you?

Abba, sustain me in the journey to deeper union with you.

For more: *The Signature of Jesus* by Brennan Manning

When You Fail, as You Must

"There is no failure except in no longer trying."

—Albert Hubbard

"It is by going down into the abyss that we recover the treasures of life. Where you stumble, there lies your treasure."

—Joseph Campbell

"It is always possible to make a new start by means of repentance. 'You fell ... now arise' (cf. Prov. 24:16). And if you fall again, then rise again, without despairing at all of your salvation, no matter what happens.... Should we fall, we should not despair and so estrange ourselves from the Lord's love.... We should not cut ourselves off from Him … nor should we lose heart when we fall short of our goal … let us always be ready to make a new start. If you fall, rise up. If you fall again, rise up again. Only do not abandon your Physician…. Wait on Him, and He will be merciful …."[241]

—St. Peter of Damascus

"The weakness which is serviceable is the weakness which seeks the aid of a physician."

—Bernard of Clairvaux

"Do all in your power not to fall, for the strong athlete should not fall. But if you do fall, get up again at once and continue the contest. Even if you fall a thousand times … rise up again each time, and keep on doing this until the day of your death."[242]

—John of Karpathos

"The path of descent is the path of transformation. Darkness, failure, relapse, death, and woundedness are our primary teachers, rather than ideas or doctrines."[243]

—Richard Rohr

"The Lord is like a father to his children,
tender and compassionate to those who fear him.
For he knows how weak we are;
he remembers we are only dust."
Psalm 103:13, 14 NLT

- The Lord remembers that you are "weak." Do you?

- Does failures cause you to hide from God or seek the divine physician?

- Even when you fail the same test a thousand times, can you determine not to lose heart? . . . to rise again?

- Failure, including repeated failure, is one of God's "primary teachers." What might God be teaching you in your falling down?

Abba, a righteous man falls seven times, and rises again. May I be that man.

For more: *Set Your Heart Free* by Francis de Sales

The Danger of the Spotlight . . . and Success

"No one can be a public person, without risk to his soul, unless first he is a private person. No one can be a speaker, without risk to his soul, unless first he is fulfilled when he says nothing. . . . Who enjoys tranquility? The one who doesn't take seriously either praise or lack of it from people."

—Thomas a Kempis

"Blessed is that servant who does not think himself better when he is praised and exalted by men, than when he is despised and considered simple and good-for-nothing, for what a man is in the sight of God, this he is and no more."

—Francis of Assisi

"Prosperity knits a man to the World. He feels that he is 'finding his place in it', while really it is finding its place in him."[244]

—C. S. Lewis

"There was no weight there [below the waterline in his sailboat]. In a moment when a well-designed keel and adequate ballast might have saved the ship they were nowhere to be found."[245]

—Gordon MacDonald

"If you think you are standing strong,
be careful not to fall."
1 Corinthians 10:12 NLT

- Do you need affirmation and approval to feel good about yourself? When someone praises you, do you take it seriously? Assess the level of danger you are in based on your answers.

- "What a man is in the sight of God, this he is and no more." That's convicting. Is the part of your life which is above the water line and seen by others, kept safe by weight below the water line–an adequate "ballast?" What is your ballast?

- A "disruptive moment" (MacDonald) is certain to come. Are you preparing yourself for the inevitable? If yes, how?

Abba, help me to focus on who I am in your sight, on having weight, on being ready for crisis. May integrity and uprightness protect me, because I hope in you.

For more: *The Life God Blesses* by Gordon MacDonald

Community, Stability, and Spirituality

"Everything in life, contrary to Madison Avenue's guarantees, can't be cured or resolved or eliminated. Some things must simply be endured. Some things must simply be borne. Some things must simply be accepted. Community and relationships enable us to do that.... It is in community where we find out who we really are. It is life with another that shows my impatience and life with another that demonstrates my possessiveness and life with another that gives notice to my nagging devotion to the self. Life with someone else, in other words, doesn't show me nearly as much about his or her shortcomings as it does about my own. In human relationships I learn how to soften my hard spots and how to reconcile and how to care for someone else besides myself. In human relationships I learn that theory is no substitute for love. It is easy to talk about the love of God; it is another thing to practice it. That's how relationships sanctify me. They show me where holiness is for me. That's how relationships develop me. They show me where growth is for me.... Alone, I am what I am, but in community I have the chance to become everything that I can be. And so, stability bonds me to this group of people and to these relationships so that resting in the security of each other we can afford to stumble and search, knowing that we will be caught if we fall and we will be led where we cannot see by those who have been there before us."[246]

—Joan Chittister

"Iron sharpens iron,
So one man sharpens another."
Proverbs 27:17 NASB

- Are you discovering who you really are through your life in community-perhaps as a spouse, sibling, parent, roommate, employee, church member, or neighbor? What about you needs to change?

- Have you discovered in your relationships that some things won't change and must simply be endured? Have you accepted that?

- Are you tempted to leave when really instead you need to change?

Abba, help me to submit to this messy but essential part of spirituality.

For more: *Wisdom Distilled From the Daily* by Joan Chittister

---

The Divine Gaze

"Jacob's theophany, his dream of angels on a stairway to heaven, strikes me as an appealing tale of unmerited grace. Here's a man who has just deceived his father and cheated his brother out of an inheritance. But God's response to finding Jacob vulnerable, sleeping all alone in open country, is not to strike him down for his sins but to give him a blessing.... Jacob's exclamation is ... a reminder that God can choose to dwell everywhere and anywhere we go. One morning this past spring I noticed a young couple with an infant at an airport departure gate. The baby was staring intently at other people, and as soon as he recognized a human face, no matter whose it was, no matter if it was young or old, pretty or ugly, bored or happy or worried-looking he would respond with absolute delight. It was beautiful to see. Our drab departure gate had become the gate of heaven. And as I watched that baby play with any adult who would allow it, I felt awe-struck as Jacob, because I realized that this is how God looks at us, staring into our faces in order to be delighted, to see the creature he made and called good, along with the rest of creation. And, as Psalm 139 puts it, darkness is as nothing to God, who can look right through whatever evil we've done in our lives to the creature made in the divine image."[247]

—Kathleen Norris

"Then Jacob awoke from his sleep and said,
'Surely the Lord is in this place, and I did not know it.

. . . How awesome is this place!
This is none other than the house of God,
and this is the gate of heaven."
Genesis 28:16–17 NLT

- The "God of Jacob" is, of necessity, a God of grace. What feelings arise when you consider that the God of Jacob is your God? (Psalm 46)

- God gazes into our faces "in order to be delighted." What feelings does God intend for you as you ponder this?

- Imagine how your grandchild gazes at you, or your child going off to war, or your spouse as you're taken into surgery. Now imagine God gazing at you. Feel it, don't analyze it.

Abba, never hide from me the light of your face.

For more: *Amazing Grace* by Kathleen Norris

Unable to Answer the Knock at Midnight

"A theology of love cannot afford to be sentimental. It cannot afford to preach edifying generalities about charity, while identifying 'peace' with mere established power and legalized violence against the oppressed. A theology of love cannot be allowed merely to serve the interests of the rich and powerful, justifying their wars, their violence, and their bombs, while exhorting the poor and underprivileged to practice patience, meekness, long-suffering and to solve their problems, if at all, non-violently. The theology of love must seek to deal drastically with evil and injustice in the world, and not merely to compromise with them. . . . Theology does not exist merely to appease the already too untroubled conscience of the powerful and the established. A theology of love may also conceivably turn out to be a theology of revolution. In any case, it is a theology of resistance, a refusal of the evil that reduces a brother to homicidal desperation."[248]

—Thomas Merton

"In the terrible midnight of war men have knocked on the door of the church to ask for the bread of peace, but the church has often disappointed them. What more pathetically reveals the irrelevancy of the church in present-day world affairs than its witness regarding war? In a world gone mad with arms buildups, chauvinistic passions, and imperialistic exploitation, the church has either endorsed these activities or remained appallingly silent....A weary world, pleading desperately for peace, has often found the church morally sanctioning war....And those who have gone to the church to seek the bread of economic justice have been left in the frustrating midnight of economic deprivation. In many instances the church has so aligned itself with the privileged classes and so defended the status quo that it has been unwilling to answer the knock at midnight."[249]

—Martin Luther King, Jr.

"A person who seeks to honor
the one who sent him
speaks truth, not lies."
John 7:18 NLT

- Is your theology of love a "theology of resistance?"
- Is your church aligned with the privileged classes and the status quo?
- Where in our day, might the church be guilty of appeasing "the already too untroubled?"

Abba, keep me from conforming to this world, or allowing others to do so in peace.

For more: *Faith and Violence* by Thomas Merton

Catastrophic Loss and the Growth of the Soul

"If normal, natural, reversible loss is like a broken limb, then catastrophic loss is like an amputation....Catastrophic loss by definition precludes recovery. It will transform us or destroy us, but it will never leave us the same. There is no going back to the past, which is gone forever, only going ahead to the future, which has yet to be discovered. Whatever that future is, it will, and must, include the pain of the past with it. Sorrow never entirely leaves the soul of those who have suffered a severe loss. If anything, it may keep going deeper. But this depth of sorrow is the sign of a healthy soul, not a sick soul. It does not have to be morbid and fatalistic. It is not something to escape but something to embrace. Jesus said, 'Blessed are those who mourn, for they will be comforted.' Sorrow indicates that people who have suffered loss are living authentically in a world of misery, and it expresses the emotional anguish of people who feel pain for themselves and others. Sorrow is noble and gracious. It enlarges the soul until the soul is capable of mourning and rejoicing simultaneously [just like God], of feeling the world's pain and hoping for the world's healing at the same time [just like God]. However painful, sorrow is good for the soul. . . . No matter how deep the pit into which I descend, I keep finding God there. He is not aloof from my suffering but draws near to me when I suffer."[250]

—Jerry Sittser [bracketed phrases by Pete Scazzero]

"In this world you will have trouble.
But take heart! I have overcome the world."
John 16:33 NIV

- Is your sorrow ever-present? Is it destroying you or transforming you?
- Has your loss been "a grace disguised?" If so, how so?
- Has your soul been enlarged? Are you more capable of mourning and rejoicing simultaneously–just like God? . . . more capable of feeling the world's pain and hoping for the world's healing at the same time–just like God?

Abba, thank you for your sometimes exceedingly painful gifts. I depend on your drawing near in the pit. Help me to love authentically in a world of misery.

For more: *A Grace Disguised* by Jerry Sittser

It's Not Always About You

"If people don't have some lightness in their lives then they end up taking themselves too seriously and are unable to move outside themselves. And a great deal of spirituality lies in putting yourself in an appropriate place in the universe. Those who can laugh at themselves can also look at themselves critically, but not harshly, a key element of emotional growth."[251]

—David Robb

"The truly holy are humble because they know their place before God. But how, with our accomplishments and our egos, especially in a culture that tells us that we have to be on top, to be number one, to be successful, do we keep that humility before us? Self-deprecating humor . . . is one way to do this. Laughing at yourself, not taking yourself too seriously, not making every situation about you, not demanding that life adjust itself to suit your needs, and laughing at yourself when you forget all this are good places to start."[252]

—James Martin

"Laugh. For this laughter is an acknowledgment that you are a human being. An acknowledgment that is itself the beginning of the acknowledgment of God. For how else is a person to acknowledge God except for admitting in his life and by means of his life that he himself is not God but a creature that has his times–a time to weep and a time to laugh, and the one is not the other. A praising of God is what laughter is, because it lets a human being be human."[253]

—Karl Rahner

"Our mouths were filled with laughter,
our tongues with songs of joy.
Then it was said among the nations,
'The Lord has done great things for them.'"
Psalm 126:2 NIV

- Is laughter in your repertoire? If so, how does it help you keep things in perspective?

- If you can laugh at yourself, you can look at yourself critically but not harshly which is a key element of emotional growth. *Can* you laugh at yourself?
- It's not about you. You're not in control. Can you laugh at yourself when you forget all this, and let humor bring you back to your senses and proper place before God?

Abba, keep me from taking myself or others too seriously.

For more: *Between Heaven and Mirth* by James Martin

Knowing Self, Knowing God

"All people have three characters, that which they exhibit, that which they are, and that which they think they are."

—Alphonse Karr

"True and sound wisdom, consists of two parts: the knowledge of God and of ourselves. But while joined by many bonds, which one precedes and brings forth the other is not easy to discern. In the first place, no one can look upon himself without immediately turning his thoughts to the contemplation of God, in whom he 'lives and moves' [Acts 17:28].... The knowledge of ourselves not only arouses us to seek God, but also, as it were, leads us by the hand to find him. Again, it is certain that man never achieves a clear knowledge of himself unless he has first looked upon God's face, and then descends from contemplating him to scrutinize himself."[254]

—John Calvin

"If I find God I will find myself and if I find my true self I will find God."[255]

—Thomas Merton

"Contemplation is also the response to a call ... from Him Who has no voice, and yet Who speaks in everything that is, and Who, most of all, speaks in the depths of our own being ...."[256]

—Thomas Merton

"I will give them a heart to know Me, for I am the LORD;
and they will be My people, and I will be their God . . . ."
Jeremiah 24:7a NASB

Calvin insists that "sound and true wisdom" consists in essentially two things–knowing ourselves and knowing God. We must know ourselves intimately to know God properly, and we must know God intimately to know ourselves properly.

- Are you devoting as much effort to knowing yourself as you are to knowing God? Can you imagine truly knowing one and not the other?

- Have you been aroused to seek God or find him in a new way through "scrutiny of yourself?"

- Are you responding to the "call from Him Who has no voice, and yet Who speaks in everything?" Do you to listen for his voice "in the depths of your own being?"

Abba, lead me, as it were, by the hand, into a deeper experience of knowing myself . . . and you.

For more: *Seeds: Thomas Merton* edited by Robert Inchausti

May 6   November 3

Sabbath and the Trance of Overwork

"Sabbath is not dependent upon our readiness to stop. We do not stop when we are finished. We do not stop when we complete our phone calls, finish our project, get through this stack of messages, or get out this report that is due tomorrow. We stop because it is time to stop. . . . Sabbath dissolves the artificial urgency of our days, because it liberates us from the need to be finished. . . . In the trance of overwork, we take everything for granted. We consume things, people, and information. We do not have time to savor this life, nor to care deeply and gently for ourselves, our loved ones, or our world; rather with increasingly dizzying haste, we use them all up, and throw them away."[257]

—Wayne Muller

"To gain control of the world of space is certainly one of our tasks. The danger begins when in gaining power in the realm of space we forfeit all aspirations in the realm of time. *There is a realm of time where the goal is not to have but to be, not to own but to give, not to control but to share, not to subdue but to be in accord.* Life goes wrong when the control of space, the acquisition of things of space, becomes our sole concern."[258]

—Abraham Joshua Heschel

Sabbath "…invites us to rest. It asks us to notice that while we rest, the world continues without our help."[259]

—Wendell Berry

"Sabbath is about withdrawal from the anxiety system of Pharaoh, the refusal to let one's life be defined by production."[260]

—Walter Brueggemann

"Set me free from the laziness that goes about disguised as activity when activity is not demanded of me …"

—Thomas Merton

"Then Jesus said,
'Let's go off by ourselves to a quiet place
and rest awhile.'"
Mark 6:31a NLT

- Are you in an overwork-induced trance? Is your urgency necessary or artificial? Would Jesus agree?

- Is your life characterized by a "dizzying haste?" Do you have the freedom to care deeply and gently for yourself and your loved ones?

- Do you stop only when you're "finished?" If so, what does that say about you? Do you ever really stop?

Abba, subvert my artificial urgency. Deliver me from the anxiety system that surrounds me.

For more: *Sabbath* by Wayne Muller

A Life of Constant Repentance

"Forgive us for the evil we have done, and the evil done on our behalf."

—The Episcopal Liturgy

"There is so much evil done on our behalf [as Americans]....A racist criminal justice and penal system. War, drones and torture. Systemic poverty, the absence of worker protections or living wage laws, the constriction of unions. Oppression of the poor, immigrants, people of color. Globalized capitalism and sweatshop labor. The abuse and exploitation of the environment for financial gain and our financial ease. Racial injustice. Environmental injustice. Injustice anywhere is a threat to justice everywhere, King once said, and his words ring true. For, in today's world, injustice isn't just anywhere. It's everywhere."[261]

—David Henson

"It is the work of Christians in the world to minister in word and deed and to gather together to do justice....A life poured out in doing justice for the poor, is the inevitable sign of any real, true gospel faith."[262]

—Tim Keller

"Contemplation, at its highest intensity, becomes a reservoir of spiritual vitality that pours itself out in the most telling social action."[263]

—Thomas Merton

"Learn to do good; seek justice, reprove the ruthless,
defend the orphan, plead for the widow."
Isaiah 1:17 NASB

- One church tradition may emphasize the need for repentance for "the evil we have done" and another for "the evil done on our behalf." Which is your tradition? If you listen, can you hear God speaking in both traditions? What is lost by listening to only one or the other?

- Does your tradition have a place for the words of the prophet Isaiah? How does your church (or church tradition) "seek justice?" How does it "reprove the ruthless?"

- Do you agree that, as Christians, we should repent for "the evil done on our behalf?" Is that even possible? If so, what would it look like? What would be the point? Would it be unpatriotic?
- Can your heart be moved by the call to each of these kinds of repentance?

Abba, help me to live a life of constant repentance, full of doing good to those in need.

For more: *Generous Justice* by Tim Keller

The Most Important (And Difficult) Thing You'll Ever Do

"One learns to love God by loving men and women."

—Charles deFoucauld

"For one human being to love another: that is perhaps the most difficult of all our tasks, the ultimate, the last test and proof, the work for which all other is but preparation."[264]

—Rainer Maria Rilke

"Love is 'to reveal the beauty of another person to themselves,' wrote Jean Vanier. Jesus did that with each person he met. This ability to really listen and pay attention to people was at the very heart of Jesus' mission, and it could not help but move him to compassion. In the same way, out of our contemplative time with God, we too are invited to be prayerfully present to people, revealing their beauty to them. Unfortunately, the religious leaders of Jesus' day, the 'church leaders' of that time, never made that connection. They were diligent, zealous, and absolutely committed to having God as Lord of their lives. They memorized the entire books of Genesis, Exodus, Leviticus, Numbers, and Deuteronomy. They prayed five times a day. They tithed all their income and gave money to the poor. They evangelized. But they never delighted in people. They did not link loving God with the need to be diligent, zealous, and absolutely committed to growing in their ability to love people."[265]

—Pete Scazzero

"Ministry is simply about loving the person in front of you. It's about stopping for the one and being the very fragrance of Jesus to a lost and dying world."[266]

—Heidi Baker

"What value has compassion that does not take its object in its arms?"

—Antoine de Saint-Exupery

"Whoever does not love their brother and sister, whom they have seen, cannot love God, whom they have not seen."
1 John 4:20b NIV

- Are you determined to grow in your ability to love people?
- How can you practice being prayerfully present to whoever is "in front of you?"
- Have you been distracted by something else, no matter how noble, from doing the most difficult–and important–of all tasks?

Abba, I want to completely focus on people I'm with. I want them to feel my love and your love for them. I want to see for myself, and reveal to them, the beauty they possess as your beloved ones.

For more: *Emotionally Healthy Spirituality* by Peter Scazzero

---

Setting An Intention For Worship

"We prepare the children before they go in [to Children's church] with the expectations as to what it means to enter that space: 'Are you ready to be with God?' They take their shoes off, and they look you in the eye, and if they say 'No' then they can wiggle out in the hall until they're ready, and when they say 'Yes' they're expected to take a seat and listen and participate.... Oh, I would love to start church that way. ...We haven't really trained people on how do you help people prepare to be in a worshipful state of mind. There is more attention to that in a yoga session than there is in worship. People will come and be present, and do some breathing, and prepare themselves to be in their bodies and fully present to what's happening in yoga more than they would in a worship service. In my opinion, in the many thousands of worship services I have attended in my life, very few start with 'setting an intention.'"[267]

"Considering God not so much as an 'object' outside of ourselves, for whose greater glory we undertake all our different works, but rather as a 'subject' alive within and around us, a divine Presence, 'in whom we live and move and have our being,' is a notion explored [by] Thomas Merton. Merton ... makes a distinction between two kinds of intention, a *right* intention and a *simple* intention. When we have a *right* intention ... 'we seek to do God's will' but 'we consider the work and ourselves apart from God and outside of Him.' But 'when we have a *simple* intention, we ... do all that we do not only *for* God but, so to speak, *in* Him. We are more aware of Him who works in us than of ourselves or of our work.'"[268]

—Paul Murray

*"You will fill me with joy
in your presence."*
Psalm 16:11 NIV

- Is your intention to drop your guardedness and give God access to your life?
- Can you tell God that when you arrive for worship?
- In what other ways can you "set an intention" for worship?

Lord, let me be done with absent-mindedly going through the motions of worship.

For more: *The New Wine of Dominican Spirituality* by Paul Murray

The Community of Sinners and Saints

"Forgiveness flounders because I exclude the enemy from the community of humans even as I exclude myself from the community of sinners. But no one can be in the presence of the God of the crucified Messiah for long without overcoming this double exclusion–without transposing the enemy from the sphere of monstrous inhumanity into the sphere of shared humanity and herself from the sphere of proud innocence into the sphere of common sinfulness. When one knows that the torturer will not eternally triumph over the victim, one is free to rediscover that person's humanity and imitate God's love for him. And when one knows that God's love is greater than all sin, one is free to see oneself in the light of God's justice and so rediscover one's own sinfulness."[269]

—Miroslav Volf

"Strong hate, the hate that takes joy in hating, is strong because it does not believe itself to be unworthy and alone. It feels the support of a justifying God, of an idol of war, an avenging and destroying spirit. From such blood-drinking gods the human race was once liberated, with great toil and terrible sorrow, by the death of a God Who delivered Himself to the Cross and suffered pathological cruelty of His own creatures out of pity for them. In conquering death He opened their eyes to the reality of a love which asks no questions about worthiness, a love which overcomes hatred and destroys death. But men have now come to reject this divine revelation of pardons and they are consequently returning to the old war gods, the gods that insatiably drink blood and eat the flesh of men.... To serve the hate-gods, one has only to be blinded by collective passion. To serve the God of Love one must be free, one must face the terrible responsibility of the decision to love in spite of all unworthiness whether in oneself or in one's neighbor."[270]

—Thomas Merton

"Love your enemies"
Luke 6:27a NASB

- Do you see your enemy as God does–sharing both their sinfulness and humanity with you?

- Do you see yourself like them, not as innocent, but included in "the community of sinners?"
- Can you practice "a love that asks no questions about worthiness?"

Abba, may I overcome hatred with love.

For more: *Exclusion and Embrace* by Miroslav Volf

You Have to Do the Stuff

"What we see in many of the Eastern religions is not an emphasis upon verbal orthodoxy, but instead an emphasis upon practices and lifestyles that, if you do them (not think about them, but do them), your consciousness will gradually change. …Here at the [Center for Action and Contemplation] we want to emphasize the importance of praxis over theory, of orthopraxy over orthodoxy. We are not saying that theory and orthodoxy are not important; like Saint Francis, we feel that what is ours to do has more to do with our practical engagements, and the way we live our daily lives than making verbal assent to this or that idea. … In the last fifty years, education theory has come to recognize that listening to lectures and reading are among the least effective forms of learning. They are highly passive, individualistic, do not necessarily integrate head with heart or body, but leave both the ego (and the shadow self) in their well-defended positions, virtually untouched. As long as our ego self is in the driver's seat, nothing really new or challenging is going to happen. Remember our ego is committed to not changing, and is highly defensive by its very nature. And our shadow self entirely relies upon delusion and denial. Only the world of practical relationships exposes both of these. The form of education which most changes people in lasting ways has to touch them at a broader level than the thinking, reading mind can do. … Somehow we need to engage in hands-on experience, emotional risk-taking, moving outside of our comfort zones, with different people than our usual flattering friends. We need some expanded level of spiritual seeing or nothing really changes at a cellular or emotional level. Within minutes or hours of entertaining a new idea, we quickly return to our old friends, our assured roles, our familiar neural grooves, our ego patterns of response, and we are back to business as usual."[271]

—Richard Rohr

"Faith without works is dead."
James 2:26b NASB

- Have you experienced the limits of "orthodoxy?"
- You learn to love in a soup kitchen like you never would from a sermon. Have you experienced what Rohr calls "living into a new way of thinking?"

Abba, renew my mind, but don't stop there!

For more: *Radical Grace* by Richard Rohr

The Sorrows and Joys of Parenting

"Then Simeon blessed them, and he said to Mary, the baby's mother, 'This child is destined to cause many in Israel to fall, but he will be a joy to many others. He has been sent as a sign from God, but many will oppose him. As a result, the deepest thoughts of many hearts will be revealed. And a sword will pierce your very soul.'"
Luke 2:34–36

"Since mothers share in the sufferings of the children of their womb, those prophetic words of old Simeon could be appropriately addressed to every mother at the conclusion of her infant's baptism. Not simply mothering, but all parenting is painful as every mother and father knows. Still they are called to live lives of joy while enduring the sorrows of their children. Whatever your state in life; married, single, vowed religious, or ordained, it is essential to find a balance between joy and those sorrows that seem so unavoidable in this life. This balancing act is easier if you live the art of the famous three: giving thanks constantly, praying always, and rejoicing always. Give thanks constantly by expressing true gratitude for every small daily

171

domestic kindness. Pray always by living as consciously as possible in the presence of God as that mystery unfolds within your home. And rejoice always by searching for something good, the potential of happiness, hidden in every event–even those that are sorrowful. The last discovery of a joy hidden in some misfortune requires trusting God. Faith encourages you to open yourself to God's creative ability to convert darkness into light, to generate life out of death, to convert anger into peace and sorrow into joy."[272]

—Edward Hays

"And Mary said,
'My soul magnifies the Lord,
and my spirit rejoices in God my Savior.'"
Luke 1:46, 47 ESV

- Can you keep your eyes peeled for "every small daily domestic kindness" and give thanks for each one?

- Are you learning to be conscious of the mystery of God's presence unfolding in you home?

- Can you commit yourself to searching for something good hidden in every event–even the sorrowful? . . . to making your home a place where each one looks to God for God's transforming work?

Abba, I rely daily upon the loving, mysterious work of your presence in my home.

For more: *Chasing Joy* by Edward Hays

This Confusion of Images and Myths

"Contrary to common belief … Huxley [Brave New World] and Orwell [1984] did not prophesy the same thing. Orwell warns that we will be overcome by an externally imposed oppression. But in Huxley's vision, no Big Brother is required to deprive people of their autonomy, maturity and history. As he saw it, people will come to love their oppression, to adore the technologies that undo their capacities to think.

What Orwell feared were those who would ban books. What Huxley feared was that there would be no reason to ban a book, for there would be no one who wanted to read one. Orwell feared those who would deprive us of information. Huxley feared those who would give us so much that we would be reduced to passivity and egoism. Orwell feared that the truth would be concealed from us. Huxley feared the truth would be drowned in a sea of irrelevance. Orwell feared we would become a captive culture. Huxley feared we would become a trivial culture, preoccupied with some equivalent of the feelies, the orgy porgy, and the centrifugal bumblepuppy.... In 1984, Huxley added, people are controlled by inflicting pain. In Brave New World, they are controlled by inflicting pleasure. In short, Orwell feared that what we hate will ruin us. Huxley feared that what we love will ruin us. This book is about the possibility that Huxley, not Orwell, was right."[273]

—Neil Postman

"But how does one stop to separate the truth from the half-truth, the event from the pseudo-event, reality from the manufactured image? It is in this confusion of images and myths, superstitions and ideologies that the 'powers of the air' govern our thinking.... Where there is no critical perspective, no detached observation, no time to ask the pertinent questions, how can one avoid being deluded and confused?"[274]

—Thomas Merton

"What is truth?"
John 18:38 ESV

- Do you have enough leisure to develop some "critical perspective?"
- Are you sufficiently separated from the culture for "detached observation"–or so immersed that you can't help being "deluded and confused?" Be realistic.
- What exactly would detaching more look like for you?

Abba, help me as I attempt to "opt out" of the daily misinformation campaign of my world.

For more: Amusing Ourselves to Death by Neil Postman

Moving Upstream For Social Change

"Imagine a large river with a high waterfall. At the bottom of this waterfall hundreds of people are working frantically trying to save those who have fallen into the river and have fallen down the waterfall, many of them drowning. As the people along the shore are trying to rescue as many as possible one individual looks up and sees a seemingly never-ending stream of people falling down the waterfall and begins to run upstream. One of other rescuers hollers, 'Where are you going? There are so many people that need help here.' To which the man replied, 'I'm going upstream to find out why so many people are falling into the river.'"[275]

—Saul Alinsky

"[Other] rescuers notice that while there are too many babies coming floating down the river to save them all, the chubby ones float pretty well, so they focus on pulling out the skinny ones. One of the rescuers jumps in and starts teaching the babies in the river how to swim."

—Janey Skinner

"I will not tire of declaring that if we really want an effective end to violence we must remove the violence that lies at the root of all violence: structural violence, social injustice, exclusion of citizens from the management of the country, repression. All this is what constitutes the primal cause, from which the rest flows naturally."[276]

—Oscar Romero

"We are not to simply bandage the wounds of victims beneath the *wheels* of injustice, we are to drive *a spoke* into the *wheel* itself."

—Dietrich Bonhoeffer

"*Take away from Me the noise of your songs;*
I will not even listen to the sound of your harps.
But let justice roll down like waters
And righteousness like an ever-flowing stream."
Amos 5:23, 24 NASB

- Are you good at worship ("songs and harps") and weak on seeing to justice? How about your church?
- Have you ventured into the river to try to help its victims?
- Have you ventured upstream to try to discover the cause of the crisis?
- Is all your time and energy invested in "pulling out the skinny ones" and "teaching babies how to swim?"

Abba, make my religion one of doing, not only of thinking and believing. Make my attempts to help others wise ones, not only sincere and determined ones.

For more: *Welcoming Justice* by Charles Marsh and John Perkins

May 15

November 12

Wonder At the Wonder of Our Universe

"The whole of Creation is but one sacred temple of the One who created it."

—Gregory of Nyssa

"Look at the fruit of the Osage orange tree, big as a grapefruit, green, convoluted as any human brain. Or look at a rotifer's translucent gut: something orange and powerful is surging up and down like a piston, and something small and round is spinning in place like a flywheel. Look, in short, at practically anything—the coot's feet, the mantis's face, a banana, the human ear—and see that not only did the creator create everything, but that he is apt to create *anything*. He'll stop at nothing. There is no one standing with a blue pencil to say, 'Now that one, there, is absolutely ridiculous, and I won't have it.'… The world is full of creatures that for some reason seem stranger to us than others, and libraries are full of books describing them—hagfish, platypuses, lizardlike pangolins four feet long with bright green, lapped scares like umbrella-tree leaves on a bush hut roof, butterflies emerging from anthills, spiderlings wafting through the air clutching tiny silken balloons, horseshoe crabs … the creator creates … he creates everything and anything.… Of all known forms of life, only about ten percent are still living today. All other forms—fantastic plants, ordinary plants, living animals with unimaginably various wings, tails, teeth, brains–are utterly and forever gone. That is a great many forms that have been created. Multiplying ten times the number of living forms today yields a profusion that is quite beyond what I consider thinkable.... The creator goes off on one wild, specific tangent after another, or millions simultaneously, with an exuberance that would seem to be unwarranted, and with an abandoned energy sprung from an unfathomable font."[277]

—Annie Dillard

"The heavens declare the glory of God . . . ."
Psalm 19:1 ESV

- Did this quote make you smile? . . . worship? . . . give thanks?
- Are you aware of the wonder all around you? Are you in awe?
- When is the last time you really experienced nature for yourself?

Abba, thank you for the wonder of your creation.

For more: *Pilgrim at Tinker Creek* by Annie Dillard

The Pinnacle of God's Creation

"You have made us for yourself, O Lord, and our hearts are restless until they rest in you."

—Augustine

"As the New Testament and the church tradition teach, the *life* of God is nothing other than the perfect love that eternally unites the Father, Son, and Holy Spirit, and this Triune God spoke creation into being with the ultimate goal of inviting humans to share in this *life*.... [Jonathan] Edwards painted a portrait of the Trinity in which the love and joy of the three divine persons was so full and intense, it simply could not be contained. God's fullness thus yearned to be expressed and replicated by sharing it with others. So this fullness overflowed, as it were, as God brought forth a creation that mirrored his triune beauty. And the pinnacle of this creation is created beings whose yearning for God mirrors, in a small way, his yearning for them.

176

But whereas God's yearning comes out of his fullness, our yearning comes out of emptiness. It's a beautiful arrangement. The God of overflowing love longs to pour his love into others, so he creates beings that long for his love to be poured into them. But in my opinion … it wasn't God's original intention for us to ever go a moment with this longing unsatisfied. Living without the fullness of God's love is a reality we have brought on ourselves through our rebellion, and it's completely unnatural to us. And try as we may to run from it or numb it, the pain of our unnatural emptiness is acute and incurable. The profundity of our emptiness is the negative reflection of the profundity of the fullness of the One we long for."[278]

—Gregory Boyd

"And may you have the power to understand . . .
how wide, how long, how high, and how deep [God's] love is."
Ephesians 3:18 NLT

- Imagine the triune God choosing to make a home in you. How does that feel?

- Have you ever thought of your yearning for intimacy with God as mirroring God's yearning for intimacy with you?

- Have you ever thought of your longing for more as an indicator of God's longing to give you more?

Abba, how can it be that you have made your home in me?

For more: *Benefit of the Doubt* by Gregory Boyd

"Fun Jesus"

"When I imagine Jesus, it is not simply as a person who heals the sick, raises the dead, stills the storm, and preaches the good news. It's also as a man of great goodwill and compassion, with a zest for life … brimming with generous good humor. Full of high spirits. Playful. Even fun. Interestingly, in the past few decades two images of a joyful Jesus have enjoyed some popularity. The first is "*The Laughing Christ*" by Willis Wheatley, a sketch that shows Jesus's head thrown back in open-mouthed laughter. The second is "*The Risen Christ By the Sea*," a colorful portrait of Jesus wearing a broad smile and standing beside a fishing net, painted by Jack Jewell, a seascape artist, in the 1990s. These two paintings, among others, serve to counteract countless images of the gloomy Messiah.... But I wonder if some eschew these portraits [because they do] not for the quality of the artistry, but rather for their subject material. Is there something about a smiling Jesus that threatens our understanding of the man?"[279]

—James Martin

"Jesus frequently called together His disciples, His followers and often strangers to dine with him. It doesn't take too much imagination to picture these as joyful events—just think of enjoyable dinner parties and celebrations in your own life, full of laughter and good cheer, everyone delighting in one another's company. There is a reason that one enduring image of heaven is a banquet. Maureen O'Connell, an assistant professor of theology at Fordham University, says, 'At my house, we often laugh ourselves sick around the dinner table. Isn't this the point of dinner parties?'"[280]

—James Martin

"The Son of Man came eating and drinking, and they say,
'Here is a glutton and a drunkard,
a friend of tax collectors and sinners.'"
Matthew 11:18 NIV

- Are you uncomfortable with a Jesus who is "fun?" If so, can you say why?

- Have you perhaps created a Jesus in your own image—serious and humorless?

- It's interesting to me that a *woman* says "we often laugh ourselves sick." Statistically men have fewer friends than women, and die younger. Men, in the future, will you regret not "lightening up" more—being so serious so much of the time?

Abba, help me not to take myself, or my life, so seriously.

For more: *Between Heaven and Mirth by James Martin*

Your Enemy the Savage

"It took me a long time to learn that God is not the enemy of my enemies. He is not even the enemy of His enemies."

—Martin Niemöller

"Today, if African American protests turn into riots, the offenders are often referred to as 'animals.' In the early American West, native Americans were called 'savages,' and wartime slurs dehumanized Jews, Germans, and Japanese. Richard Rohr reminds us that we all have a viewpoint, and that each viewpoint is 'a view from a point.' Consequently, he says 'We need to critique our own perspective if we are to see and follow the full truth.' To love our enemies, as Jesus commands, and to escape our own unconscious biases, we will need such a critique."

—William Britton

"Do not be too quick to assume your enemy is a savage just because he is your enemy. Perhaps he is your enemy because he thinks you are savage. Or perhaps he is afraid of you because he feels that you are afraid of him. And perhaps if he believed you were capable of loving him he would no longer be your enemy. Do not be too quick to assume that your enemy is an enemy of God just because he is your enemy. Perhaps he is your enemy precisely because he can find nothing in you that gives glory to God. Perhaps he fears you because he can find nothing in you of God's love and God's kindness and God's patience and mercy and understanding of the weaknesses of men."[281]

—Thomas Merton

"I tell you, love your enemies
and pray for those who persecute you,
that you may be children of your Father in heaven."
Matthew 5:44, 45b NIV

- Do you understand your enemy well enough to understand his motives, for instance, the reasons he may fear you?

- Can you understand the forces in your world (historical, political, religious, racial, economic) that might make another person see you as an enemy?

- Does faith as you practice it tend to disarm others, or to make them suspicious and defensive?

- Do you approach those of other faiths or persuasions based on prejudices and stereotypes–perhaps the way they do with you?

Abba, may practiced love transform my enemy into my friend.

For more: *Seeds* by Thomas Merton

Busy Being Born Again . . . Again

"When we visited the makeshift tent city, I was angry. Oh yes–angry with God, angry with the world, angry with my own self. How is this place even possible in our world? I could not bear the smell, the sights, the truth of the place, and I saw babies the age of my tinies there. . . . And all of my carefully reasoned understandings about how everyone has a different calling and some of us are just called to different things than poverty relief and caring for orphans stank rank like heresy. I walked the rubble and nodded my gentle French Canadian bonsoir to their Creole bonswa as dusk gathered, and suddenly a thought broke into my mind: I would be terrified here. I would be so scared in the darkness. How did these women bear it? And one of our guides told me how before the United Nations installed spotlights it was literally a 'rape camp.' And then we stood in that very same tent city, among our Haitian brothers and sisters, babies in our laps, and we sang the canvas roof off: 'Glory, glory, glory to God; he's been good to us! Amen! Amen!' Me? I want to throw things when I am disappointed in my nice life. I pout, and I do not sing praise, because apparently, I expect my life to be perfect and clean and ideal and as pretty as Pinterest. I didn't want to cry in their church, out of respect, and so I sneaked my tears down my face. . . . I think I got born again, all over again, that night, and now God smells like sweat, like open sewage ditches, like charcoal and avocados in addition to my northern lakes and pine trees, clean air, and water."[282]

—Sarah Bessey

"I will sing praises to your name."
2 Samuel 22:50 NLT

- Are you a privileged person? How often to you think about it?
- Would you be afraid to leave home and perhaps be "born again" all over again?
- Are you quick to pout and slow to praise? What does your answer say about you?

Abba, the poor can teach me, and I have a lot to learn.

For more: *Jesus Feminist* by Sarah Bessey

Leaving Church

"Writing *Searching for Sunday* forced me to consider that perhaps real maturity is exhibited not in thinking myself above other Christians and organized religion, but in humbly recognizing the reality that I can't escape my own cultural situatedness and life experiences, nor do I want to escape the good gift of my (dysfunctional, beautiful, necessary) faith community.... The truth is, I am a Christian, which means I am religious. And I am an American, which means my Christianity is profoundly affected by privilege, by Western philosophy, by 17th century Puritanism, and by Psalty the Singing Songbook. My American Christian heritage includes both Martin Luther King Jr. and the white segregationists who opposed him—a reality that is both empowering and uncomfortable, but one I can't escape, one I want to look squarely in the eyes. Loving the Church means both critiquing it and celebrating it. We don't have to choose between those two things. But we cannot imagine ourselves to be so far above the Church that we are not a part of it. Like it or not, those of us who continue to follow Jesus will have to do so with our adopted siblings by our side. Yes, we are called to grow and mature, and yes, our convictions and denominational affiliations will likely change, but I've found I'm a better writer–and a better person–when I'm more focused on outgrowing the old me than I am on outgrowing other people in my community. After all, this is Kingdom growth. There aren't ladders, only trellises."[283]

—Rachel Held Evans

"I will build my church,
and the gates of hell
shall not prevail against it."
Matthew 16:18b ESV

- Have you decided you must either only celebrate or critique the church?
- "Those of us who continue to follow Jesus will have to do so with our adopted siblings by our side." Hasn't this always been the hard but inescapable reality about the church? It's often hard to bear with others–but then remember that old joke: "If you find a perfect church, don't go there. You'll only ruin it!" Are you trying to escape inescapable reality?
- Are you focused more on outgrowing the "old you" than on outgrowing other people in your community? If not, why not?

Loving Lord who loves us, teach us to love one another.

For more: *Searching for Sunday* by Rachel Held Evans

Tell Me

"When I ask, 'How are you?' that is really what I want to know. I am not asking how many items are on your to-do list, nor asking how many items are in your inbox. I want to know how your heart is doing, at this very moment. Tell me. Tell me your heart is joyous, tell me your heart is aching, tell me your heart is sad, tell me your heart craves a human touch. Examine your own heart, explore your soul, and then tell me something about your heart and your soul. Tell me you remember you are still a human being, not just a human doing. Tell me you're more than just a machine, checking off items from your to-do list. Have that conversation, that glance, that touch. Be a healing conversation, one filled with grace and presence. Put your hand on my arm, look me in the eye, and connect with me for one second. Tell me something about your heart, and awaken my heart. Help me remember that I too am a full and complete human being, a human being who also craves a human touch."[284]

—Omid Safi

"Let us tell our neighbors the truth,
for we are all parts of the same body."
Ephesians 4:25b NLT

- Are you aware of the state of your heart?
- Do you reveal the state of your heart to anyone?
- Are you available for an honest human connection?
- Should your life with God make you more available for an honest human connection? Why?

Abba, make me a safe person for others who want to be real.

For more: "Tell Me"[285] by Bob Dylan

First-Century Faith Today

"As much as contemporary believers might find similarities between our time and that of Christianity in ancient Rome, the two are not the same. The ancient Mediterranean world that Rome once ruled was a vast, culturally diverse set of societies, unrelated by languages, economics, religions, and histories, all forced into political unity by a brutal military. Vast numbers of people who inhabited the Roman Empire resented or hated Roman rule and experienced few, if any, benefits from its social and economic structures. The empire was not in any modern way even vaguely democratic or inclusive; instead, it was a rigidly hierarchical and status-based world of haves and have-nots, of masters and slaves. Unlike a Hollywood sword-and-sandal film, the ancient world was not a pleasant place absent conveniences such as sewer systems and running water. As sociologist Rodney Stark describes, 'Greco-Roman cities were small, extremely crowded, filthy beyond imagining, disorderly, filled with strangers, and afflicted with frequent catastrophes—fires, plagues, conquests, and earthquakes.' Unlike Western urban life today, where even the poor have access to marginally acceptable services, 'life in antiquity abounded in anxiety and misery' for nearly everyone."[286]

—Diane Butler Bass

"Three times I was shipwrecked. Once I spent a whole night and a day adrift at sea. I have traveled on many long journeys. I have faced danger from rivers and from robbers. I have faced danger from my own people, the Jews, as well as from the Gentiles. I have faced danger in the cities, in the deserts, and on the seas. And I have faced danger from men who claim to be believers but are not. I have worked hard and long, enduring many sleepless nights. I have been hungry and thirsty and have often gone without food. I have shivered in the cold, without enough clothing to keep me warm."
2 Corinthians 11:25–27 NLT

- Is your faith deep enough that it would sustain you in a world like the one described?

- Is the gospel you trust in and share with others sufficient for such a world? Would it make sense? Would it be heard as good news?

- Imagine yourself living in that world. What would it mean to live like Jesus there?

Abba, thank you for all I have. Show me what you expect of me in my privileged time and place.

For more: *A People's History of Christianity* by Diana Butler Bass

The Descent Of God

"The Son of God came down and was made humble.... God was made humble for you."

—Augustine

"This is the truth unknown to philosophy.... not found in Epicureans, Stoics, Manichees, or Platonists. Although discovering the best precepts of custom and discipline, they never find humility. This comes only from Christ who became humble even to death on the cross. The humility exhibited by the Word in the Incarnation is the cure for pride, the worst of all sins. Only divine humility is true medicine for *superbia* [haughtiness].... It is indeed correct to say that, for Augustine, 'it is the humility of Christ which is the most striking feature of the Incarnation.' Augustine has grasped precisely that the core of Christian faith is an acceptance of the divine kenosis in Jesus of Nazareth. To get a sense of the impression Phil. 2:6–8 made on Augustine one should consult the Index at the end of [his *Corpus Christianorum*] . ... There are two hundred or more citations or allusions to this text in *De Trinitate* alone. Even more impressive is the fact that in Augustine's entire corpus he cites part or all of this passage 422 times, and alludes to it 563 times. Thus he had it in mind nearly a thousand times when he wrote."[287]

—Joseph Hallman

"Though he was God, he did not think of equality with God
as something to cling to. Instead, he gave up his divine privileges;
he took the humble position of a slave and was born as a human being.
When he appeared in human form, he humbled himself in obedience to God
and died a criminal's death on a cross." Philippians 2:6–8 NLT

- When you look at today's church–today's Christian–at yourself in the mirror–do you see humility?

- Consider the practices of silence, Sabbath, listening well, loving well, receiving instruction, simplicity–think how each of these requires or teaches humility.

- How formative is the incarnation of Jesus in your life? Has what he did for you in that way ever really gripped you?

Abba, I think often of how your son humbled himself for me–and it changes me.

For more: The Descent of God by Joseph M. Hallman

Opening Up Space For God In Your Life

"Dallas Willard once wrote that the secret of the easy yoke is to live your life as Jesus would it he were in your place. How do you do that? I believe the first step is to slow down the pace. That allows you to be fully present, to be mindful, to be intentional, to create space, and to notice where God is working and join him in that work.... My focus is] on three Christian practices that help us live as Jesus would if he were in our place: simplicity, slowing, and Sabbath-keeping.... Notice that these three create space for practices such as solitude, service, prayer, meditation on Scripture, and others.... Any spiritual practice, from solitude to service, must be approached in an unhurried fashion or the benefits of the practice itself will be lost. Connection with God, which is the reason for any spiritual practice, begins with changing our focus (from ourselves and our problems to God and his sufficiency) and changing our pace (from hurried and distracted to deliberate and focused). That is what simplicity, slowing, and Sabbath-keeping force us to do. They move us toward a life, an easy yoke, which if you let it, will open up space for God.... [to redirect] you toward a simpler lifestyle with more of God in it and to help you find rest for your soul and lighten your burden."[288]

—Keri Wyatt Kent

"Resting in the presence of God, without work or speech ... one becomes more aware of the companionship, grace, and love of God than one has been of the companionship, demands, and duties associated with other people.... Contemplative practices ... are exercised more or less in solitude, making the first cluster [solitude, Sabbath, and silence] in many ways the key to the rest."[289]

—Brian Mclaren

"The burden I give you
is light."
Matthew 11:30b NLT

- Imagine Jesus living your life. What would change?

- Imagine "opening up space for God" in your life. What would that require?

- Can you begin some new practices in one of the areas mentioned above–solitude, silence, etc?

Jesus, I want to be always aware of your companionship with me.

For more: *Breathe* by Keri Wyatt Kent

Living in the Present

"I got out of bed on two strong legs.
It might have been otherwise.
I ate cereal, sweet milk, ripe, flawless peach.
It might have been otherwise.
I took the dog uphill to the birch wood.
All morning I did the work I love.
At noon I lay down with my mate.
It might have been otherwise.
We ate dinner together at a table with silver candlesticks.
It might have been otherwise.
I slept in a bed in a room with paintings on the walls,
and planned another day just like this day.
But one day, I know, it will be otherwise."[290]

—Jane Kenyon

"We are living in a culture entirely hypnotized by the illusion of time, in which the so-called present moment is felt as nothing but an infinitesimal hairline between an all-powerfully causative past and an absorbingly important future. We have no present. Our consciousness is almost completely preoccupied with memory and expectation. We do not realize that there never was, is, nor will be any other experience than present experience. We are therefore out of touch with reality. We confuse the world as talked about, described, and measured with the world which actually is."[291]

—Alan Watts

"The spiritual life can only be lived in the present moment, in the now. All the great religious traditions insist upon this simple but difficult truth. When we go rushing ahead into the future or shrinking back into the past, we miss the hand of God, which can only touch us in the now."[292]

—Cynthia Bourgeault

"This is the day that the Lord has made . . . ."
Psalm 118:24b ESV

- What's happening to you now? Are you opening your heart to God? . . . relaxing in God's unconditional acceptance? . . . experiencing a rootedness that will inform your day?

- Some present moment might turn out to be the most formative or strategic of your day. Imagine being oblivious to it due to what seemed an "all-powerfully causative past . . . [or] an absorbingly important future."

Abba, today may my soul be "as light as a feather, as fluid as water, simple as a child, as easily moved as a ball, so as to receive and follow all the impressions of grace." J. P. de Caussade

For more: *Collected Poems* by Jane Kenyon

Disruptive Jesus

"The gentleman arrested Thursday and tried before Pontius Pilate had a troubled background. Born (possibly out of wedlock?) in a stable, this jobless thirty-something of Middle Eastern origin had had previous run-ins with local authorities for disturbing the peace, and had become increasingly associated with the members of a fringe religious group. He spent the majority of his time in the company of sex workers and criminals. He had had prior run-ins with local authorities—most notably, an incident of vandalism in a community center when he wrecked the tables of several licensed money-lenders and bird-sellers. He had used violent language, too, claiming that he could destroy a gathering place and rebuild it. At the time of his arrest, he had not held a fixed residence for years. Instead, he led an itinerant lifestyle, staying at the homes of friends and advocating the redistribution of wealth. He had come to the attention of the authorities more than once for his unauthorized distribution of food [and] disruptive public behavior.... Some say that his brutal punishment at the hands of the state was out of proportion to and unrelated to any of these incidents in his record. But after all, he was no angel."[293]

—Alexandra Petri

"I am a Jew, but I am enthralled by the luminous figure of the Nazarene.... No one can read the Gospels without feeling the actual presence of Jesus. His personality pulsates in every word. No myth is filled with such life."[294]

—Albert Einstein

"I am an historian, I am not a believer, but I must confess as a historian that this penniless preacher from Nazareth is irrevocably the very center of history. Jesus Christ is easily the most dominant figure in all history."[295]

—H. G. Wells

"He was despised and rejected . . . ."
Isaiah 53:3a ESV

- What would you think of an outsider like Jesus today?
- Has the story of Jesus made you more aware of the long and seemingly universal history of the suppression of dissent?
- The religious and political leaders of the day condemned Jesus as dangerous and subversive because of their own self-interest. Should the story of Jesus made you more skeptical of authority—both political and religious?

Abba, thank you for the luminous Nazarene. I want to follow him.

For more: *Mere Christianity* by C. S. Lewis

A King Clothed in Rags

"To the hard of hearing you shout, and for the almost-blind you draw large and startling figures."[296]

—Flannery O'Connor

"We need to be shaken out of our expectations.... God is never what Pharoah, Ahab, and Herod expect. There's a shocking, almost comic quality about the annunciations one finds in scripture. Angels announce to shepherds standing in a field of sheep dung the birth of a king clothed in rags. A figure clad in white announces to John of the Apocalypse the majestic Lion of the Tribe of Judah, but when he turn to look there's only a slain and bloody lamb (Rev. 5:5–6). In biblical experience what you see isn't necessarily what you get. This is the mystery of God as *Deus absconditus*. The God of scripture is equally revealed in vulnerability and in triumph. This is because both actions are rooted in love. God wills us to be broken for the sake of a strength to make whole. Divine love is incessantly restless until it turns all woundedness into health, all deformity into beauty, all embarrassment into laughter. In biblical faith, brokenness is never celebrated as an end in itself. God's brokenness is but an expression of a love on its way to completion. Hence we never can accept, much less romanticize, the plight of a people rejected by the world as aberrant and unfit. They invite us to share in the 'groaning of all creation' for a redemption yet to be revealed (Rom. 8:19–21). The paradox of the grotesque is that it summons those who are whole to be broken and longs for those who are broken to be made whole."[297]

—Belden Lane

"*His appearance was marred more than any man*
And His form more than the sons of men."
Isaiah 52:14 NASB

- Are you familiar with the vulnerable God of the Bible?
- Do you think of God's love as "incessantly restless until it turns all woundedness into health, all deformity into beauty, all embarrassment into laughter?" Is God doing that for you?

- In what ways are you whole needing to be broken? . . . broken needing to be make whole?

Abba, thank you for your love that will not rest until I am whole.

For more: *The Solace of Fierce Landscapes* by Belden Lane

"My Loneliness Blesses Me"

"Man finds nothing so intolerable as to be in a state of complete rest, without passions, without occupation, without diversion, without effort. Then he faces his nullity, loneliness, inadequacy, dependence, helplessness, emptiness. And at once there well up from the depths of his soul boredom, gloom, depression, chagrin, resentment, despair."[298]

—Blaise Pascal

"My loneliness attracts me to the feet of Jesus. Like a magnet I am drawn there, longing to be all one with God. The separateness I keep choosing makes me desperately homesick, and so I am willing, at last, to surrender my divided heart. I am homesick to be one with God. Union with God is the only heaven there is, and it begins here on earth. . . . There is someone I must become. There is someone I must be grafted onto, and how lonely I am until it is accomplished. My loneliness blesses me because it shows me that I'm not enough all by myself, and so I am impelled to reach out my arms and heart to God and to others. My loneliness blesses me because it encourages me to allow myself to be vulnerable. My loneliness blesses me because it won't let me hide in the illusion of my self-sufficiency."[299]

—Macrina Wiederkehr

"Fear, guilt and shame can be useful on your spiritual journey. When you experience these, follow the trail back to the idea, notion, belief or concept that was the source. When you find it, divest all your belief in it, and let it go. Never return to it. Do this as many times as is necessary."[300]

—Jim Palmer

191

"Whom have in heaven but you?
I desire you more than anything on earth.
My health may fail,
and my spirit may grow weak,
but God remains the strength of my heart;
he is mine forever."
Psalm 73:25, 26 NLT

- Do you sometimes feel desperately homesick? . . . desperately afraid of something (or many things) out of your control?
- Can you "follow the trail" of that feeling back to the belief or concept that was the source? Pause now, and try that.
- Is there a way that your desperation–your loneliness, your fear, your powerlessness–"blesses" you?

Abba, in my loneliness and fear I turn to you . . . and you find me.

For more: *A Tree Full of Angels* by Macrina Wiederkehr

Interruptions!

"There is an old story about a wise man living on one of China's vast frontiers. One day, for no apparent reason, a young man's horse ran away and was taken by nomads across the border. Everyone tried to offer consolation for the man's bad fortune, but his father, a wise man, said, 'What makes you so sure this is not a blessing?' Months later, his horse returned, bringing with her a magnificent stallion. This time everyone was full of congratulations for the son's good fortune. But now his father said, 'What makes you so sure this isn't a disaster?' Their household was made richer by this fine horse the son loved to ride. But one day he fell off his horse and broke his hip. Once again, everyone offered their consolation for his bad luck, but his father said, 'What makes you so sure this is not a blessing?' A year later nomads invaded across the border, and every able-bodied man was required to take up his bow and go into battle. The Chinese families living on the border lost nine of every ten men. Only because the son was lame did father and son survive to take care of each other."301

—Peter Scazzero

"The great thing, if one can, is to stop regarding all the unpleasant things as interruptions of one's 'own', or 'real' life. The truth is of course that what one calls the interruptions are precisely one's real life–the life God is sending one day by day: what one calls one's 'real life' is a phantom of one's own imagination."302

—C. S. Lewis

"God is right there in the thick of our day-by-day lives.... trying to get messages through our blindness as we move around down here knee-deep in the fragrant muck and misery and marvel of the world."303

—Frederick Buechner

> "Do not boast [or worry, or despair] about tomorrow,
> For you do not know what a day may bring forth."
> Proverbs 27:1 NASB

- What is your usual response to interruptions? Do you know what is best?
- Are you obsessed with being in control? Is that working for you?
- Can you approach the next few days as "the life that God is sending you day-by-day?"

Abba, may I remember to look for you in the thick of my day-by-day life.

For more: *Secrets in the Dark* by Frederick Buechner

The Person For Others

"To become free does not mean becoming great in the world, not becoming free from your brother, nor even free from God, but to become free from oneself, one's lie. It means to become free from thinking only of myself, from being the center of my world, from hate, by which I despise God's creation. It means to be free to be for the other: the person for others. Only God's truth can enable me to see the other as he really is. It tears out the twisted image that I have of the other within me and shows him to me in a new light. And insofar as God's truth does that, it bestows upon me the action, the love, the grace of God. It destroys our lies and creates the truth. It destroys hatred and creates love. God's truth is God's love and God's love makes us free from ourselves for others. To be free means nothing less than to be in love. And to be in love means nothing less than being in the truth of God. The man who loves because he has been made free by God is the most revolutionary man on earth. He challenges all values. He is the explosive material of human society. He is a dangerous man. For he recognizes that the human race is in the depths of falsehood. And he is always ready to let the light of truth fall upon his darkness; and he will do this because of his love."[304]

—Dietrich Bonhoeffer

"Use your freedom
to serve one another in love."
Galatians 5:13 NLT

- Do you sometimes have a twisted image of others–perhaps based on race, religion or social status?
- Will you let God's truth free you to see the other as he or she really is?
- What would it mean for you to be "the person for others?"
- Are you free enough from narcissism and hate–to be that person?

Abba, free me of lies I tell myself that cause me to hate.

For more: *Dietrich Bonhoeffer's Christmas Sermons* edited by Edwin Robertson

Glory Without the Big Splash

"How hard it is to see real glory when we think glory is all about making a splash! We miss the real thing. . . . John has a different view of glory. In his Gospel, Jesus changes water to wine at a wedding to make people joyful. He washes his disciples' feet, hoping to model and ignite a heart of service in them. He feeds the disciples bread at the table where they reclined–including Judas–and then submits himself to arrest. In all three cases–the wine (chap. 2), the bathwater (chap. 13), the bread for a traitor (chap. 13)–the evangelist tells us that it was a sign of his glory. This is a glory he shares with his Father. Jesus makes lots of wine at Cana because he comes from a wine making family. Every Fall God turns water into wine in France and Chile and the Napa Valley. . . . Jesus on his knees before his disciples is just doing what he sees his Father doing, and the gospel finds glory here, because it is so much like God humbly to clean people up. . . . Jesus hands Judas a piece of bread because he just does what he sees his Father doing, and the gospel finds glory here, because it is so much like God to feed enemies even while you oppose their evil. The gospel finds glory where we are not looking–in the wine, and the water, and the bread, and even in the blood of Jesus. The Son of Man will die and fall into the earth in an event so devastating that it will seem to turn creation back into chaos; but Jesus says that this is the hour in which the Son of Man will be glorified."[305]

—Cornelius Plantinga, Jr.

"The Son of Man came not to be served
but to serve . . . ."
Matthew 20:28a ESV

- Are you still hoping to make a big splash?
- Are you learning to look for God's glory in unexpected, unnoticed places?
- Are you trusting and expecting God to work gloriously, although perhaps subtly, in your day? . . . your situation? . . . your world?

Abba, open my eyes to your glory all around me.

For more: *Feasting on the Gospels: John* edited by Cynthia A. Jarvis and Elizabeth E. Johnson

---

Letting the Bible Read You

"What if instead of reading the Bible, you let the Bible read you?"[306]

—Brian McLaren

"Hal … only had three fingers on his left hand. There should have been four. He lost one legitimately while working with his skilsaw. The second finger was lost while showing a friend how he lost the first. After that he let his wife tell folks about the accident(s). Hal was known for reading the Bible. Before he retired and back when he had all ten fingers, he was known for flipping through the well-worn pages of his Bible really fast so he'd be the first in the congregation to locate the sermon text.… When Hal retired he decided to become more serious and systematic with his Bible reading. He bought one of those 'Read-the-Bible-in-a-Year' Bibles, and he did just that. And apparently he really enjoyed it because on New Year's Eve the following year he determined to read all the way through the Bible in a month. And he did. Apparently Hal liked that as well, because he resolved to read the Bible through once per month for every month of that new year. And he did. From all his Bible reading, Hal thought he had figured out that God seemed to be partial to some numbers more than others. The numbers 3, 7, 12, 40, and 144 seemed particularly important to God, and this gave Hal an idea. He determined that he would continue reading the Bible through once each month until he had read from cover to cover 144 times. And he did! When Hal died, he was known for being one of the meanest, angriest, and most hateful people you could ever meet. Hal made a mistake. He got all the way through the Bible many times, but he never got certain key passages all the way through himself."[307]

—Gary Moon

"Give me life
through your word."
Psalm 119:37b NLT

- As time goes by, is your thirst for the Bible growing? Are you in it daily?
- Do you read the Bible in such a way that it gets through to you?
- What would it mean to let the Bible "read you?"[308]

Beyond the sacred page I seek thee Lord.

For more: *Apprenticeship with Jesus* by Gary Moon

Downward Mobility

"We use the word cross in our hymns, in our piety, in our prayers, and in our pastoral language. But we use it too cheaply. We say that a person has to live with some sort of suffering in life: a sickness that cannot be cured, an unresolvable personality conflict within the family, poverty, or some other unexplainable or unchangeable suffering. Then we say, 'That person has a cross to bear.' Granted, whatever kind of suffering we have is suffering that we can bear in confidence that God is with us. But the cross that Jesus had to face, because he chose to face it, was not–like sickness, something that strikes you without explanation. It was not some continuing difficulty in his social life. It was not an accident or catastrophe that just happened to hit him when it could have hit somebody else. Jesus' cross was the price to pay for being the kind of person he was in the kind of world he was in; the cross that he chose was the price of his representing a new way of life in a world that did not want a new way of life. That is what he called his followers to do."[309]

—John Howard Yoder

"The servant leader is the leader who is being led to unknown, undesirable, and painful places. The way of the Christian leader is not the way of upward mobility in which our world has invested so much, but the way of downward mobility ending on the cross.... It is not a leadership of power and control, but a leadership of power-lessness and humility in which the suffering servant of God, Jesus Christ, is made manifest."[310]

—Henri Nouwen

197

*"In what I am suffering for you . . . I fill up in my flesh
what is still lacking in regard to Christ's afflictions,
for the sake of his body, which is the church."*
Colossians 1:24 NIV

- What would it mean for you to suffer in filling up what is lacking in Christ's afflictions? Is any of your suffering redemptive?
- Are you willing to be led by God to unfamiliar, painful places?
- Is your discipleship at all "radical?"

Abba, may my life advance your redemptive work in this world, even it if costs.

For more: *Radical Christian Discipleship* by John Howard Yoder

---

June 3   December 1

The Pregnant Pause

"Those who love their own noise are impatient of everything else . . . ."[311]

—Thomas Merton

"When a pro interviewer feels a subject is holding something back on a particular topic, they'll often use the power of silence at the end of the answer to draw out more information. Here's how journalist Jim Lehrer describes it: 'If you resist the temptation to respond too quickly to the answer, you'll discover something almost magical. The other person will either expand on what he's already said or he'll go in a different direction.' Try counting to three–or five if you can stand it–after your subject answers a tough or thoughtful question. This method can seem agonizing at first, but–used with empathy–it works wonders to develop a deeper rapport between two people. . . . Of course we'd all like to think of ourselves as attentive, curious students of the world, but one little thing gets in the way: our own egos. It's not our fault–we're hardwired that way. After all, talking about ourselves feels as good to our brains as money or sex. That's why ego suspension is so essential to cultivating the kind of curiosity that lets you connect with others. Robin Dreeke . . . explains: 'Most times, when two individuals engage in a conversation, each patiently waits for the other person to be done with whatever story he or she is telling. Then, the other person tells his or her own story, usually on a related topic and often times in an attempt to have a better and more interesting story. Individuals practicing good ego suspension would continue to encourage the other individual to talk about his or her story, neglecting their own need to share what they think is a great story."[312]

—Courtney Siete

- Are you just waiting for the other person to finish?
- How often are you turning the conversation back to you?
- Do you use silence to draw others out? . . . to develop rapport?
- Are you aware of what can be lost by "filling the silence" when you should be still?

Abba, make me wise about silence.

For more: "Top Ten FAQs about Practicing Silence"[313]

Speechless Before the Cross

"A man dies when he refuses to stand up for that which is right. A man dies when he refuses to stand up for justice. A man dies when he refuses to take a stand for that which is true."[314]

—Martin Luther King, Jr.

"When that Word fell silent on Golgotha—when, after a loud cry, both the high sound of his nervous system, and the low sound of his beating heart stopped—the earth shook with grief. Rocks made the only sound they could, slitting open with small explosions that were their best version of tears. The veil in the temple was torn from top to bottom, with a sound of such ripping that those who heard it thought it was the sky. The whole inanimate world leapt in to fill that silence, while poor, dumb humanity stood speechless before the cross."[315]

—Barbara Brown Taylor

"The people passing by shouted abuse, shaking their heads in mockery. 'Look at you now!' they yelled at him. 'You said you were going to destroy the Temple and rebuild it in three days. Well then, if you are the Son of God, save yourself and come down from the cross!' The leading priests, the teachers of religious law, and the elders also mocked Jesus. 'He saved others,' they scoffed, 'but he can't save himself! So he is the King of Israel, is he? Let him come down from the cross right now, and we will believe in him! He trusted God, so let God rescue him now if he wants him! For he said, "I am the Son of God."' Even the revolutionaries who were crucified with him ridiculed him in the same way."
Matthew 27:39–44 NLT

- Can you think of a shameful moment when everyone was silent and you regretted later that you hadn't leapt in to speak? . . . perhaps to speak up for Jesus, or as Jesus would have, for someone else?

- Can you think of a holy moment when you should have stood speechless–with no desire or attempt to speak? Did you?

- What does it take for you to stop talking? Are you filling sacred spaces with unhelpful words? Can you stop talking long enough to worship?

Abba, teach me when to speak and when to be silent.

For more: *When God is Silent* by Barbara Brown Taylor

We Are Made By What Would Break Us

"By trying to handle all suffering through willpower denial, medication, or even therapy, we have forgotten something that should be obvious: we do not handle suffering; *suffering handles us*–in deep and mysterious ways that become the very matrix of life and especially new life. Only suffering and certain kinds of awe lead us into genuinely new experiences. All the rest is merely the confirmation of old experience."[316]

—Richard Rohr

"I'm not surprised by the fact that inexplicable and terrible things happen in a cosmos as complicated as ours, with sentient beings like us running the show. But I am emboldened by the fact that surprise is the only constant. We are never really running the show, never really in control, and nothing will go quite as we imagined it. Our highest ambitions will be off, but so will our worst prognostications. I am emboldened by the puzzling, redemptive truth to which each and every one of my conversations has added nuance, that we are made by what would break us. Birth itself is a triumph through a bloody, treacherous process. We only learn to walk when we risk falling down, and this equation holds—with commensurately more complex dynamics—our whole lives long. I have heard endless variations on this theme—the battle with illness that saves the life that follows; the childhood pain that leads to vocation; the disability that opens into wholeness and a presence to the hidden wholeness of others. You have your own stories, the dramatic and more ordinary moments where what has gone wrong becomes an opening to more of yourself and part of your gift to the world. This is the beginning of wisdom."[317]

—Krista Tippett

"Joyful is the person who finds wisdom,
the one who gains understanding."
Proverbs 3:13 NLT

- Have you experienced being made by what would break you?
- In what ways have terrible difficulties in your life become "an opening to more of yourself?" How would you describe that new self?
- Have difficulties or tragedies helped to shape your "gift to the world?" What do you understand as your gift to the world?
- If you haven't been shaped or made more valuable by great difficulties in your life, why is that?

Abba, make me a good student of the mystery and art of living.

For more: *Becoming Wise* by Krista Tippett

I Hit the Bottom and Escape

"Beyond all knowing and unknowing, disregarding the pain, confusion and doubt, I sink into the Great Darkness, down through its waters to the depths of the very depths. In that place answers, explanations and expectations–having indeed become irrelevant, irreverent and useless–have ceased to exist. And I exist without them–sinking, resting, abiding in that Darkness. Beside me, abides the Unseen One, and in the presence of that One, I nearly cease to be. I enter a death barely short of death, and a well of life otherwise out of reach. Beyond the reach of words, with nothing to choose but stillness, with no support of any kind–save the invisible, unsensed loving arms of the Eternal One, I come to rest on the bottom. And whereas I had expected my destruction and death, instead I find new breath, new space, and new hope. O God, who is beyond and above all things, who draws near in mystery, confusion, and contradiction–cradle me, renew me, deliver me."

—William Britton

"Hence I observe how needful it is for me to enter into the darkness, and to admit the coincidence of opposites, beyond all the grasp of reason, and there to seek the truth where impossibility meeteth me.... And the more that dark impossibility is recognised as dark and impossible, the more truly doth His Necessity shine forth, and is more unveiledly present and draweth nigh."[318]

—Nicholas of Cusa

"Sanctity ... may mean learning, from God, to be without anxiety in the midst of anxiety.... living in a silence which so reconciles the contradictions within us that, although they remain within us, they cease to be a problem. Contradictions have always existed in the soul of man. But it is only when we prefer analysis to silence that they become a constant and insoluble problem. We are not meant to resolve all contradictions but to live with them and rise above them ...."[319]

—Thomas Merton

"Moses approached the thick darkness
where God was."
Exodus 20:21 NIV

- Can you rest in a place beyond explanation? . . . live with contradiction?
- Can you simply be with God and let God can cradle you, and renew you?

Thank you Abba, you draw nigh in my impossibilities.

For more: *Thomas Merton* edited by M. Basil Pennington

Those Who Are Hardest to Love

"Those who are hardest to love need it most."

—Socrates

"Don't say 'That person bothers me'. Think: 'That person sanctifies me.'"

—St. Josémaria Escriva

"When you love someone, you do not love them all the time, in exactly the same way, from moment to moment. It is an impossibility. It is even a lie to pretend to. And yet, this is exactly what most of us demand. We have so little faith in the ebb and flow of life, of love, of relationships. We leap at the flow of time and resist in terror its ebb. We are afraid it will never return. We insist on permanency, on duration, on continuity; when the only continuity possible in life, as in love, is in growth, in fluidity–in freedom. The only real security is not in owning or possessing, not in demanding or expecting, not in hoping, even. Security in a relationship lies neither in looking back to what it was, nor forward to what it might be, but living in the present and accepting it as it is now. For relationships, too, must be like islands. One must accept them for what they are here and now, within their limits–islands surrounded and interrupted by the sea, continuously visited and abandoned by the tides."[320]

—Anne Morrow Lindberg

"The beginning of love is the will to let those we love be perfectly themselves, the resolution not to twist them to fit our own image. If in loving them we do not love what they are, but only their potential likeness to ourselves, then we do not love them: we only love the reflection of ourselves we find in them."[321]

—Thomas Merton

> *"Be kind to each other,*
> *tenderhearted, forgiving one another,*
> *just as God through Christ has forgiven you."*
> Ephesians 4:22 NLT

- Can you look deeply enough at someone to discover beauty others have missed?
- Read through Lindberg's words again. Can you ask God to show you where you might be straying off course?
- Have you ever thought of the one who is hardest for you to love as the one who needs your love the most? Can you name that person?

Loving Abba, may your love for me inform my love for others–especially that one who is hardest to love.

For more: *Gift From the Sea* by Anne Morrow Lindberg

How Good a Christian Are You?

"John [the apostle] sums up the matter bluntly. 'Those who say, "I love God," and hate their brothers or sisters, are liars' (1 John 4:20). To truly love God includes loving others with the same love God has for us and the same love God has for them. This is part of what it means to be a participant in the divine nature. It is, in fact, what it means to be Christian (Christ-like). 'Whoever does not love,' John wrote, 'does not know God, for God is love' (1 John 4:8). Our capacity to love–to fulfill the greatest two commandments–is the definitive evidence that we are in fact abiding in Christ and participating in the perfect love of the triune God. Christians sometimes try to assess how they or others are doing on the basis of such things as how success-fully they conquer a particular sin, how much prayer and Bible study they do, how regularly they attend and give to church, and so forth. But rarely do we honestly ask the question that Scripture places at the center of everything: Are we growing in our capacity to love all people? Do we have an increasing love for our sisters and brothers in Christ as well as for those for whom Christ died who are yet outside the church? Are we increasing in our capacity to ascribe unsurpassable worth to people whom society judges to have no worth? If there is any distinguishing mark of the true disciple from a biblical perspective, this is it!"[322]

—Gregory Boyd

"If we love our brothers and sisters who are believers,
it proves that we have passed from death to life . . . ."
1 John 3:14a NLT

- How do you measure your maturity as a Christian?
- Do you focus on your beliefs? . . . the opinions of others? . . . abstaining from big sins? . . . practicing spiritual disciplines? . . . tireless service for Christ?
- How would you do if the question was, "Am I growing in my capacity to love all people?"

Abba, I'm sometimes good at loving those who love me. It's when it comes to those who dislike, disregard, or disrespect me that I'm often failing. Help me Lord. May that be my practice.

For more: *Repenting of Religion* by Gregory Boyd

A Life Uncluttered by Ambition

"Anyone who thinks that his time is too valuable to spend keeping quiet will eventually have no time for God and his brother, but only for himself and for his own follies."[323]

—Dietrich Bonhoeffer

"Responding to God's presence like a child who trusted completely in a loving Parent, his relationship with God was spontaneous, uncluttered by ambition and calculation. Rather than promote his own agenda or hide behind fear, anxiousness, and other barriers to trust, [Saint] Francis humbly accepted the mystery of his life and relied on the guidance of the Spirit."[324]

—Wayne Simsic

"At some point when we've made ourselves available for any kind of ministry, the question will arise, 'Is this the best use of my time?' It's both an unsurprising and provocative query. And just look at what underlies that question: ego, drivenness, a sense of hurry–striving. But in truth, as Francis demonstrated, it's not necessary to keep busy– only to 'trust completely.' It's not necessary to accomplish anything–only to 'humbly accept the mystery' of my life. It's not necessary to be productive–only to 'rely on the guidance of the Spirit.' My time is not so valuable. I'm not so necessary as I think. Any equation will be essentially unchanged by my absence. The way of St. Francis, 'spontaneous, uncluttered by ambition and calculation' rebukes my anxious way–my craving for an agenda, my insistence on significance. And Bonhoeffer's insight is critical: 'keeping quiet'–seemingly doing nothing, accomplishing nothing, producing nothing, is not only essential, but if ignored leads only to fruitlessness and folly. The ego always lurks nearby, insidious, subtly undoing the best intentions. Both St. Francis and Bonhoeffer insist upon, and themselves lived, a contemplative life of faith–a life of 'keeping quiet' and 'making time for God.' Only such lives create a spaciousness where God can meet us in our folly, take us again into the clutch of his parental love, and purify us–making us useful after all–as God did with both of them."

—William Britton

"I do not even judge myself."
1 Corinthians 4:3 NIV

- Are you aware of unconscious forces affecting your behavior?
- Do you overemphasize "productivity?"
- Can you look less to your agenda and more to the guidance of the Spirit?

Abba, teach me the "folly" of St. Francis.

For more: *Living The Wisdom of St. Francis* by Wayne Simsic

Never a Man Like This

"Perhaps it is no wonder that the women were … last at the Cross [and first at the tomb!]. They had never known a man like this Man—there never has been such another. A prophet and teacher who never nagged at them, never flattered or coaxed or patronized: … who rebuked without querulousness and praised without condescension; who took their questions and arguments seriously; who never mapped out their sphere for them, never urged them to be feminine or jeered at them for being female; who had no axe to grind and no uneasy male dignity to defend; who took them as he found them and was completely unself-conscious. There is no act, no sermon, no parable in the whole Gospel that borrows its pungency from female perversity; nobody could possibly guess from the words and deeds of Jesus that there was anything 'funny' about woman's nature."[325]

—Dorothy Sayers

"After years of reading the Gospels and the full canon of Scripture, here is, very simply, what I learned about Jesus and the ladies: he loves us. He loves us. On our own terms. He treats us as equals to the men around him; he listens; he does not belittle; he honors us; he challenges us; he teaches us; he includes us—calls us all beloved. Gloriously, this flies in the face of the cultural expectations of his time—and even our own time."[326]

—Sara Bessey

"Women aged fifteen through forty-five are more likely to be maimed or die from male violence than from cancer, malaria, traffic accidents, and war combined. One-third of women face abuse at home. … in most countries, between 30 and 60 percent of women had experienced physical or sexual violence by a husband or a boyfriend. Up to 70 percent of female murder victims are killed by their male partners."[327]

—Sara Bessey

"So God created human beings in his own image.
In the image of God he created them;
male and female he created them."
Genesis 1:27 NLT

- Is this the attitude toward women seen in your home? . . . in your church?
- Men, is your goal to be like Jesus when it comes to women?

Abba, help me be like Jesus in my relationships with women.

For more: *Jesus Feminist* by Sara Bessey

Living Out Wholeness

"I am that to which I gave short shrift and that to which I attended. I am my descent into darkness and my arising into light, my betrayals and my fidelities, my failures and my successes. I am my ignorance and my insight, my doubts and my convictions, my fears and my hopes. Wholeness does not mean perfection: It means embracing brokenness as an integral part of life."[328]

—Parker Palmer

"Having made us, he knows our weaknesses—our fear, our self-pity, our self-regarding anger, our moral paralysis, our randomness, our indiscipline, our suicidal self-loathing. As gently as a shepherd taking up a lamb out of the brambles or a mother taking her infant to her breast, he will take us up and work with us—not to indulge our egoism, however, but to cure it. We must realize that we are in the hands of the Great Physician, whose goal it is, not to make us comfortable invalids, but to restore us to moral health and wholeness. And we must understand that his principal method of treating us, his petulant patients, is hard and constant exercise in a world which under his providence becomes a moral and spiritual gymnasium for us."[329]

—J. I. Packer

"The weakness which is serviceable is the weakness which seeks the aid of a physician."

—Bernard of Clairvaux

"Remember, Lord, your great mercy and love,
for they are from of old.
Do not remember the sins of my youth
and my rebellious ways;
according to your love remember me,
for you, Lord, are good. . . .
Guard my life and rescue me;
do not let me be put to shame,
for I take refuge in you.
May integrity and uprightness protect me,
because my hope, Lord, is in you."
Psalm 25: 6, 7, 20, 21

- Do you think of yourself as a person of wholeness and "integrity?"

- Can you do so in spite of your brokenness and failures? How is that?

- Does your weakness cause you to "seek the aid of a physician" (the Great Physician)? Can you see how that physician uses even your brokenness–and therefore is unsurprised by it and in one sense even intends it?

Abba, take all I am, and all I have done. Make me real, whole, and useful to you and others.

For more: *Christianity The True Humanism* by J. I. Packer

Concerning the Inner Life

"The beginning, then, of a strong and fruitful inner life … requires, not merely the acceptance but the full first-hand apprehension, of the ruling truth of the richly living spaceless and unchanging God; blazing in the spiritual sky, yet intimately present within the world of events, moulding and conditioning every phase of life. The religion of the priest, if it is to give power and convey certitude, must be from first to last a theocentric religion; and it must be fed by a devotional practice based upon that objective Power and Presence, and neither on your own subjective feelings, cravings, and needs, nor on the feelings, cravings, and needs of those among whom you work.... Only a spirituality which thus puts the whole emphasis on the Reality of God, perpetually turning to Him, losing itself in Him, refusing to allow even the most pressing work or practical problems, even sin and failure, to distract from God, only this is a safe foundation for spiritual work.... The inner life means an ever-deepening awareness of all this: the slowly growing and concrete realization of a Life and a Spirit within us immeasurably exceeding our own, and absorbing, transmuting, supernaturalizing our lives by all ways and at all times. It means the loving sense of God, as so immeasurably beyond us as to keep us in a constant attitude of humblest awe and yet so deeply and closely with us, as to invite our clinging trust and loyal love."[330]

—Evelyn Underhill

"Apart from me
you can do nothing."
John 15:5 ESV

- Are you perpetually turning to God, losing yourself in Him?
- Will you refuse to allow neither pressing work nor sinful failure to move your attention from God himself?
- Is the life that you offer to others that which immeasurably exceeds your own?
- Is your life and ministry supernaturalized "by all ways and at all times?"

Abba, may my faith be theocentric, my life supernaturalized, my heart perpetually turning to you.

For more: *Concerning the Inner Life* by Evelyn Underhill

Living Life . . . Inside a Bubble

"Never forget that justice is what love looks like in public."

—Cornel West

"Often I am ill-prepared for action in a dark world of injustice because I have gotten used to a little lie within my mind. I have gotten used to the idea that the fair garden that I have worked so hard to carve out for myself and my family is normal. I have gradually adjusted to the idea that 'the world' into which Christ has sent his disciples is actually a reasonably pleasant backyard patio. [but] . . . The outcome in the twentieth century would be described [otherwise] . . . I would just call it an open-mouthed grave: an entire generation of European youth composting the World War I battlefields of Verdun and the Somme, Hitler's six million Jews, Stalin's twenty million Soviet citizens, Mao's tens of millions of political enemies and peasant famine victims, Pol Pot's two million Cambodians, the Interhamwe's million Tutsi Rwandans, and the millions of lives wasted away during apartheid's forty-year reign. We can easily forget that the same spirit of darkness rules our present age... . Outside the affluent West ... in the Two-Thirds World where most of the children God created actually live, the Fall is being played out in ways more familiar to the biblical writers: it is manifest in a world of brutal injustice. . . . All those Scriptures about 'the world,' which seemed rather melodramatic when I heard them in my suburban church as a kid, turned out to be much more worthy of my attention than I ever knew."[331]

—Gary Haugen

"Their feet rush into sin;
they are swift to shed innocent blood."
Isaiah 59:7 NIV

- If you live in a "first world" nation, has that made you oblivious to the plight of the majority of people who don't share your good fortune?
- When we used to talk about worldliness it was about dancing, drinking and smoking. Imagine how much bigger, darker and more important the concept is.

Abba, when I obtain a service without paying a bribe, when the legal system works for me, when my daughter walks home from school without being kidnapped for a life of prostitution in a faraway city–may I remember the multitudes whose lives are not like mine.

For more: *Good News About Injustice* by Gary Haugen

June 14   December 12

Wherever You Go . . . There You Are

"We are, perhaps, uniquely among the earth's creatures, the worrying animal. We worry away our lives. We worry away our lives, fearing the future, discontent with the present, unable to take in the idea of dying, unable to sit still."[332]

—Lewis Thomas

"Your sadness, your loneliness, your fear, and your anxiety are not mistakes. They are not obstacles on your path. They *are* the path. The freedom you are longing for is not found in the eradication of these, but in the information they carry. You need not transcend anything here, but be willing to become deeply intimate with your lived, embodied experience. . . . Nothing is missing, nothing is out of place, nothing need be sent away."[333]

—Matt Licata

"We don't like the way reality is *now* and therefore wish it would go away fast. But what we find . . . is that nothing ever goes away until it has taught us what we need to know. Even if we run a hundred miles an hour to the other side of the continent, we find the very same problem awaiting us when we arrive. It keeps returning with new names, forms, and manifestations until we learn whatever it has to teach us: Where are we separating ourselves from reality? How are we pulling back instead of opening up? How are we closing down instead of allowing ourselves to experience fully whatever we encounter?"

—Pema Chödrön

"We dare not get rid of the pain before we have learned what it has to teach us. . . . Fixing something doesn't usually transform us. We try to change events in order to avoid changing ourselves. We avoid God, who works in the darkness–where we are not in control! Maybe that is the secret: relinquishing control. We must learn to stay with the pain of life, without answers, without conclusions, and some days without meaning."[334]

—Richard Rohr

"Does not wisdom call out?
Does not understanding raise her voice?"
Proverbs 8:1 NIV

- Can you stop avoiding your feelings, and instead allow yourself to "feel" them–to hear what they are telling you?
- We shouldn't be controlled by emotions, but they are a source of revelation. Are you listening?
- What are your present feelings telling you?

Abba, keep me on the path. Listening. Learning. Growing.

For more: *Everything Belongs* by Richard Rohr

Dangerous Jesus

"The experience that Jesus had in Gethsemane ... is the experience of assent. The cup of suffering becomes the cup of strengthening. Whoever empties that cup has conquered all fear. The one who at the end returns from prayer to the sleeping disciples is a different person from the one who went off to pray. He is clear-eyed and awake; he trembles no longer. 'It is enough; the hour has come. Rise, let us be going."

—Dorothee Soelle

"In that gruesome and interminable night, waiting revealed itself as a true ally, a bulwark against fear. And Jesus became the most radically free and dangerous man of all, the one who embodies hope in the face of death and is afraid of nothing."[335]

—Kathleen Norris

"Another will is greater, wiser and more intelligent than my own. So I wait. Waiting means that there is Another whom I trust and from whom I receive. My will, important and essential as it is, finds a Will that is more important, more essential. . . . In prayer we are aware that God is in action and that when the circumstances are ready, when others are in the right place and when my heart is prepared, I will be called into action. Waiting in prayer is a disciplined refusal to act before God acts. Waiting is our participation in the process that results in the 'time fulfilled.'"[336]

—Eugene Peterson

"Then he returned to the disciples and said to them, 'Are you still sleeping and resting? Look, the hour has come, and the Son of Man is delivered into the hands of sinners. Rise! Let us go! Here comes my betrayer!'" Matthew 26:45, 46 NIV

- Suffering, waiting, assent–these activities transform us. When extreme suffering engulfs you, can you do what Jesus did and allow the cup of suffering to become the cup of strengthening?

- If Jesus sought out solitude and prayer in his darkest hour, is your need any less?

- Will you learn how to wait and give assent to God in prayer before trouble comes, or hope to learn it when crisis strikes? What practices can help you learn it now?

Abba, deliver me from my fears to be a radically free and dangerously courageous man.

For more: *Acedia And Me* by Kathleen Norris

God, the Promiscuous Lover

"Through meal-sharing, preaching, teaching, and healing, Jesus acted out His understanding of the Father's indiscriminate love—a love that causes His sun to rise on bad men as well as good, and His rain to fall on honest and dishonest men alike (Matthew 5:45).... The absolute unpardonable thing was not his concern for the sick, the cripples, the lepers, the possessed ... not even his partnership for the poor, humble people. The real trouble was that he got involved with moral failures, with obviously irreligious and immoral people.... What kind of dangerous and naive love is this, which does not know its limits: the frontiers between fellow countrymen and foreigners, party members and non-members, between neighbors and distant people, between honorable and dishonorable callings, between moral and immoral, good and bad people? As if dissociation were not absolutely necessary here. As if we ought not to judge in these cases. As if we could always forgive in these circumstances."[337]

—Hans Küng

"The sign of true love, we remember, is that it is universal love, love to all, without exception, not just to a chosen few or to a special coterie of particular Christians."[338]

—Hannah Hurnard

"Christ's love cannot be limited by human qualities, character, sins, weaknesses or boundaries but stretches beyond all limits."

—Hans Urs von Balthasar

"If you love those who love you, what reward will you get?
Are not even the tax collectors doing that?
And if you greet only your own people,
what are you doing more than others?
Do not even pagans do that?
Be perfect, therefore,
as your heavenly Father is perfect."
Matthew 5:43–48 NIV

- God's love "stretches beyond all limits." It's "universal . . . without exception." It's indiscriminate. It's promiscuous. Does this seem "dangerous" or "naive" to you? Does it make you uncomfortable?

- How do you do when it comes to showing love that crosses boundaries of race, religion, political party, social status, gender, or sexual orientation? Are you also promiscuous? If not, what does that say about you?

- How can you be more indiscriminate with your love at work, in your neighborhood, at church?

Abba, where would I be without your promiscuous love?

For more: *On Being a Christian* by Hans Küng

Loving the One in Pain

"One of the hardest things we must do sometimes is to be present to another person's pain without trying to 'fix' it, to simply stand respectfully at the edge of that person's mystery and misery. Standing there, we feel useless and powerless . . . and our unconscious need as Job's comforters is to reassure ourselves that we are not like the sad soul before us. In an effort to avoid those feelings, I give advice, which sets me, not you, free."[339]

—Parker Palmer

"When we hold space for one another, we are fully present to the other's pain—to their mystery and misery. We are not trying to rush in to fill the circle of discomfort a friend or acquaintance feels, but instead we are fully present in the moment and in the sharing. We are witnesses to human experience. Holding space goes so much farther than offering words of advice. Our silence is the act of holding someone up, without words. Silence in this context is beautiful and non-judgmental, and it goes so much farther in offering comfort than our words could ever hope to offer. Holding space is such a hard practice at first, because it is in our nature to want to rush into the center of the hurt and to do something about it."[340]

—Heidi Metrakoudes-Hewett

"When Job's three friends . . . heard about all the troubles that had come upon him,
they set out from their homes and met together by agreement to go and sym-
pathize with him and comfort him. When they saw him from a distance, they
could hardly recognize him; they began to weep aloud, and they tore their
robes and sprinkled dust on their heads. Then they sat on the ground with
him for seven days and seven nights.
No one said a word to him . . . ."
Job 2:11–13 NIV

- Have you ever experienced being held up "without words?"

- We're usually very hard on Job's friends, often forgetting that they started by sitting in silence with Job for seven days and seven nights! Have you ever done anything like that? Has anyone done it for you?

- Have you ever regretted later the words of comfort you offered someone?

Abba, help me love my suffering friend with my loving presence not my philosophy or advice.

For more: *Let Your Life Speak* by Parker Palmer

The Backbone of the World

"Father is a name which implies personal and affectional relations. It embodies the highest conception of God which can be gathered from our knowledge of earthly relationships. It is the divine name which constituted the most distinct contribution of Jesus to religious thought. . . . Tennyson says that to take it away is to 'take away the backbone of the world.' The God who is over all is the Father of all; the God who is through all is the Father of all; the God who is in all is the Father of all. This is the God to whom every man may come, claiming a child's place, a child's privileges, a child's blessing."[341]

—James Campbell

"Imagine God thinking about you. What do you assume God feels when you come to mind? [Many people say disappointment or anger.] ... In both cases, these people are convinced that it is their sin that first catches God's attention.... The truth is that when God thinks of you, love swells in God's heart and a smile comes to God's face. God bursts with love for humans. God is far from being emotionally uninvolved with creation. God's bias toward us is strong, persistent and positive. The Christian God chooses to be known as Love, and that love pervades every aspect of God's relationship with us."[342]

—David Benner

"So don't be misled, my dear brothers and sisters.
Whatever is good and perfect
comes down to us from God our Father,
who created all the lights in the heavens. . . .
And we, out of all creation, became his prized possession."
James 1:16–18 NLT

- Do you think of God as one to whom you can come "claiming a child's place, a child's privileges, a child's blessing?" Can you think of yourself as God's "prized possession?"

- If instead, you feel God must be disappointed or angry with you, can you quiet yourself daily to listen for God's voice to you, letting God confirm his love? . . . God's "bias" towards you? That's probably the only way you'll ever feel it.

- Can you dare to believe that "when God thinks of you, love swells in God's heart and a smile comes to God's face?"

Abba, may I live into and out of that smile for me on your face.

For more: *Surrender to Love* by David G. Benner

The Preposterous Idea of "Worthiness"

"One of the keys to real religious experience is the shattering realization that no matter how hateful we are to ourselves, we are not hateful to God. This realization helps us to understand the difference between our love and His. Our love is a need, His a gift. We need to see good in ourselves in order to love ourselves. He does not. He loves us not because we are good, but because He is. But as long as we worship a God who is only a projection of ourselves, we fear a tremendous and insatiable power who *needs to see goodness* in us and who, for all the infinite clarity of His vision, finds nothing but evil ...."[343]

—Thomas Merton

"If I make anything out of the fact that I am Thomas Merton, I am dead. And if you make anything out of the fact that you are in charge of the pig barn, you are dead. Quit keeping score altogether and surrender yourself with all your sinfulness to God who sees neither the score nor the scorekeeper but only his child redeemed by Christ."[344]

—Merton

"God is asking me, the unworthy, to forget my unworthiness and that of my brothers, and dare to advance in the love which has redeemed and renewed us all in God's likeness. And to laugh, after all at the preposterous idea of 'worthi-ness.'"[345]

— Merton

"Faith is the courage to accept acceptance, to accept that God loves me as I am and not as I should be, because I'm never going to be as I should be."[346]

—Paul Tillich

> *"Who dares accuse us whom God has chosen for his own?*
> *No one–for God himself has given us right standing with himself.*
> *Who then will condemn us?*
> *No one–for God himself has given us right standing with himself."*
> Romans 8:33, 34a NLT

- Is it true that in this life you're "never going to be as you should be?" Do you hate yourself for that? Should you? Does God hate you for that?

- Do you think that fear of judgment will keep you in line better than unconditional love? Can you trace that idea to its source and critique it?

- Can you quit keeping score? Do you laugh at the preposterous idea of worthiness?

For more: *Merton's Palace of Nowhere* by James Finley

Disillusionment in the Church

"A great disillusionment with others, with Christians in general, and, if we are fortunate, with ourselves, is bound to overwhelm us as surely as God desires to lead us to an understanding of genuine Christian community. By sheer grace God will not permit us to live in a dream world even for a few weeks and to abandon ourselves to those blissful experiences and exalted moods that sweep over us like a wave of rapture.... Only that community which enters into the experience of this great disillusionment with all its unpleasant and evil appearances begins to be what it should be in God's sight, begins to grasp in faith the promise that is given to it. The sooner this moment of disillusionment comes over the individual and the community, the better for both.... Every human idealized image that is brought into the Christian community is a hindrance to genuine community and must be broken up so that genuine community can survive. Those who love their dream of a Christian community more than the Christian community itself become destroyers of that Christian community even though their personal intentions may be ever so honest, earnest, and sacrificial."[347]

—Dietrich Bonhoeffer

"Parker Palmer ... says community is the place where the person you least want to live with always lives. So community is not like a place where you love each other sort of freely and warmly and affectionately. Community is in fact the place where you are purified, where your love is tested, where your childhood of God is constantly put through the mill of human relationships. That is what community is. Community is a place where Judas always is and sometimes it is just you."[348]

—Henri Nouwen

> *"But we have this treasure in jars of clay to show that*
> *this all-surpassing power is from God and not from us."*
> 2 Corinthians 4:7 NIV

- Is God at work to break you of your illusions about the church in general–and your church in particular? Why would God do that?

- Do you have idealized expectations for your church that make you a danger to genuine community–even though you're earnest in your support of it?

- Do you have what it takes according to Nouwen to participate in community?

For more: *Life Together* by Dietrich Bonhoeffer

Don't Just Do Something, Stand There!

"Nothing was ever accomplished in a stampede."

—Baron von Hugel

"Our busyness–whether of body or of mind–is often a distraction, a way of avoiding others, avoiding intimacy, avoiding ourselves. We keep busy to push back our fears, our loneliness, our self-doubt, our questions about purposes and ends. We want to know we matter, we want to know our lives are worthwhile. And when we're not sure, we work that much harder, we worry that much more. In the face of our uncertainty, we keep busy. . . . What is it, then, that restores us to a better version of ourselves, that returns us to our firm sense of goodness–both our own and the world's? Perhaps it's a question of grace: a reflected sunset flares in the windows of a skyscraper, a sheet of newspaper takes flight down an empty street, and suddenly we find ourselves in a world made luminous with wonder. . . . And so it is: the world itself can call us out of our preoccupations, our worries, our lists and agendas. In such moments our attention is arrested, quite literally stopped, and the world seems to say to us: 'Don't just do something, stand there.'"[349]

—Philip Simmons

"Take a long, scrutinizing look at what God is doing. This requires patient attentiveness and energetic concentration. Everybody else is noisier than God. The headlines and neon lights and amplifying systems of the world announce human works. But what of God's works? They are unadvertised but also inescapable, if we simply look. They are everywhere. They are marvelous. But God has no public relations agency. He mounts no publicity campaign to get our attention. He simply invites us to look."[350]

—Eugene Peterson

"It is a commonplace of the spiritual masters that the deepest part of the soul likes to go slow, since it seeks to savor rather than to accomplish; it wants to rest in and contemplate the good rather than to hurry off to another place."[351]

—Robert Barron

"Come, behold the works of the Lord."
Psalm 46:8 ESV

- Are you able to just stand in wonder?
- Are you always hurrying off to another place? If so, why?
- Does your pace of life allow for seeing what God is doing? . . . for awe?

Abba, slow me down for wonder.

For more: *Learning to Fall* by Philip Simmons

The Christian as World Citizen

"Sister Janelle plays 'My Country 'Tis of Thee' on the organ, but no one belts out the words. I do not think this is because the sisters are unpatriotic, nor do I think they don't love and bless this country. But to be a monastic is to live as a citizen of the world. It requires love for every country on the planet."[352]

—Judith Valente

"The nation is the most pervasive of all the gods, in any time, in any culture. True patriotism is not worship of our nation but rather, in the light of our worship of the God of justice, to conform our nation's ways to justice.... We can insist on a distinction between our country and our government.... Let it be clear: it is because we say Yes to what *our country* ought to represent ('liberty and justice for all'), that we must say No to what *our government* has come to represent ('truth...on the scaffold, wrong...on the throne'). When a government traduces the ideals of a country, it is an act of loyalty to oppose the government. Let us never concede that because people have been elected to public office they are exempt from challenge and critique; on the contrary they are more than ever subject to challenge, and critique, because they now speak and act...for all of us...."[353]

—Robert McAfee Brown

"I am the sort of Christian whose patriotism might be called into question by some on the grounds that I do not take the United States to be more beloved of God than France, let us say, or Russia, or Argentina, or Iran. I experience religious dread whenever I find myself thinking that I know the limits of God's grace, since I am utterly certain it exceeds any imagination a human being might have of it. God does, after all, so love the world.... Making God a tribal deity, our local Baal, is embarrassing and disgraceful."[354]

—Marilynne Robinson

"Give to Caesar what belongs to Caesar,
and give to God what belongs to God."
Mark 12:17 NLT

- Is *your* patriotism ever questioned?
- Is *your* God a "tribal deity?"
- Does *your* faith require holding government accountable?

Abba, guide my allegiances.

For more: *Unexpected News* by Robert McAfee Brown

The Laboratory of the Spirit

"Closer is he than breathing
and nearer than hands and feet."

—Alfred Lord Tennyson

"Our need of [God] is but an echo of His need of us."[355]

—Abraham Heschel

"Just as in earthly life lovers long for the moment when they are able to breathe forth their love for each other, to let their souls blend in a soft whisper, so the mystic longs for the moment when in prayer he can, as it were, creep into God."[356]

—*Søren* Kierkegaard

"Retirement is the laboratory of the spirit; interior solitude and silence are its two wings. All great works were prepared in the desert, including the redemption of the world. The precursors, the followers, the Master Himself, all obeyed or have to obey one and the same law. Prophets, apostles, preachers, martyrs, pioneers of knowledge, inspired artists in every art, ordinary men and the Man-God, all pay tribute to loneliness, to the life of silence, to the night."

—A. Gilbert Sertillanges

"Just imagine how different your life would be if moment by moment you were constantly open to God. Think of how much your experience of yourself, others and the world would change if you were continuously attuned to the loving presence of God and allowed the life of God to flow into and through you with each breath.... It holds the possibility of helping us move from occasional acts of praying to a life of prayer."[357]

—David Benner

"For in him we live and move and exist . . . ."
Acts 17:28 NIV

- Can you imagine a God who "aches for you?"(Heschel, who is an expert in the Hebrew prophets where idea recurs, uses this phrase.)

224

- Try to imagine a God who is closer to you "than your hands and feet." ... in whom you "live and move and exist." Can you let that reality become your reality?

- Does the aspiration to "creep into God" express your desire for deeper intimacy with God? What, specifically, can you do to develop such intimacy?

Abba, by interior solitude and silence may I creep into your felt presence Lord.

For more: *Opening to God* by David Benner

Wisdom Through the Awful Grace of God

"Even in our sleep, pain which cannot forget
falls drop by drop upon the heart
until, in our own despair, against our will,
comes wisdom through the awful grace of God."

—Aeschylus

"Misfortunes leave wounds which bleed drop by drop even in sleep; thus little by little they train man by force and dispose him to wisdom in spite of himself. Man must learn to think of himself as a limited and dependent being; and only suffering teaches him this."[358]

—Simone Weil

"Suffering can be a path to awakening when we engage it with receptivity to the gifts it holds rather than simply attempt to endure it. One of those gifts is that suffering has unique capacity to help us soften and release attachments and move toward a life of non-attachment. Simone Weil said that suffering that does not detach us is wasted suffering. Don't waste suffering. It's always a shame to have to repeat lessons because we don't get their point but suffering is a particularly bad lesson to be slow to get."[359]

—David Benner

"Spirituality is about what we do with our pain."[360]

—Richard Rohr

"The sad reality is that most of us will not go forward until the pain of staying where we are is unbearable."[361]

—Peter Scazzero

"Do not become upset when difficulty comes your way. Laugh in its face and know that you are in the arms of God."

—Francis de Sales

> *"Do not be like a senseless horse or mule*
> *that needs a bit and bridle*
> *to keep it under control."*
> Psalm 32:9 NLT

- Are you waiting until things become "unbearable" before changing?
- Are you at risk of needing to repeat difficult lessons that the "awful grace of God" has been trying to teach you?
- The next time you are suffering, can you remember that you're "in the arms of God?"

Abba, help me to embrace the gifts of your frequently painful grace.

For more: *Spirituality and the Awakened Self* by David Benner

---

A Good-news Gospel

"This past winter, we had unusually cold weather.... Some nights, temperatures plummeted below zero. Dashing from a warm car through the cold into a warm house, I thought of the dozens of people ... near our University, who had no warm place to sleep. I couldn't imagine how difficult it would be to try to survive overnight in the cold. The physical cold might be unbearable, but for me, the more painful reality would be that no one loved me enough to invite me inside on such a cold night. I grew up in a Christian environment, but as a child and teenager, I heard very little about God's heart for those in need. I'm not sure how we missed it, because the Bible is full of passages speaking about God's justice, compassion, and faithful love for those who have nothing, who are marginalized or oppressed. God is pleased when His church acts like Him, showing compassion for those in need, and God can use this generosity to lead those who don't know Him to a saving knowledge of our Lord Jesus Christ. Social justice is not the gospel, but it is a natural consequence of the gospel taking root in our hearts. Jesus' half-brother James … explains that true devotion to God results in taking action to care for those who could never repay us: "orphans and widows in their affliction" (James 1:27, ESV).... In Isaiah 58, the children of Israel are rebuked because of their lack of response to the oppressed, the hungry, and the homeless. The children of Israel were repeatedly commanded to care for those who were displaced or in need, because the Israelites themselves were once immigrants in need. Now they were practicing outward religious activities such as fasting, but they were not demonstrating any evidence of a heart like God's heart."[362]

—Matt McAlack

"Though he was rich,
yet for your sakes he became poor . . . ."
2 Corinthians 8:9 NLT

- If you were freezing on the sidewalk, ignored by people walking past, would you feel loved by God?
- If a gospel fails the "justice test," can it really be good news?
- Are you developing a heart like God's heart–including on the street?

Abba, may love give credence to my gospel.

For more: *The Prodigal God* by Tim Keller

Beholding My Brokenness

"In prayer we seek what John Cassian (360–430) called 'integrity of heart' or 'integral wholeness'. But when you're honest before God, that can feel far off. Here's Cassian's self-diagnosis in his *Institutes and Conferences*–lethargy, sleeplessness, unsettling dreams, impulsive urges, self-justification, seething emotions, sexual fantasies, pious pretense that masked as virtue, self-deception, clerical ambition and the desire to dominate, crushing despair, confusion, wild mood swings, flattery, and the dreaded 'noonday demon' of acedia ("a wearied or anxious heart" that suggests close parallels to clinical depression). Cassian further admits that 'there are many things that lie hidden in my conscience which are known and manifest to God, even though they may be unknown and obscure to me'. And this is a monk who had devoted his entire life to prayer!"[363]

—Daniel Clendenin

"I get so tired of beholding my brokenness. But the deeper I go into the depths of it, the deeper I experience my belovedness too."[364]

—Jonathan Martin

"The man who does not permit his spirit to be beaten down and upset by dryness and helplessness, but who lets God lead him peacefully through the wilderness, and desires no other support or guidance than that of pure faith and trust in God alone, will be brought to the Promised Land."[365]

—Thomas Merton

"I belong to my beloved,
and his desire is for me."
Song of Songs 7:10 NIV

- I can never help but smile reading Cassian's list–it's so honest–and so familiar at points. Are you in touch with your "dryness and helplessness" like Cassian, Martin and Merton?

- Do you keep seeking God in prayer even when you're overwhelmed by your brokenness? Even when you're beaten down?

- Have you attempted to let the experience of brokenness move you into a deeper experience of belovedness? . . . into the Promised Land?

"Beloved Silence: Thank you for listening to my confessions and failures. Under the shadow of your light, my darkness is no more."[366] (Peter Traben Haas)

For more: *Centering Prayers* by Peter Traben Haas

Unperturbed in Jerusalem

"Now when Jesus was born in Bethlehem of Judea in the days of Herod the king, behold, there came wise men from the east to Jerusalem, saying, 'Where is he that is born King of the Jews? For we have seen his star in the east, and are come to worship him.'"
Matthew 2:1–2 KJV

"Although the scribes could explain where the Messiah should be born, they remained quite unperturbed in Jerusalem. They did not accompany the Wise Men to seek him. Similarly we may know the whole of Christianity, yet make no *movement*. The power that moved Heaven and Earth leaves us completely unmoved. What a difference! The three kings had only a rumor to go by. But it moved them to make that long journey. The scribes were much better informed, much better versed. They sat and studied the Scriptures like so many dons, but it did not make them move. Who had the more truth? The three kings who followed a rumor, or the scribes who remained sitting with all their knowledge? What a vexation it must have been for the kings, that the scribes who gave them the news they wanted remained quiet in Jerusalem! We are being mocked, the kings might have thought. For indeed what an atrocious self-contradiction that the scribes should have the knowledge and yet remain still. This is as bad as if a person knows all about Christ and his teachings, and his own life expresses the opposite. We are tempted to suppose that such a person wishes to fool us, unless we admit that he is only fooling himself."[367]

—Søren Kierkegaard

- Sometimes it takes an outsider to help us see our mistakes. Are you open to the voices of those from outside your usual circle? . . . even, as in the story, from outside your religion?

- Everyone is wrong somewhere, and everyone is right somewhere. Are you as good at learning from others as you are pointing out the wrongs of others?

- Could you be described as "sitting" with all your knowledge? What needs to change?

Abba, don't let me fool myself about myself.

For more: *Meditations from Kierkegaard* translated and edited by T. H. Croxall

---

Only Love Can Do That

"Where love rules, there is no will to power; and where power predominates, there love is lacking."[368]

—Carl Jung

"Violence is any way we have of violating the integrity of the other. Racism and sexism are violence. Derogatory labeling of any sort constitutes violence. Rendering other people invisible or irrelevant is an act of violence. So is manipulating people towards our ends as if they were objects that existed only to serve our purposes... . Violence is not just about bombing or shooting or hitting people. To create peace in our lives—and our world—we need to be able to sit with frustration and hold the tension of opposite views."[369]

—Parker Palmer

"The ultimate weakness of violence is that it is a descending spiral, begetting the very thing it seeks to destroy. Instead of diminishing evil, it multiplies it. Through violence you may murder the liar, but you cannot murder the lie, nor establish the truth. Through violence you may murder the hater, but you do not murder hate. In fact, violence merely increases hate. So it goes. Returning violence for violence multiplies violence, adding deeper darkness to a night already devoid of stars.

Darkness cannot drive out darkness: only light can do that. Hate cannot drive out hate: only love can do that."[370]

—Martin Luther King, Jr.

"The child is totally available in the present because he has relatively little to remember, his experience of evil is as yet brief, and his anticipation of the future does not extend very far. The Christian, in his humility and faith, must be as totally available to his brother, to his world, in the present, as the child is. But he cannot see the world with childlike innocence and simplicity unless his memory is cleared of past evils by forgiveness, and his anticipation of the future is hopefully free of craft and calculation. For this reason, the humility of Christian nonviolence is at once patient and uncalculating."[371]

—Thomas Merton

"How I wish today that you of all people
would understand the way to peace."
Luke 19:42 NLT

- Do you have enough humility to hold opposing views in tension?
- Is your past flooded with forgiveness so that, like a child, you have little to remember?
- Have you determined never to return violence for violence?

Abba, help me live the way of peace.

For more: *Faith and Violence* by Thomas Merton

Just Fade Away

"Perhaps some man will say, 'How can a man carry his cross? How can a man who is alive be crucified?' Hear, briefly, how this thing may be.... One who is crucified no longer has the power of moving or turning his limbs in any direction as he pleases, so we ought to fix our wishes and desires, not in accordance with what is pleasant and delightful to us now, but in accordance with the law of the Lord in whatsoever direction it constrain us. Also, he who is fastened to a cross no longer considers things present, nor thinks about his likings, nor is perplexed with anxiety or care for the morrow, [nor] is inflamed by any pride, or strife, or rivalry, grieves not at present insults, nor remembers past ones. While he is still breathing in the body, he is dead to all earthly things, and sends his heart on to that place to which he doubts not he shall shortly come. So we, when we are crucified by the fear of the Lord, ought to be dead to all these things. We die not only to carnal vices, but to all earthly things, even to those indifferent. We fix our minds there whither we hope at every moment we are to go."[372]

—James Hanney

> *"May I never boast about anything*
> *except the cross of our Lord Jesus Christ.*
> *Because of that cross,*
> *my interest in this world has been crucified,*
> *and the world's interest in me has also died."*
> Galatians 6:14 NLT

- Imagine finding consolation for the very difficult circumstances of your life in the fact that you will soon be leaving this life for heaven.

- Now imagine that you intentionally created the difficult circumstances of your life as the desert hermits did, to escape the faith-wrecking pull of earthly things–and not only sinful ones.

- Does the Christianity you know encourage you to die to much of what this world considers important? Has your interest in this world been "crucified" in some measurable way?

- It seems like we take spiritual matters so lightly compared to the desert fathers. Why do you suppose that is?

Abba, help me learn from these ancient fathers what I may not learn otherwise today.

For more: *The Wisdom of the Desert* by James Hannay

Come-and-See Evangelism

"Your life is your theology and your sermon. Don't preach the good news, but be the good news.... Preach as you go! Preach the gospel at all times, and when necessary, use words."

—Francis of Assisi

"The general tendency in Emergence Christian theology is to question with real vigor and precision whether or not the connection between faith and doctrinal precision is essential to the soul's salvation. Dogma, yes, but doctrine, not so much. That is, do one's brainwaves and verbal utterances actually make one's faith? Emergence Christians can often take this even a step further and reference those places of spiritual primacy where Jesus taught (as in his judgment of the nations as told in the Gospel of Matthew, for example) that a life is what constitutes and demonstrates a disciple, rather than a mind-set."[373]

—Phyllis Tickle

"For postmodern evangelism, this means that truth is best communicated as it is lived in the life of a body of Christ out of its (his)story and its stories, not one-on-one combat via evidentiary apologetic. Instead, the church itself becomes the apologetic. As the truth of the gospel is worked out in the real lives of people living together in community, its veracity cannot be debated or individualized, it's reality is something into which we may simply invite others to 'come and see' and the church thereby becomes the center for evangelism. Evangelicals often preach that what the culture needs is absolute truth, but what the culture needs is a church that believes the truth so absolutely it actually lives it out."[374]

—David Fitch

"Silence every radio and television preacher, stop every evangelical book or tract from being published, take down every evangelical website from the net and simply ask Christians to show one tangible expression of Jesus's love to another person every day. We would be far better off."[375]

—David Di Sabatino

"Come, see a man who told me everything I ever did.
Could this be the Messiah?"
John 4:29 NIV

- What will make you more persuasive with people–absolute truth, or unconditional love?

- Are people more or less interested in God after they spend time with you?

- If you showed one tangible expression of Jesus's love to someone every day, how different would that be from what you're doing now?

Abba, may my faith transcend just a mindset.

For more: *The Great Giveaway* by David Fitch

The Crippling Effect of Discontent

"'Look at the birds of the air,' Jesus said to the crowds gathered around him (Matt. 6:26). I've been looking at the birds lately, and it strikes me that today our lives are more akin to the frantic scurrying of rats and the disciplined marching of ants than to the contented and joyous singing of birds....Cultures of postindustrial societies encourage and reward scurrying and marching more than they do rejoicing. They reach into what seems like the most intimate regions of our hearts, and by affecting our desires and our sense of responsibility, they disturb the peace of contentment and suppress the buoyancy of joy ....'The eye is not satisfied with seeing, or the ear filled with hearing,' writes the author of Ecclesiastes (1:7–8), describing the ancient experience of insatiability. We are finite, but our desire is infinite ....Insatiability is a human condition–but one that the modern market economy magnifies. According to Kenneth Galbraith, the modern market doesn't so much respond to existing needs by supplying goods, but rather 'creates the wants the goods are presumed to satisfy.' Desire, hunger, and dissatisfaction are the market economy's fuel. The more fuel it has, the faster it can run, and so it creates the void it seeks to fill. The result is a rushing stream of both amazing and not-so-amazing goods and services–along with a perpetual lack of contentment and diminished capacity for joy. The relation between joy and contentment at any given moment is straightforward: the less content you are, the less joy you will have (though discontentment often precedes joy). Joy celebrates the goodness of what is, what was, or is to come; the market economy fuels insatiability and malcontent, systematically erodes the goodness of what is, and cripples joy."[376]

—Miroslav Volf

"I have learned how to be content
with whatever I have."
Philippians 4:11 NLT

- Does scurrying seem normal or good?
- Are you an "insatiable" consumer? If so, why?
- Can you recognize and reject artificially created needs?
- Are you willing to be a person who has less than others?

Abba, may I be motivated, not by anxiety, greed or ego, but by gratitude and the desire to serve you and others.

For more: *The Living God and the Fullness of Life* by *Jürgen* Moltmann

Spirituality as Balance

"Esther de Waal, in her book *Living with Contradiction: An Introduction to Bene-dictine Spirituality*, uses the language of paradox and contradiction to describe Benedict's genius as he interprets the Gospel of Jesus Christ into everyday life. We are called to find God in this place and to seek the peace and discipline of stability, yet we are also called to grow and change and be willing to move. We are called to welcome strangers and accept them for who they are, yet we are not called to change our own priorities as we welcome them. Many, including de Waal, use the word 'bal-ance' to describe the life patterns laid out by Benedict. We are called to prayer, work, study, and rest in fairly equal proportions. Each is important, but to overemphasize any one of them would be unhealthy. Benedict invites us to embrace the balance between community, where we live and work, and time alone for prayer and reflection. Benedict encourages us to engage in self-reflection without self-absorption and to strive for sincere repentance without dwelling excessively on our shortcomings. Benedict calls us to a radical obedience that sees all of life as a response to God's voice and God's initiative, yet we are not encouraged to strain for that kind of obedience. In fact, Benedict encourages us to accept that we will fail as often as we succeed. We are called to believe that we have enough today, in this moment, while we also acknowledge that we are looking to heaven for our ultimate fulfillment. The grace of God overflows in every moment, in every place, and in every human life, and Benedict's balance is firmly rooted in God's character and God's presence with us."[377]

—Lynne Baab

"We have seen his glory, the glory of the one and only Son,
who came from the Father, full of grace and truth."
John 1:14 NIV

- Where do you still need better balance?
- Do you practice self-reflection without self-absorption?
- Can you seek to practice radical obedience without "striving?" What does that mean?
- Can you let the grace of God overflow in your life "in every moment and every place?"

Abba, help me as I recalibrate daily, in my balancing act with you and my world.

For more: *Living with Contradiction* by Esther de Waal

February 29 (Leap Year)   December 31

The Quiet Member of the Trinity

"It is generally safe to say that noise and turmoil in the interior life are signs that proceed from our own emotion or from some spirit that is anything but holy. The

236

inspirations of the Holy Ghost are quiet, for God speaks in the silent depths of the spirit. His voice brings peace. It does not arouse excitement, but allays it because excitement belongs to uncertainty. The voice of God is certitude. If he moves us to action, we go forward with peaceful strength. More often than not his inspirations teach us to sit still. They show us the emptiness and confusion of projects we thought we had undertaken for his glory. He saves us from the impulses that would throw us into wild competition with other men. He delivers us from ambition. The Holy Spirit is most easily recognized where he inspires obedience and humility. No one really knows Him who has not tasted the tranquillity that comes from the renunciation of our own will, our own pleasure, our own interests, without glory, without notice, without approval, for the interests of some other person. The inspirations of the Spirit of God are not grandiose. They are simple. They move us to see God in works that are difficult without being spectacular."[378]

—Thomas Merton

"You know him, because he lives with you now
and later will be in you."
John 14:17b NIV

- Are you aware of the seemingly universal tendancy to look for the Holy Spirit in what is grandiose and spectacular? What might one miss doing that?

- Are you acquainted with the Spirit's voice telling you to sit still? Are you able to identify the dark side of ambition?

- Do you minister and make sacrifices for others even when it will certainly be "without glory, without notice, without approval?"

- How do you protect yourself from "noise and turmoil in the interior life?"

"Spirit of God, descend upon my heart; Wean it from earth; through all its pulses move; Stoop to my weakness, mighty as Thou art; And make me love Thee as I ought to love." (George Croly)

For More: *The Ascent to Truth* by Thomas Merton

Endnotes

1. Gateley, *Margins.*
2. Williams, "Contemplation."
3. Martin, *Heaven.*
4. Rohr, *Radical.*
5. Ortberg, *Me.*
6. Rohr, *Everything.*
7. Willard, *Disciplines.*
8. Willard, *Omission.*
9. Lewis, *Basic.*
10. Ortberg, *Life.*
11. Willard, *Conspiracy.*
12. Ibid.
13. Manning, *Furious.*
14. Whyte, "Art."
15. Adapted from Rohr, *Eager.*
16. Willard, *Disciplines.*
17. Twitter post by Willard: https://twitter.com/renovareusa/status/905516202239385601.
18. Ghezzi, *Voices.*
19. Merton, *World.*
20. Ghezzi, *Voices.*
21. Bruni, review of *Quiet.*
22. Foster, *Celebration.*
23. Cunningham, *Search.*
24. Ortberg, *Life.*
25. Hervey, *Works.*
26. Swindoll, *Laugh.*
27. Bonhoeffer, *Life.*
28. Jerry Seinfeld in an episode of "Comedians in Cars Going For Coffee."
29. Benner, *Spirituality.*
30. Adapted from Rohr, *Radical.*
31. de Vinck, *Nouwen.*
32. Foster, *Finding.*
33. Fretheim, *Suffering.*
34. Pearsall, *Toxic.*
35. Moltmann, *Experiences.*
36. Merton, *Island.*
37. Scazzero, "Thy Kingdom Come" (This is my transcription from a presently unavailable podcast.)
38. Harter, *Hearts.*
39. Manning, *Ragmuffin.*
40. Nouwen, *Genesee.*
41. Küng, *Being.*
42. Rohr, *Falling.*
43. Baldwin, *Fire.*
44. Lewis, *Grief.*
45. Rohr, *Yes.*
46. Nouwen, *Beloved.*
47. Buechner, *Magnificent.*
48. Lewis, *Basic.*
49. I owe this image to Father Greg Boyle, who says that working side-by-side is how men are healed, instead of face-to-face, which he believes is more the way it works with women.
50. Smith, *Quaker.*
51. Rohr, *Yes.*
52. Coles, *Spiritual.*
53. Merton, *Raids.*
54. Buchanan, *Rest.*
55. Rauschenbusch, *Prayers.*
56. Yancey, *Survivor.*
57. Scott, *Conversations.*
58. Norris, *Silence.*
59. Jonas, *Essential.*
60. Flowers, "Non-Anxious."
61. Francis, "Silence."
62. Barton, *Invitation.*
63. Alfred, *Donne.*
64. MacDonald, "Cultivating."
65. Ibid.
66. Schaefer, *Family?*
67. Whyte, *Marriages.*
68. Crabb, *Community.*
69. Buri, *Wife.*
70. Rohr, *Return.*
71. Beck, "Intelligence."
72. Verhey, *Ephesians.*
73. de Sales, *Loving.*
74. Merton, *Island.*
75. Brown, *Unexpected.*
76. Moltmann, *Church.*
77. McCullough, *Consolations.*
78. O'Malley, *Prayers.*
79. Francis, *Conversations.*
80. Allender, *Told.*
81. Chesterton, *Francis.*
82. Buechner, *Whistling.*
83. Rohr, *Radical.*
84. Miller, *Table.*

85. Morgan, *Promise.*
86. Nouwen, *Reaching.*
87. Ibid.
88. Lawrence, *Practice.*
89. Newell, *Celtic.*
90. de Mello, *Meditations.*
91. Scazzero, *Office.*
92. Shafir, *Listening.*
93. Nouwen, *Bread.*
94. Küng, *Being.*
95. Rohr, *Everything.*
96. Buechner, *Secrets.*
97. Day, *Praying.*
98. Peterson, *Contemplative.*
99. Yancey, *Disappointment.*
100. Ortberg, *Life.*
101. Nouwen, *Selfless.*
102. Whyte, *Consolations.*
103. Barth, *Dogmatics.*
104. Thanks for this phrase to Emily Freeman.
105. Whyte, *Consolations.*
106. Cushing, "Human."
107. Ibid.
108. Fretheim, *Suffering.*
109. Ibid.
110. Kirvan, *Heart.*
111. Chalmers, *Affection.*
112. Benner, *Surrender.*
113. Bounds, *Works.*
114. Chambers, *Not Knowing.*
115. Manning, *Abba's.*
116. Peterson, *Plant.*
117. Willard, *Omission.*
118. Cairns, *Endless.*
119. Nouwen, *Way.*
120. Bonhoeffer, *Life.*
121. Manning, *Abba's.*
122. Ibid.
123. Boyle, *Calling.*
124. Merton, *Seeds.*
125. Kirvan, *Nothing.*
126. Peterson, *Contemplative.*
127. Simpson, *Holy.*
128. Rampy, "Waiting"
129. Peterson, *Leap.*
130. Ibid.
131. Roazzi, *Success.*
132. DeYoung, *Crazy.*
133. Foster, *Celebration.*
134. Barton, *Invitation.*

135. Nouwen, *Genesee.*
136. Tozer, *Pursuit.*
137. Millay, *Poems.*
138. Fitzgerald, *Habit.*
139. Whyte, "Thoughts"
140. Kirvan, *Nothing.*
141. Scazzero, "Slow."
142. Lefton, "The Gifts."
143. Keller, *Walking.*
144. Yancey, *Bible.*
145. Merton, *New Seeds.*
146. Ghezzi, *Voices.*
147. Thomas, "Clown."
148. de Mello, *Song.*
149. de Mello, *Way.*
150. Norris, *Dakota.*
151. Bonhoeffer, *Discipleship.*
152. Norris, *Amazing.*
153. Kazantzakis, *Zorba.*
154. Palmer, *Hidden.*
155. Hansel, *Dancin'.*
156. Ghezzi, *Saints.*
157. Scazzero, *Office.*
158. Taylor, *Altar.*
159. Ibid.
160. Huxley, *Perennial.*
161. Valente, *Atchison.*
162. Allegri, *Conversations.*
163. Angelou, *Journey.*
164. Smith, *Quaker.*
165. Postman, *Amusing.*
166. Merton, *Mountain.*
167. Merton, *Contemplation.*
168. Chomsky, "Essentially."
169. Gopnik, "1984."
170. Baldwin, *Ticket.*
171. Rohr, "Bias."
172. Bruteau, *Optimism.*
173. Scazzero, "Body."
174. Ibid.
175. Campbell, *Paul.*
176. Ibid.
177. Barton, *Invitation.*
178. Demaray, *Imitation.*
179. McCullough, *Consolations.*
180. Orwell, *1984.*
181. Kierkegaard, *Either/Or.*
182. Palmer, *Listen.*
183. Thurman, *Deep.*
184. Scazzero, *Quit!*
185. Barton, *Rhythms.*

186. Jones, *Soul.*
187. Cardenal. *Abide.*
188. Muller, *Sabbath.*
189. Buchanan, *Rest.*
190. Foster and Smith, *Devotional Classics.*
191. Keating, *Human.*
192. Buechner, *Whistling.*
193. White, *Serious.*
194. de Wall, *Seeking.*
195. Nouwen, *Reaching.*
196. Haugen, *News.*
197. Peck, *Road.*
198. White, *Nones.*
199. Fadling, *Unhurried.*
200. Peterson, *Contemplative.*
201. Baab, *Sabbath.*
202. Buchanan, *Rest.*
203. Lewis, *Weight.*
204. Martin, *Heaven.*
205. Heschel, *Prophets.*
206. Heschel, *Between.*
207. Brown, *Saying.*
208. Sherwin, *Heschel.*
209. Palmer, *Healing.*
210. Norris, *Dakota.*
211. Taylor, *Altar.*
212. Nouwen, *Waiting.*
213. Peterson, *Earth.*
214. Flowers, "Non-Anxious"
215. Cunningham, *Merton.*
216. Nouwen, *Mourning.*
217. McCullough, *Consolations.*
218. Foster, *Challenge.*
219. Merton, *Life.*
220. Schaef, *Meditations.*
221. Kierkegaard, *Purity.*
222. Jones, *Soul.*
223. Chödrön, *Things.*
224. Rohr, "Egoic."
225. Palmer, *Nobodies.*
226. May, *Addiction.*
227. Fretheim, *Suffering.*
228. Ibid.
229. Crabb, *Inside.*
230. Buechner, *Journey.*
231. Norris, *Acedia.*
232. Forest, "Dorothy."
233. Rohr, "Motives."
234. Clendenin, "Reviews."
235. O'Connell, *Essays.*
236. Merton, *Seeds.*
237. de Vinck, *Powerless.*
238. Buchanan, *Rest.*
239. Taylor, *Learning.*
240. Manning, *Signature.*
241. Smith, *Philokalia.*
242. Papanagiotou, *Restoration.*
243. Rohr, *Yes.*
244. Lewis, *Screwtape.*
245. MacDonald, *Life.*
246. Chittister, *Wisdom.*
247. Norris, *Amazing.*
248. Merton, *Faith.*
249. King, *Knock.*
250. Sittser, *Disguised.*
251. Martin, *Heaven.*
252. Ibid.
253. Holt, *Thirsty.*
254. McNeill, *Institutes.*
255. Merton, *Seeds.*
256. Ibid.
257. Muller. *Sabbath.*
258. Heschel, *Sabbath.*
259. Wirzba, *Sabbath.*
260. Brueggemann, *Common.*
261. Henson, "Behalf."
262. Keller, *Justice.*
263. Merton, "Contemplative."
264. Rilke, *Letters.*
265. Scazzero, *Unleash.*
266. Baker, *Compelled.*
267. My transcript from a "Homebrewed Christianity" podcast.
268. Murray, *Wine.*
269. Volf, *Exclusion.*
270. Merton, *New Seeds.*
271. Rohr, "Orthopraxy."
272. Hays, *Joy.*
273. Postman, *Amusing.*
274. Merton, *Faith.*
275. Shelden and Macallair, *Justice.*
276. McCarty, *Disappeared.*
277. Dillard, *Pilgrim.*
278. Boyd, *Doubt.*
279. Martin, *Heaven.*
280. Ibid.
281. Inchausti, *Seeds.*
282. Bessey, *Feminist.*
283. Evans, "Outgrowing."
284. Safi, *Disease.*
285. Dylan, "Tell Me."

286. Bass, *History.*
287. Hallman, *Descent.*
288. Kent, *Breathe.*
289. McLaren, *Finding.*
290. Kenyon, "Otherwise."
291. Edmondson, *Navigate.*
292. Bourgeault, *Mystical.*
293. Petri, "Crucified." Used with permission.
294. Viereck, *Glimpses.*
295. Hodge, *World Religions.*
296. O'Connor, *Mystery.*
297. Lane, *Solace.*
298. Pascal, *Pensees.*
299. Wiederkehr, *Tree.*
300. Palmer, "Fear."
301. Scazzero, *Office.*
302. Lewis, *Letters.*
303. Buechner, *Secrets.*
304. Robertson, *Christmas.*
305. Jarvis and Johnson, *Feasting.*
306. McLaren, *New.*
307. Moon, *Apprenticeship.*
308. See McLaren, *New,* 56–58.
309. Yoder, *Radical.*
310. Nouwen, *Name.*
311. Merton, *Island.*
312. Siete, *Communication.*
313. Scazzero, *Relationships.* See appendix C.
314. Mayer, *Narrative.*
315. Taylor, *Silent.*
316. Rohr, *Return.*
317. Tippett, *Wise.*
318. Cusa, *Vision.*
319. Pennington, *Merton.*
320. Lindberg, *Gift.*
321. Merton, *Island.*
322. Boyd, *Repenting.*
323. Bonhoeffer, *Life.*
324. Simsic, *Francis.*
325. Sayers, *Women.*
326. Besey, *Feminist.*
327. Ibid.
328. Palmer, "Brink."
329. Packer and Howard, *Humanism.*
330. Underhill, *Inner.*
331. Haugen, *Injustice.* Used with permission.
332. Habyarimana, *Quotes.*
333. Licata, *Confusion.*
334. Rohr, *Everything.*
335. Norris, *Acedia.*
336. Peterson, *Earth.*
337. Küng, *Christian.*
338. Hurnard, *Winged.*
339. Parker, *Speak.*
340. Metrakoudes-Hewett, "Sacred Space."
341. Campbell, *Paul.*
342. Benner, *Surrender.*
343. Merton, *New Man.*
344. Finley, *Nowhere.*
345. Ibid.
346. Tillich, *Foundations.*
347. Bonhoeffer, *Life.*
348. Nouwen, *Discovering.*
349. Simmons, *Learning.*
350. Peterson, *Altar.*
351. Barron, *Heaven.*
352. Valente, *Atchison.*
353. Brown, *Unexpected.*
354. Robinson, *Read.*
355. Heschel, *Between.*
356. Kierkegaard, *Either/Or.*
357. Benner, *Opening.*
358. Weil, *Source.*
359. Benner, *Awakened.*
360. Rohr, *Adam's.*
361. Scazzero, *Unleash.*
362. McAlack, "Grateful."
363. Clendenin, "Weak."
364. Martin @theboyonthebike
365. Merton, *New Seeds.*
366. Traben Hass, *Centering.*
367. Kierkegaard, *Meditations.*
368. Jung, *Unconscious.*
369. Palmer, *Violence.*
370. King, *Where?*
371. Merton, *Faith.*
372. Hannay, *Desert.*
373. Tickle, *Age.*
374. Fitch, *Giveaway.*
375. Weber, *Younger.*
376. Volf, "Good?"
377. Baab, "Benedictine."
378. Merton, *Ascent.*

Bibliography

Allegri, Renzo. *Conversations with Mother Teresa: A Personal Portrait of the Saint, Her Mission, and Her Great Love for God.* Frederick: The Word Among Us, 2011.

Allender, Dan. *To Be Told: God Invites You to Coauthor Your Future.* Colorado Springs: WalterBrook, 2005.

Angelou, Maya. *Wouldn't Take Nothing for My Journey Now.* New York: Bantam, 1993.

Baab, Lynne. "Benedictine Spirituality: Balance and Paradox." http://www.lynnebaab.com/blog/benedictine-spirituality-balance-and-par.

———. *Sabbath Keeping: Finding Freedom in the Rhythms of Rest.* Downers Grove: InterVarsity, 2005.

Baker, Heidi. *Compelled by Love.* Lake Mary: Charisma House, 2008.

Baldwin, James. *The Fire Next Time.* New York: Dial, 1963.

———. *The Price of the Ticket: Collected Nonfiction, 1948–1985.* New York: St. Martin's, 1985.

Barron, Richard. *Heaven in Stone and Glass: The Spirituality of Gothic Cathedrals.* Chestnut Ridge, NY: Crossroad, 2000.

Bart, Karl. *Church Dogmatics: The Doctine of Creation. (Vol. 3, Part 4).* New York: T & T Clark, 2009.

Barton, Ruth Haley. *Invitation to Solitude and Silence: Experiencing God's Transforming Presence.* Downers Grove: InterVarsity, 2014.

———. "Sacred Rhythms in the Life of the Leader." http://www.christianitytoday.com/pastors/2016/july-web-exclusives/sacred-rhythms-in-life-of-leader.html.

Bass, Diane Butler. *A People's History of Christianity: The Other Side of the Story.* New York: HarperCollins, 2009.

Beck, Richard. "Emotional Intelligence and Sola Scriptura." http://experimentaltheology.blogspot.com/2015/10/emotional-intelligence-and-sola.html.

Benner, David. "Brokenness and Wholeness." http://www.drdavidgbenner.ca/brokenness-and-wholeness/.

———. *Opening to God: Lectio Divina and Life as Prayer.* Downers Grove: InterVarsity Press, 2010.

———. *Spirituality and the Awakening Self: The Sacred Journey of Transformation.* Grand Rapids: Brazos, 2012.

———. *Surrender to Love: Discovering the Heart of Christian Spirituality.* Downers Grove: InterVarsity, 2015.

Bessey, Sarah. *Jesus Feminist: An Invitation to Revisit the Bible's View of Women.* New York: Howard, 2013.

Bonhoeffer, Dietrich. *The Cost of Discipleship.* New York: Touchstone, 1995.

———. *Life Together.* New York: HarperCollins, 1954.

Bounds, E. M. *The Complete Words of E. M. Bounds.* Radford: Wilder, 2008.

Bourgeault, Cynthia. *Mystical Hope: Trusting in the Mercy of God.* Lanham: Rowman & Littlefield, 2001.

Boyd, Gregory. *Benefit of the Doubt: Breaking the Idol of Certainty.* Grand Rapids: Baker, 2013.

———. *Repenting of Religion: Turning from Judgment to the Love of God.* Grand Rapids: Baker, 2004.

Boyle, Gregory. "The Calling of Delight: Gangs, Service, and Kinship." https://onbeing. org/programs/greg-boyle-the-calling-of-delight-gangs-service-and-kinship/.

Brown, Robert McAfee Brown. *Saying Yes and Saying No: On Rendering to God and Caesar.* Louisville: Westminster John Knox, 1986.

———. *Unexpected News: Reading the Bible with Third World Eyes.* Louisville: Westminster John Knox, 1984.

Brueggemann, Walter. *Journey To the Common Good.* Louisville: John Knox, 2010.

———. *The Prophetic Imagination: Preaching an Emancipating Word.* Minneapolis: Fortress, 2012.

Bruni, Frank. Review of *Quiet,* by Susan Cain. New York Times, June 9, 2014.

Bruteau, Beatrice. *Radical Optimism: Practical Spirituality in an Uncertain World.* Boulder: Sentient, 2004.

Buchanan, Mark. *The Rest of God: Restoring Your Soul by Restoring Sabbath.* Nashville: Thomas Nelson, 2006.

Buechner, Frederick. *The Magnificent Defeat.* New York: HarperCollins, 1966.

———. *The Sacred Journey: A Memoir of Early Days.* New York: HaperCollins, 1982.

———. *Secrets in the Dark: A Life in Sermons.* New York: HarperCollins, 2006.

———. *Whistling in the Dark: A Doubter's Dictionary.* San Francisco: Harper, 1988.

Buri, John. *How to Love Your Wife.* Mustang: Tate, 2006.

Cairns, Scott. *Endless Life: Poems of the Mystics.* Brewster: Paraclete, 2015.

Campbell, James M. *Paul the Mystic: A Study In Apostolic Experience.* London: Forgotten Books, 2015.

Cardenal, Ernesto. *Abide In Love.* Maryknoll: Orbis, 1995.

Carson, Clayborne and Peter Holloran, eds. *A Knock At Midnight: Inspiration From the Great Sermons of Reverend Martin Luther King, Jr.* New York: Warner, 2000.

Chalmers, Thomas. *The Expulsive Power of a New Affection.* Edinburgh: Constable, 1855.

Chambers, Oswald. *Not Knowing Whither: The Steps of Abraham's Faith.* London: Simpkin Marshall, 1934.

Chesterton, G. K. *St. Francis of Assisi.* New York: Doubleday, 1957.

Chittister, Joan. *Wisdom Distilled From the Daily: Living the Rule of St. Benedict Today.* New York: HarperCollins, 1990.

Chödrön, Pema. *Comfortable with Uncertainty: 108 Teachings on Cultivating Fearlessness and Compassion.* Boston: Shambhala, 2002.

———. *When Things Fall Apart: Heart Advice for Difficult Times.* Boulder: Shambhala, 1997.

Chomsky, Norm. "The United States Has Essentially a One-Party System: Noam Chomsky Interviewed by Gabor Steingart" https://chomsky.info/20081010/.

Clendenin, Daniel. "Book Reviews: Richard Rohr, Eager to Love; The Alternative Way of Francis of Assisi." https://www.journeywithjesus.net/BookNotes/Richard_Rohr_Eager_To_Love.shtml.

———. "For the Weak and the Weary: A Spirituality of Imperfection." https://www.journeywithjesus.net/Essays/20060130JJ.shtml.

Coles, Robert. *The Spiritual Life of Children.* Boston: Houghton Mifflin Harcourt, 1990.

Crabb, Larry. *Becoming a True Christian Community: A Profound Vision of What the Church Can Be.* Nashville: Thomas Nelson, 1999.

———. *Inside, Out.* Colorado Springs: NavPress, 1988.

Croxall, T. H. ed. and trans. *Meditations from Kierkegaard.* Philadelphia: Westminster, 1955.

Cunningham, Lawrence S., ed. *A Search for Solitude: Pursuing the Monk's True Life. The Journals of Thomas Merton, Volume 3: 1952–1960.* San Francisco: HarperCollins, 1997.

———. *Thomas Merton: Spiritual Master: The Essential Writings.* Mahwah: Paulist, 1992.

Cushing, Pamela. "To Be Fully Human." http://www.jean-vanier.org/en/his_message/jean_vanier_on_becoming_human/to_be_fully_human.

Day, Dorothy and David E. Scott. *Praying in the Presence of Our Lord with Dorothy Day.* U.S.: Our Sunday Visitor, 2002.

de Botton, Alain. *The Course of Love: A Novel.* New York: Simon & Schuster, 2016.

de Mello, Anthony. *The Song of the Bird.* New York: Doubleday, 1982.

———. *The Way to God: The Last Meditations of Anthony de Mello.* New York: Doubleday, 1995.

———. *The Way to Love.* New York: Doubleday, 2012.

de Sales, Francis. *Set Your Heart Free.* Notre Dame: Ave Maria, 2008.

de Vinck, Christopher. *Nouwen Then.* Grand Rapids: Zondervan, 1999.

———. *The Power of the Powerless.* Grand Rapids: Zondervan, 1988

de Waal, Esther. *Seeking God: The Way of St. Benedict.* Collegeville: Liturgical, 1984.

Demaray, Donald E., ed. *The Imitation of Christ: Paraphrased.* New York: Alba House, 1997.

DeYoung, Kevin. *Crazy Busy: A (Mercifully) Short Book About a (Really) Big Problem.* Wheaton: Crossway, 2013.

Dillard, Annie. *Pilgrim at Tinker Creek.* New York: HarperPerennial, 2013.

Donne, John. *The Complete Works of John Donne.* London: Parker, 1839.

Dylan, Bob. *The Lyrics: 1961–2012.* New York: Simon & Schuster, 2016.

Edmondson, Michael. *Navigate the Chaos: 365 Strategies for Personal Growth and Professional Development.* Lulu.com, 2017.

Evans, Rachel Held. "On 'Outgrowing' American Christianity." https://rachelheldevans.com/blog/outgrowing-american-christianity.

Fadling, Alan. *An Unhurried Life: Following Jesus' Rhythms of Work and Rest.* Downers Grove, InterVarsity, 2013.

Finley, James. *Merton's Palace of Nowhere.* Notre Dame: Ave Maria, 1978.

Fitch, David. *The Great Giveaway: Reclaiming the Mission of the Church from Big Business, Parachurch Organizations, Psychotherapy, Consumer Capitalism, and Other Modern Maladies.* Grand Rapids: Baker, 2005.

Fitzgerald, Sally, ed. *The Habit Of Being: Letters of Flannery O'Connor.* New York: Farrar, Straus & Giroux, 1988.

Flowers, David K. "On Being a Non-Anxious Presence." http://davidkflowers. com/2012/02/non-anxious-presence/.

Forest, Jim. "A Harsh and Dreadful Love: Dorothy Day's Witness to the Gospel." http:// jimandnancyforest.com/2005/01/a-harsh-and-dreadful-love/.

Foster, Richard J. *Celebration of Discipline: The Path to Spiritual Growth.* New York: Harper and Row, 1988.

———. *The Challenge of the Disciplined Life: Christian Reflections on Money, Sex & Power.* New York: HarperCollins, 1985.

———. *Prayer: Finding the Heart's True Home.* San Francisco: Harper, 1992.

Foster, Richard J. and James Bryan Smith, eds. *Devotional Classics: Selected Readings for Individuals & Groups.* New York: HarperCollins, 1993.

Francis, Pope. *God Is Always Near: Conversations with Pope Francis.* U.S.: Our Sunday Visitor, 2015.

———. "Silence Guards One's Relationship With God." http://en.radiovaticana.va/ storico/2013/12/20/pope_silence_guards_ones_relationship_with_god/en1– 757349.

Freeman, Emily. *Grace for the Good Girl: Letting Go of the Try-Hard Life.* Grand Rapids: Revell, 2007.

Fretheim, Terrence. *The Suffering Of God: An Old Testament Perspective.* Philadelphia: Fortress, 1984.

Gateley, Edwina and Robert Lentz. *Christ In the Margins.* New York: Orbis, 2003.

Ghezzi, Bert. *Saints at Heart: How Fault-Filled, Problem-Prone, Imperfect People Like Us Can Be Holy.* Chicago: Loyola, 2007.

———. *The Voices of the Saints: A Year of Readings.* New York: Random House, 2000.

Gopnik, Adam. "Orwell's '1984' and Trump's America." https://www.newyorker.com/ news/daily-comment/orwells-1984-and-trumps-america.

Habyarimana, Bangambiki. *Inspirational Quotes For All Occasions.* U.S.: Createspace, 2003.

Hallman, Joseph. *The Descent of God: Divine Suffering in History and Theology.* Eugene: Wipf and Stock, 2004.

Hannay, James O. *The Wisdom of the Desert.* Mesa: Scriptoria, 2014.

Hansel, Tim. *You Gotta Keep Dancin'.* Colorado Springs: David C Cook, 1985.

Harter, Michael, ed. *Hearts on Fire: Praying With Jesuits.* Chicago: Loyola, 2004.

Hass, Peter Traben. *Centering Prayers: A One-Year Daily Companion for Going Deeper into the Love of God.* Brewster: Paraclete, 2013.

Haugen, Gary. *The Good News About Injustice: A Witness of Courage in a Hurting World.* Downers Grove: InterVarsity, 2009.

Hays, Edward. *Chasing Joy: Musings on Life in a Bittersweet World.* Notre Dame: Ave Maria, 2007.

Henson, David. "On Our Behalf." https://www.christiancentury.org/blogs/ archive/2013–02/our-behalf.

Hervey, James. *Whole Works of the Late Rev. James Hervey, Volume 4.* London: Forgotten Books, 2018.

Heschel, Abraham. *Between God and Man: An Interpretation of Judaism.* New York: Harper & Row, 1959.

———. *The Insecurity of Freedom: Essays on Human Existence.* New York: First Noonday, 1969.

———. *The Prophets.* Peabody: Prince, 2000.

Hodge, Bodie and Roger Patterson. *World Religions and Cults, Volume 2: Moralistic, Mythical and Mysticism Religions*. Green Forest: New Leaf, 2016.

Holt, Bradley P. *Thirsty For God: A Brief History of Christian Spirituality*. Minneapolis: Fortress, 2005.

Hooper, Walter, ed. *The Letters of C. S. Lewis to Arthur Greeves, 1914–1963*. New York: Macmillan, 1979.

Hurnard, Hannah. *The Winged Life*. Wheaton: Tyndale, 1987.

Huxley, Aldous. *The Perennial Philosophy*. New York: Harper & Brothers, 1945.

Imbelli, Robert P. "A Visit with Avery Dulles." https://www.commonwealmagazine.org/visit-avery-dulles.

Inchausti, Robert, ed. *Seeds: Thomas Merton*. Boston: Shambhala, 2002.

Jarvis, Cynthia A. and E. Elizabeth Johnson, eds. *Feasting on the Gospels: John, Volume 1*. Louisville: Westminster John Knox, 2015.

Jonas, Robert A., ed. *The Essential Henri Nouwen*. Boston: Shambhala, 2009.

Jones, Alan. *Soul Making: The Desert Way of Spirituality*. New York: HarperCollins, 1985.

Jung, Carl. *The Psychology of the Unconscious*. Mineola: Dover, 2002.

Kavanaugh, Kieran, ed. *John of the Cross: Selected Writings*. Mahwah: Paulist, 1987.

Kazantzakis, Nikos. *Zorba the Greek*. New York: Simon Schuster, 1952.

Keating, Thomas. *The Human Condition: Contemplation and Transformation*. Mahwah: Paulist, 1999.

Keller, Tim. *Generous Justice: How God's Grace Makes Us Just*. New York: Dutton, 2010.

———. *Walking With God Through Pain and Suffering*. New York: Riverhead, 2015.

Kent, Keri Wyatt. *Breathe: Creating Space for God in a Hectic Life*. Hoffmann Estates, IL: A Powerful Story, 2014.

Kenyon, Jane. *Collected Poems*. St. Paul: Graywolf, 2005.

Kierkegaard, **Søren.** *Either/Or: A Fragment of Life.* **New York: Princeton University Press, 1944.**

———. *Purity of Heart Is To Will One Thing*. Radford: Wilder, 2008.

King Jr., Martin Luther. *Where Do We Go from Here: Chaos or Community?* Boston: Beacon, 1968.

Kirvan, John, ed. *The Art of Loving God: Simple Virtues for the Christian Life*. Manchester, N.H.: Sophia, 1998.

———. *Let Nothing Disturb You: Teresa of Avila. (30 Days With a Great Spiritual Teacher)*. Notre Dame: Ave Maria, 2008.

———. *Set Your Heart Free: Francis de Sales. (30 Days With a Great Spiritual Teacher)*. Notre Dame: Ave Maria, 2008.

Küng, Hans. *On Being a Christian*. Garden City: Doubleday, 1984.

Lampy, Leah. "A Time For Waiting." http://myemail.constantcontact.com/December-2014—-A-Time-for-Waiting.html?soid=1101779658792&aid=YnmMJUd4DRU.

Lane, Belden. *The Solace Of Fierce Landscapes: Exploring Desert and Mountain Spirituality*. New York: Oxford, 1988.

Lawrence, Brother. *The Practice of the Presence of God: Being the Conversations and Letters of Nicholas Herman of Lorraine (Brother Lawrence)*. U.S.: CreateSpace, 2012.

Lefton, Andréana. "The Gifts of Hibernation" https://onbeing.org/blog/the-gifts-of-hibernation/.

Lewis, C. S. *A Grief Observed*. New York: HarperCollins, 2001.

———. *Mere Christianity*. New York: Macmillan, 1960.

———. *Screwtape Letters*. New York: HarperCollins, 2001.

———. *The Weight of Glory*. New York: HarperCollins, 2001.

Licata, Matt. "Your Confusion Is Not Pathology." https://manyvoices.soundstrue.com/confusion-pathology-path/#.UmApjPkQaCk.

Lindberg, Anne Morrow. *Gift From the Sea*. New York: Pantheon, 2003.

MacDonald, Gordon. "Cultivating the Soul–Spiritual Formation with Gordon MacDonald." https://mrclm.wordpress.com/2005/11/28/cultivating-the-soul-spiritual-formation-with-gordon-macdonald/.

———. *The Life God Blesses: Weathering the Storms of Life That Threaten the Soul*. Nashville: Thomas Nelson, 1997.

Manning, Brennan. *Abba's Child: A Cry of the Heart for Intimate Belonging*. Colorado Springs: Navpress, 2015.

———. *The Furious Longing of God*. Colorado Springs: David C Cook, 2009.

Martin, James. *Between Heaven and Mirth: Why Joy, Humor, and Laughter Are at the Heart of the Spiritual Life*. New York: HarperCollins, 2012.

May, Gerald G. *Addiction and Grace: Love and Spirituality in the Healing of Addictions*. New York: HarperCollins, 1991.

Mayer, Frederick W. *Narrative Politics: Stories and Collective Action*. New York: Oxford, 2014.

McAlack, Matt. "Grateful Generosity." http://magazine.cairn.edu/2015/06/grateful-generosity/.

McCarty, Jimmy. "Jon Stewart: 'How Oscar Romero Got Disappeared by Right-Wingers . . . for the Second Time.'" https://sojo.net/articles/jon-stewart-how-oscar-romero-got-disappeared-right-wingersfor-second-time.

McCullough, Donald. *The Consolations of Imperfection*. Grand Rapids: Brazos, 2004.

McLaren, Brian. *Finding Our Way Again: The Return of the Ancient Practices*. Nashville: Thomas Nelson, 2008.

———. *A New Kind of Christian: A Tale of Two Friends on a Spiritual Journey*. San Francisco: Jossey-Bass, 2001.

McNeill, John T., ed. *Calvin: Institutes of the Christian Religion*. Philadelphia: Westminster, 1960.

Merton, Thomas. *The Ascent to Truth*. Wilmington: Mariner, 1981.

———. *Contemplation In a World of Action*. Notre Dame: University of Notre Dame Press, 2001.

———. "The Contemplative Life: Its Meaning and Necessity." *Dublin Review* 223 (Winter 1949) 32.

———. *Faith and Violence: Christian Teaching and Christian Practice*. Notre Dame: University of Notre Dame Press, 2015.

———. *Life and Holiness*. Trappist: The Abby of Gethsemani, 1963.

———. *The New Man*. New York: Farrar, Straus and Giroux, 1961.

———. *New Seeds of Contemplation*. New York: New Directions, 2007.

———. *No Man Is an Island*. New York: Fall River, 2003.

———. *Seeds of Contemplation*. New York: New Directions, 1987.

———. *The Seven Storey Mountain: An Autobiography of Faith*. New York: Harcourt Brace Jovanovich, 1978.

———. *Thoughts in Solitude*. New York: Farrar, Straus, and Giroux. 1999.

Metrakoudes-Hewett, Heidi. "Holding Sacred Space" https://heidiatheartspace. wordpress.com/2013/09/09/holding-space/.

Millay, Norma, ed. *Collected Poems of Edna St. Vincent Millay*. New York: Harper & Row, 1856.

Miller, Calvin. *The Table of Inwardness: Nurturing Our Inner Life in Christ*. Downers Grove: InterVarsity, 1984.

Moltmann, Jürgen. *The Church in the Power of the Spirit: A Contribution to Messianic Ecclesiology*. New York: Harper & Row, 1977.

———. *Experiences of God*. Philadelphia: Fortress, 1980.

Moon, Gary. *Apprenticeship with Jesus: Learning to Live Like the Master*. Grand Rapids: Baker, 2009.

Morgan, Gail. *Promise of Rain*. U.K.: Virago, 1985.

Muller, Wayne. *Sabbath: Finding Rest, Renewal, and Delight in Our Busy Lives*. New York: Bantam, 2000.

Murray, Paul. *The New Wine of Dominican Spirituality: A Drink Called Happiness*. London: Burns & Oats, 2006.

Newell, John Philip Newell. *Sounds of the Eternal: A Celtic Psalter*. Grand Rapids: Eerdmans, 2002.

Nicolas of Cusa. *The Vision of God*. New York: Cosimo, 1999.

Norris, Gunilla. *Inviting Silence: Universal Principles of Meditation*. New York: Blueridge, 2014.

Norris, Kathleen. *Acedia & Me: Marriage, Monks, and A Writer's Life*. New York: Riverhead, 2008.

———. *Amazing Grace: A Vocabulary of Faith*. New York: Riverhead, 1998.

———. *Dakota: A Spiritual Geography*. New York: Mariner, 1993.

Nouwen, Henri. *Bread For the Journey: A Daybook of Wisdom and Faith*. New York: HarperCollins, 2006.

———. *Discovering Our Gift Through Service to Others*. U.S.: Fadica, 1994.

———. *The Genesee Diary: Report from a Trappist Monastery*. New York: Image, 1981.

———. *In the Name of Jesus: Reflections on Christian Leadership*. Chestnut Ridge, NY: Crossroad, 1989.

———. *Life of the Beloved: Spiritual Living in a Secular World*. New York: Crossroad, 1992.

———. *Reaching Out: The Three Movements of the Spiritual Life*. New York: Doubleday, 1975.

———. *The Selfless Way of Christ: Downward Mobility and the Spiritual Life*. Maryknoll: Orbis, 2007.

———. "A Spirituality of Waiting." https://bgbc.co.uk/wp-content/uploads/2013/11/A-Spirituality-of-Waiting-by-Henri-Houwen.pdf.

———. *Turn My Mourning Into Dancing: Finding Hope In Hard Times*. Nashville: Thomas Nelson, 2001.

———. *The Way of the Heart: Desert Spirituality and Contemporary Ministry*. New York: HarperCollins, 1991.

O'Connell, Patrick F. ed. "*Thomas Merton: Selected Essays, 1947–1952*." Athens: Cistercian, 2015.

O'Connor, Flannery. *Mystery and Manners: Occasional Prose*. New York: Farrar, Straus and Giroux. 2000.

Ortberg, John. *The Life You've Always Wanted: Spiritual Disciplines for Ordinary People.* Grand Rapids: Zondervan, 2006.

———. *The Me I Want to Be: Becoming God's Best Version of You.* Grand Rapids: Zondervan, 2010.

Orwell, George. *1984.* New York: Houghton Mifflin Harcourt, 1949.

Packer, J. I. and Howard, Thomas. *Christianity The True Humanism.* Waco: Word, 1985.

Palmer, Jim. *Divine Nobodies: Shedding Religion to Find God.* Nashville: Thomas Nelson, 2006.

———. "Fear, Guilt and Shame Can Be Useful On Your Spiritual Journey." https://jimpalmerblog.wordpress.com/2013/07/26/fear-guilt-and-shame-can-be-useful-on-your-spiritual-journey/.

Palmer, Parker. *Healing the Heart of Democracy: The Courage to Create a Politics Worthy of the Human Spirit.* San Francisco: Jossey-Bass, 2011.

———. *A Hidden Wholeness: The Journey Toward an Undivided Life: Welcoming the Soul and Weaving Community in a Wounded World.* San Francisco: John Wiley & Sons, 2004.

———. *Let Your Life Speak: Listening for the Voice of Vocation.* San Francisco: Jossey-Bass, 2000.

———. "On the Brink of Everything: An Early Morning Meditation." https://onbeing.org/blog/on-the-brink-of-everything-an-early-morning-meditation/.

———. *The Violence of Our Knowledge: Toward a Spirituality of Higher Education.* Muenster: St. Peter: 1993.

Papanagiotou, Efstratios. *The Inner Restoration of Christianity.* U.S: Theosis, 2013.

Pascal, Blaise. *Pensees.* New York: Penguin Putnum, 1995.

Pearsall, Paul. *Toxic Success: How to Stop Striving and Start Thriving.* Maui: Inner Ocean, 2002.

Peck, M. Scott. *The Road Less Traveled: A New Psychology of Love, Traditional Values and Spiritual Growth.* New York: Touchstone, 2003.

Peister, John Bookser, ed. *Radical Grace: Daily Meditations by Richard Rohr.* U.S.A: St. Anthony, 1995.

Pennington, M. Basil, ed. *Thomas Merton: I Have Seen What I Was Looking For.* Hyde Park: New City, 2005.

Peterson, Eugene. *The Contemplative Pastor: Returning to the Art of Spiritual Direction.* Grand Rapds: Eerdmans, 1993.

———. *Earth and Altar: The Community of Prayer in a Self-Bound Society.* Downers Grove: InterVarsity, 1985.

———. *Leap Over a Wall: Earthy Spirituality for Everyday Christians.* New York: HarperCollins, 1997.

———. *Under the Unpredictable Plant: An Exploration in Vocational Holiness.* Grand Rapids: Eerdmans, 1992.

Petri, Alexandra. "Crucified Man Had Prior Run-in with Authorities." https://www.washingtonpost.com/blogs/compost/wp/2017/04/12/crucified-man-had-prior-run-in-with-authorities/?utm_term=.39bcad219707.

Postman, Neil. *Amusing Ourselves to Death: Public Discourse in the Age of Show Business.* New York: Penguin, 1985.

Rauschenbusch, Walter. *Prayers of the Social Awakening.* Eugene: Wipf & Stock, 2004.

Rilke, Rainer Maria. *Letters To a Young Poet.* New York: W. W. Norton & Company, 1962.

Roazzi, Vincent. *The Spirituality of Success: Getting Rich With Integrity.* Vancouver: Namaste, 2002.

Robertson, Edwin, ed. *Dietrich Bonhoeffer's Christmas Sermons.* Grand Rapids: Zondervan, 2005.

Robinson, Marilynne. *When I Was a Child I Read Books: Essays.* New York: Farrar, Straus and Giroux, 2012.

Rohr, Richard. *Adam's Return: The Five Promises of Male Initiation.* New York: Crossroad, 2017.

———. "Bias From the Bottom: Week 1." https://cac.org/the-view-from-the-bottom-2016–03-25/.

———. *Eager to Love.* Cincinnati: Franciscan: 2014.

———. "The Egoic Operating System." http://myemail.constantcontact.com/Richard-Rohr-s-Meditation—The-Egoic-Operating-System.html?soid=1103098668616&aid=KXZPfF4eSLY.

———. *Everything Belongs: The Gift of Contemplative Prayer.* New York: Crossroad, 2003.

———. *Falling Upward: A Spirituality for the Two Halves of Life.* San Francisco: Jossey-Bass, 2011.

———. "Orthopraxy: Transformative Education." http://campaign.r20.constantcontact.com/render?ca=a7a95147-c1d3–48b3-b2a1–263036a95280&c=959f7590-ef04–11e3-abca-d4ae52754db0&ch=966f48b0-ef04–11e3-ac7f-d4ae52754db0.

———. "Purifying Motivations." http://myemail.constantcontact.com/Richard-Rohr-s-Meditation—Purifying-Motivation.html?soid=1103098668616&aid=R2jxA19O7cs.

———. *Radical Grace: Daily Meditations by Richard Rohr.* Cincinnatti: Franciscan Media, 1993.

———. *Yes, and . . . : Daily Meditations.* Cincinnati: Franciscan, 2013.

Safi, Omid. "The Disease of Being Busy." https://onbeing.org/blog/the-disease-of-being-busy/.

Sayers, Dorothy. *Are Women Human?* Grand Rapids: Eerdmans, 1971.

Scazzero, Geri and Peter Scazzero. *I Quit!: Stop Pretending Everything is Fine and Change Your Life.* Grand Rapids: Zondervan, 2010.

Scazzero, Peter. *Emotionally Healthy Relationships Day by Day: A 40-Day Journey to Deeply Change Your Relationships.* Grand Rapids: Zondervan, 2017.

Scazzero, Peter. *Emotionally Healthy Spirituality Day by Day: A 40-Day Journey with the Daily Office.* Grand Rapids: Zondervan, 2014.

Scazzero, Peter. *Emotionally Healthy Spirituality: Unleash A Revolution In Your Life In Christ.* Nashville: Integrity, 2006

———. "Thy Kingdom Come" (my transcription of a presently unavailable podcast)

———. "Why Can't We Slow Down." https://www.emotionallyhealthy.org/why-cant-we-slow-down/.

———. "Your Body Is a Major, Not Minor Prophet." https://www.emotionallyhealthy.org/your-body-is-a-major-not-minor-prophet/.

Schaef, Anne Wilson. *Meditations for Women Who Do Too Much.* New York: HarperCollins, 2004.

Schaeffer, Edith. *What Is a Family?* Grand Rapids: Baker, 1975.

Shafir, Rebecca Z. *The Zen of Listening: Mindful Communication in the Age of Distraction.* Wheaton: Quest, 2011.

Shelden, Randall G. and Daniel Macallair. *Juvenile Justice In America: Problems and Prospects.* Long Grove, IL: Waveland, 2008.

Sherwin, Byron. *Abraham Joshua Heschel.* Louisville: John Knox, 1979.

Siete, Courtney. "6 Powerful Communications Tips From Some of the World's Best Interviewers." https://blog.bufferapp.com/6-powerful-communication-tricks-from-some-of-the-worlds-best-interviewers.

Simmons, Philip. *Learning To Fall: The Blessings of an Imperfect Life.* New York: Bantam, 2000.

Simpson, A. B. *The Holy Spirit or Power From On High.* Harrisburg: Christian Alliance, 1895.

Simsic, Wayne. *Living the Wisdom of St. Francis.* Mahwah: Paulist, 2001.

Sittser, Jerry. *A Grace Disguised: How the Soul Grows Through Loss.* Grand Rapids: Zondervan, 2004.

Smith, Allyne, ed. *Philokalia: The Eastern Christian Spiritual Texts: Selections Annotated & Explained.* Woodstock: SkyLight Paths, 2006.

Smith, Robert Lawrence. *A Quaker Book of Wisdom: Life Lessons in Simplicity, Service, and Common Sense.* New York: Eagle Brook, 1998.

Soelle, Dorothy. *Suffering.* Philadelphia: Fortress, 1975.

Spurgeon, Charles Haddon. *Lectures to My Students.* Peabody: Hendrickson, 2010.

Swindoll, Charles. *Laugh Again: Experience Outrageous Joy.* Dallas: Word, 1992.

Taylor, Barbara Brown. *An Altar in the World: A Geography of Faith.* New York: HarperCollins, 2010.

————. *Learning To Walk In the Dark.* New York: HarperCollins, 2015.

————. *When God Is Silent.* Lanham: Rowman & Littlefield, 1998.

Thomas, Debbie. "The Clown King." https://www.journeywithjesus.net/Essays/20150323JJ.shtml. Thurman, Howard. *Deep Is the Hunger.* New York: Harper & Row, 2000.

Tickle, Phyllis and Sweeney, Jon. *The Age of the Spirit: How the Ghost of an Ancient Controversy Is Shaping the Church.* Grand Rapids: Baker, 2014.

Tillich, Paul. *The Shaking of the Foundations.* Eugene: Wipf & Stock, 2012.

Tippett, Krista. *Becoming Wise: An Inquiry into the Mystery and Art of Living.* New York, Penguin, 2017.

Tozer, A. W. *The Pursuit of God.* South Kingston, RI: Millenium, 2014.

Underhill, Evelyn. *Concerning The Inner Life.* New York: E. P. Dutton & Co., 1947.

Valente, Judith. *Atchison Blue: A Search for Silence, a Spiritual Home, and a Living Faith.* Notre Dame: Ave Maria, 2013.

Verhey, Allen and Joseph Harvard. *Ephesians.* Louisville: John Knox, 2011.

Viereck, G. S. *Glimpses of the Great.* New York: Macauley, 1930.

Volf, Miroslav. *Exclusion and Embrace: A Theological Exploration of Identity, Otherness, and Reconciliation.* Nashville: Abingdon, 1996.

————. "What is Good? Joy and the Well-lived Life." https://www.christiancentury.org/article/2016–06/what-good.

Watts, Alan. *Behold the Spirit: A Study in the Necessity of Mystical Religion.* New York: Random House, 1971.

Webber, Robert. *The Younger Evangelicals: Facing the Challenges of the New World.* Grand Rapids: Baker, 2002.

Weil, Simone. *Le Source Grecque.* Paris: Gallimard, 1953.

White, James Emery. *The Rise of the Nones: Understanding and Reaching the Religiously Unaffiliated*. Grand Rapids: Baker, 2014.

———. *Serious Times: Making Your Life Matter in an Urgent Day*. Downers Grove: InterVarsity, 2005. .

Whyte, David. "The Art of Disappearance: Thoughts from San Miguel de Allende." https://www.facebook.com/PoetDavidWhyte/photos/a.213444315348246.68208. 213407562018588/838278782864793/?type=1&theater.

———. *Consolations: The Solace, Nourishment and Underlying Meaning of Everyday Words*. Langley: Many Rivers, 2015

———. *The Three Marriages: Reimagining Work, Self and Relationship*. New York: Riverhead, 2009.

Wiederkehr, Macrina. *A Tree Full of Angels: Seeing the Holy in the Ordinary*. New York: HarperCollins, 1990.

Willard, Dallas. *The Divine Conspiracy: Rediscovering Our Hidden Life In God*. New York: HarperCollins, 1998.

———. *The Great Omission: Reclaiming Jesus's Essential Teachings on Discipleship*. New York: HarperCollins, 2014.

———. *The Spirit of the Disciplines: Understanding How God Changes Lives*. New York: HarperCollins, 1991.

Williams, Rowan. "The Transformative, Purifying Qualities of Contemplation." https://www.theguardian.com/commentisfree/belief/2012/oct/14/why-need-contemplation-god.

Wirzba, Norman. *Living the Sabbath: Discovering the Rhythms of Rest and Delight*. Grand Rapids: Brazos, 2006.

Yancey, Philip. *The Bible Jesus Read*. Grand Rapids: Zondervan, 1999.

———. *Disappointment with God: Three Questions No One Asks Aloud*. New York: HarperCollins, 1997.

———. *Soul Survivor: How Thirteen Unlikely Mentors Helped My Faith Survive the Church*. New York: Doubleday, 2001.

Yoder, John. *Radical Discipleship*. Harrisonburg: Herald, 2012.